DESIGNING
THE SEASIDE

DESIGNING
THE SEASIDE

ARCHITECTURE, SOCIETY AND NATURE

FRED GRAY

REAKTION BOOKS

For Carol, Jack and Holly

Published by Reaktion Books Ltd
33 Great Sutton Street
London EC1V ODX, UK
www.reaktionbooks.co.uk

First published 2006

The author and publishers gratefully acknowledge support for the publication of this book
by The Paul Mellon Centre for Studies in British Art.

Printed and bound in China by Toppan Printing Co. Ltd.

British Library Cataloguing in Publication Data
Gray, Fred
    Designing the seaside: a social and architectual history of the seaside resort
    1.Seaside architecture – Great Britain – History 2.Seaside architecture – History 3.Seaside
    resorts – Great Britain – History 4.Seaside resorts – History 5.Great Britain – Social life
    and customs
    I.Title
    720.9'41

ISBN–10: 1 86189 274 8

CONTENTS

Plymouth Hoe, Devon, 1996.

INTRODUCTION

The invention of the Western seaside as a site of leisure and pleasure almost three centuries ago went hand-in-hand with the development of a novel urban form – the seaside resort – and the emergence of a new pleasure architecture beside the sea. Architecture, in varied innovative forms, became an essential ingredient fashioning the seaside. As an artificial confection designed to entice people seeking leisure and pleasure (and usually intended to generate income and a profit), architecture became the glue of individual resorts and a defining characteristic distinguishing one seaside place from another.

The most influential seaside architecture makes the most of being 'on the front' and beside the sea. Its form and function, and how it is used, help expose the fascinating relationships between society and nature found in places literally on the edge. Western seaside resorts are multi-layered places, redolent with meaning for the present and memory of the past. Whether the most fashionable and exotic sunny southern playground of the rich or a run-down and forgotten colder northern coastal pleasure town, resort architecture has become bound up with the seaside's intense sense of place and being.

The architecture of the seaside, too, has been caught up in the drift of holidaymakers swept along in the surging tides of social, economic and technological change and the ebb and flow of fashion, taste and evolving personal and social relationships. Seaside architecture has helped create, structure and define holidays by the sea and the consumption and very meaning of the seaside.

At some time in their lives most people in Western societies have, in search of leisure and pleasure, holidayed in resorts by the sea. These experiences, together with a multitude of seaside images from postcards to films, and from novels to advertisements, leave people with complex memories and feelings about the seaside. Cut through and sequenced by time and place, these might include sunburnt childhood holidays on a beach littered, depending on the place, with deckchairs and windbreaks or sun loungers and parasols; teenagers having fun in the sea or open-air lido; fumbled first sexual encounters under a pier; a family stroll along a promenade or boardwalk or through a cliff-top park; visits to seaside entertainment complexes from funfairs to casinos; or old people sitting in a seafront shelter watching the world go by. These examples, of course, are deliberately chosen to make the point that the resort experience is frequently framed and conditioned by seaside architecture: the buildings and built form, the open spaces and design detail, that go to make up resorts. But less intentionally, although not unexpectedly, the nature of the seaside – the sea itself, the marginal edge that is the beach, the weather – also emerges as a crucial part of spending time by the sea.

This book is about the Western seaside resort, with a particular emphasis on the English seaside and how it has been created and changed over time, used by holidaymakers, and represented in writing and pictures. A central argument is that a distinctive architecture helps define the seaside resort as an arena of leisure and is a significant element in the consumption of the seaside and the seaside holiday.

Collioure, France, 2004.

Seaside architecture is broadly and liberally defined to include not only obvious buildings such as piers and pavilions but also the minutiae of beach huts and promenade railings and shelters, as well as the larger scale of holiday camps, seaside parks and open spaces and complete resorts designed as a single entity. That said, at times it is impossible to separate out particular types or forms of seaside architecture since in most resorts different architectural strands merge into each other. For example, piers might carry funfairs or bathing stations or even swimming pools; beaches are the launch pad for getting into the sea; holiday camps are usually self-contained resorts, complete in themselves, with funfairs, pools and entertainment complexes.

The timescale covered in the book encompasses almost three centuries, from the appearance of the first embryonic resorts around the shores of England in the early decades of the eighteenth century to the present day, although the emphasis is on the last two centuries and the emergence of

'Rough Sea and the New Palace Pier, Brighton', postcard, c. 1905.

radical new forms of architecture by the sea that continue to help define the seaside today. Even though the geographical focus is on what is now the modern and developed Western world, at times the argument also draws on motifs and images from other 'exotic' and less-developed places that have frequently been used as elements in designing the Western seaside.

Uniting the themes of building and making, and using and representing seaside architecture, are the notions of seaside architecture as a cultural artefact, evolving over time and space through a process of cultural design. Seaside architecture is a principal component of the Western coastal resort and seaside holiday and, borrowing David Cannadine's phrase, it is one that has been 'culturally created and imaginatively constructed'.[1] The architecture of the seaside is the product of a complex and layered cultural design process: the manner in which a series of meanings attached to resorts, and their buildings and the seaside more generally, are produced and reproduced, perhaps in a drastically altered form, and have a formative and determining influence both on how people use the seaside and what they understand and envisage by it. The cultural meanings attached to architecture, the seaside and seaside resorts have evolved over time and vary over space. In particular, changing attitudes to nature and to other (often 'foreign')

Beach café, Camber Sands, Sussex, 1992.

The 'exotic' Beachcomber Bar at Butlins Holiday Camp, Bognor Regis, Sussex, in 1971.

places, questions of taste and fashion, and divides around class, gender and other social distinctions are all important elements in explaining the production and changing use of seaside architecture.

Most immediate and obvious, cultural design is the realization in built form of architectural, artistic and engineering possibilities and visions. In this physical design

The seaside advertised as society and architecture.
Blackpool, 1910, artwork by Wilton Williams.

through marketing and promotional materials such as guidebooks and publicity posters, visual media from postcards and photographs to paintings, fictional accounts in novels and film, official reports, 'expert' comment – say, from architectural critics and historians – and media reports and stories. These varied cultural representations and imaginings may be hugely influential in determining how seaside architecture, specific resorts and the seaside more generally are viewed and used, sometimes running counter to the intentions and wishes of architects, developers and others.

The flowing together of representations of seaside architecture, coastal resorts and the seaside holiday helps explain how resort architecture may assume an iconic cultural status. It may be used to define specific resorts, as with Blackpool's Tower, Brighton's Royal Pavilion, the Promenade des Anglais in Nice, the *Queen Mary* in Long Beach and Santa Monica's pier. Particular forms of architecture may capture the nature and condition of the seaside resort and seaside holiday and even culture and society in a more general way. The Edwardian pier and the 1950s holiday camp are representative (albeit partial) symbols of how the British middle and working classes, respectively, consumed the seaside during particular eras. Similarly, the Riviera hotel and villa and the Hamptons beach house are rich with resonance about holidays, class and elitist culture in European and North American societies. Over many decades varied images of the beach, revealing a changing use and architecture, encapsulate much about the West's fascination with the seaside.

process a group of crucial actors – the builders – create and manipulate resort architecture and the associated built environment. The builders include professional architects and designers and engineers, surveyors and constructors, but also extend to the individual, communal, government and corporate owners, developers and authorities making a direct contribution to building and rebuilding seaside resorts. Apart from making a physical artefact, the builders of seaside architecture also envisage and promulgate a particular view of their work and its purpose and future use. Both buildings and visions are located in the culture and society of the times and places where builders are at work, and will respect and respond to broader societal processes and the available technologies.

Designing the Seaside, however, is not simply about the design and construction of the seaside's built form. A second layer of cultural design involves the representation of the seaside and its architecture, most obviously in visual images and written texts. Such representations range

Blackpool Tower and an angel, 2004.

But a third cultural design process is also at work. As the word holiday*makers* implies, people taking holidays are not passive recipients of what they consume but instead make a direct contribution to designing the seaside, both in their practices while on holiday and in helping determine popular images and responses to the seaside resort and its architecture. Holidaymakers and other people living and working in resorts have a crucial role in the cultural design of the seaside and its architecture, making and creating it as much if not more so than the original builders.[2] At the seaside holidaymakers most obviously compose designs of their own, albeit informal and transitory, in choosing how

Plastic inflatables, Camber Sands, Sussex, 1992.

In a photographer s studio, *c.* 1906.

An early 20th-century saucy postcard.

to use the beach, including, for instance, where to sit or lie, what to do there and what beach furniture, from wind breaks to sun loungers, to bring with them. *Designing the Seaside* also provides some insights into how holidaymakers, the major consumers of the seaside, have left their marks, helping both to mould the seaside and perceptions of its architecture.

A difficulty here is that the voices of holidaymakers are often silent, drowned out by the declarations of the builders or by what those dominating in the making of cultural representations have to say. Rather than being heard clearly and directly the holidaymakers' voice may come across as a confusing Chinese whisper. The deficiency, however, is being

remedied through oral-history research exploring what people did and thought on holiday and their responses to seaside buildings and places.[3] Holidaymakers are also active participants in the production of other cultural artefacts recording the seaside and their sense of it: so, for example, twentieth-century holidaymakers actively engaged in representing their seasides through the choice of postcards (typically dominated by visual images of the resorts and their architecture) to send to relatives and friends and their messages written on the reverse side. Similarly, the invention of the cheap camera allowed people to make visual statements about the seaside experiences they considered to be worth keeping for the future. Memories of a late loved

one and their favourite seaside view could also be captured on the plaques on seaside benches and seats, recording for posterity, or at least the life of the bench, a family name and words of remembrance.

Explorations need to begin somewhere, and by way of method and illustration this book moves out from Brighton and the other English south-coast resorts I know best, to seaside towns elsewhere in Britain and other parts of Europe and so to resorts in other Western countries. The Brighton emphasis, when it occurs, is not just a matter of convenient knowledge. At times it allows drilling deeper into the life history of a specific piece of architecture, as with the resort's West Pier. Brighton is also a useful keystone because it has been the home of much innovative seaside architecture with a formative influence on styles and buildings in other resorts. As to the English emphasis, sea-bathing and the seaside resort were both English inventions,[4] associated with an array of ways of using and building for the seaside that spread to

The 1889 pier at Worthing, Sussex.
Blankenberghe, Belgium, c. 1890—1900.

other Western countries. But apart from looking at how seaside places elsewhere have copied and taken from the English experience, the book also traces how other places, societies and ideas have influenced English resort architecture. Despite these justifications, I am aware that a richer understanding of other seaside places, particularly those in the non-English-speaking Western world, would have enhanced the arguments made in this book.

My intention is to provide illustrative accounts of the cultural design of the most significant seaside architectural forms. The approach is therefore selective and fragmentary: this book is neither a compendium of seaside architecture

Yoshitora Utagawa, woodblock print showing a steam train at Takanawa seashore, Tokyo, c. 1872.

nor complete cultural geography or history, and some readers will be disappointed that their own favourite places and buildings, or those they consider especially important, are ignored. The use of material and case studies also varies: sometimes the emphasis is on the story of a particular iconic structure, elsewhere on many examples of a particular type of seaside architecture; sometimes the stress is on a written history, on other occasions visual representations come to the fore.

Ideas and material for the book have come from a range of sources. As an academic I have of course mined the professional literature. This has proved both empowering and infuriating. Empowering because it includes, for example, some brilliant studies of particular forms of seaside

architecture such as holiday camps[5] and the seaside bungalow,[6] wonderful accounts of the early development of the seaside as a place of leisure,[7] some excellent social and cultural histories of coastal resorts and holidays by the sea,[8] and some fruitful case studies from varied localities.[9] Infuriating, however, because much other academic engagement with seaside architecture is at a tangent. Where architecture is treated explicitly it is often viewed as a product of other more significant processes or as illustrations of some historical, conceptual or theoretical point. The danger is that seaside architecture becomes a cipher, with its geography and history, meaning and purpose, being abstracted and misinterpreted.

Seaside architecture rarely features as a significant object of academic study. Although there are accounts of individual iconic buildings and their architects, and particular architectural styles or periods, there has been little attempt to treat seaside architecture as a whole. The difficulty of definition and drawing of boundaries and the broad-ranging eclecticism of style and diversity of architectural form and purpose are part of the problem. Another issue is that in studying seaside architecture the empirical evidence is often fragmentary and disparate.

Although increasingly rectified in the cultural studies literature, large areas of the academy remain suspicious about studying popular culture, and this includes popular architecture by the sea. Anthony King's accusation made in the mid-1990s about the 'middle-class intellectual marginalization'[10] of the bungalow (in its Western form a building first developed for the English seaside) may be applied equally to other classic forms of seaside architecture from piers to beach huts. Seaside architecture is principally an architecture of leisure, and as John Lowerson says of the study of leisure history, 'generally, the topic is seen as not quite serious'[11] by the academy. John Walton also bemoans 'the continuing marginal status in the eyes of the historical establishment'[12] of British tourism history. Such arguments also relate to John Urry's account of how the cultural practices of the 'service class' – groups dominating in formation of opinions and cultural representations – have increasingly rendered English seaside resorts and their attractions and entertainments as 'relatively tasteless and unfashionable'.[13] It is a small step to apply this thesis to academics as a group within the service class to account for the lack of academic study, although the problem then is to explain why a few academics deviate from the dominant class practice, to engage in the tasteless and unfashionable study of (English) seaside resorts and their architecture. There is a perverse pleasure to be gained from studying what others have decried as unfashionable, and a sense that lack of popularity does not mean unimportant. The quandary is also partly resolved because, as in this book, academics can free themselves from the constraints of seaside Britain to look at coastal places and buildings on other shores.

Even so, the relative academic neglect of the seaside and its architecture remains surprising given the flow – at times an engulfing stream – of popular literature in Britain and abroad ranging from local histories of particular resorts[14] or resort regions[15] and accounts of specific iconic buildings[16] to studies of particular types of seaside building (including piers and pavilions),[17] general social histories of seaside holidays[18] and cultural histories on contextual topics, often with an international focus, including of the beach,[19] swimming pools[20] and swimming[21]. This material has informed the writing of the book.

In addition, over the last decade I have gathered together a host of textual and visual representations of the seaside, ranging from postcards, posters and adver-

tisements to fictional accounts, newspaper articles and official reports. Film and television, radio and music have also played a part in this research process. Last but not least, material has come from visits to various seaside places and buildings.

Chapter One provides a context for arguments developed later in the book. It examines how perceptions of nature at the seaside have evolved over time, played a dominant role in determining holidays and vacations by the sea, and in turn influenced the production and use of seaside architecture. The focus of chapter Two is the role of the builders creating and manipulating the built environment of resorts set against broader processes – from shifting technologies to changing class structures – that help determine the shape of seaside architecture. Chapter Three turns to cultural representations of the seaside and its architecture. In examining visual and textual representations ranging from postcards and guidebooks to novels and film, positive promotional place images in media such as guidebooks are set against alternative and contradictory images and portrayals.

The role of architecture and design in helping to turn the seaside from the ordinary into other exotic or extraordinary places is the theme of chapter Four. Using Brighton's Royal Pavilion as a starting point, it examines the use of 'Oriental' architecture to transform the seaside and the palm tree as a design motif and emblem of other locations and environments. Chapter Five turns to the design and architecture of the seaside open spaces, including the beach and seafront, promenades and boardwalks, and seaside parks and gardens. It explores how the use of the beach has evolved, and contrasts grand designs for the making of the front and seaside parks with the minutiae of seafront shelters and railings, floral beds and bandstands. Developing the theme of how changing perceptions of both nature and society at the seaside have interplayed with architecture, chapter Six turns to other beach buildings – structures often ignored or denigrated by architectural commentators, despite their immense popular significance – particularly those providing access to the sea itself. It includes a case study of the bathing machine, a unique piece of eighteenth-century vernacular architecture for the consumption of sea water, its subsequent history and its demise two centuries later, and a discussion of twentieth-century beach building, including bathing pavilions and the beach hut, an iconic structure resonating with the meaning of the contemporary seaside.

Attention is then turned, in chapter Seven, to another watery form of architecture, that of artificial structures for bathing and swimming at the seaside, from early indoor pools for sea-water treatments through the modernist open-air lidos of the inter-war years to the 'inside seaside'

and subtropical leisure pools of the present day. The unique and distinctive architecture and engineering of the seaside pier, and the transformation of mid-nineteenth-century promenade piers into pleasure piers and, more recently, funfair and heritage piers, is discussed in chapter Eight, which includes the story of Brighton's iconic West Pier. Chapter Nine examines the architecture of seaside entertainment buildings, both exploring another out-of-this-world form of seaside architecture, the amusement park and 'people's palaces' of indoor entertainment. The final chapter considers a diversity of architecture for sleeping by the sea and makes a number of contrasts, including grand hotels with boarding houses, and holiday camps with other forms of planned and complete resorts, and with self-build seaside holiday homes that eschew the professional architect and designer.

After a storm, Brighton, 2003.

CHAPTER 1
NATURE AND SEASIDE ARCHITECTURE

At the dawn of the seaside resort, pioneer visitors began to venture to the English coast in search of health, leisure and pleasure. Two of the first adventurers were the Reverend William Clarke and his wife. In the summer of 1736 they stayed for a month in Brighthelmstone, a small and declining town on the south coast of England. On 22 July Clarke wrote to his friend, a Mr Bowyer:

> We are now sunning ourselves upon the beach at Brighthelmstone . . . The place is really pleasant; I have seen nothing in its way that outdoes it. Such a tract of sea; such regions of corn; and such an extent of fine carpet, that gives your eye the command of it all. But then the mischief is, that we have little conversation besides the *clamor nauticus*, which is here a sort of treble to the plashing of the waves against the cliffs. My morning business is bathing in the sea, and then buying fish; the evening is riding out for air, viewing the remains of old Saxon camps, and counting the ships in the road, and the boats that are trawling.[1]

One of the first accounts of seaside leisure and pleasure, Clarke's activities – we know little of Mrs Clarke's holiday – are all the more remarkable in suggesting there is little new under the sun. His experiences of seaside nature included bathing in the sea, soaking up the sun on the beach, taking in the air, and extended to the sights, sounds and tastes of the sea. These sensory experiences reverberate through the subsequent history of the seaside resort and its architecture, and echo into the twenty-first century.

As an intrepid pioneer, William Clarke was free to do as he pleased. 'Society' and fashion had little interest in the coast or what people did there, and while the established inland spas provided some guidance for taking the waters, they also imposed severe social constraints. Clarke perhaps drew on a more popular sea-bathing tradition enjoyed by local working people: seaside historians have struggled to make sense of the teasing fragments of evidence from Britain, France and Germany suggesting that sea-bathing had long been used by 'common folk' for a combination of therapeutic, prophylactic, educational, festive and hedonistic purposes.[2] But for elite groups, the consumption of seaside nature had to be invented, learnt and accepted, and in one view it was Clarke who 'invented the seaside holiday'.[3] It was then codified, guided and constrained. The use of seaside nature subsequently embraced ever-larger sections of the population, changing from an elite and aristocratic activity to one with popular mass appeal. It evolved in ways that privileged specific forms of consumption – and particular forms of architecture – at particular periods.[4]

The Brighthelmstone experienced by the Clarkes was a long-established coastal town, functioning as a trading, transportation and fishing centre. But until their arrival it was not a place visited for seaside health, leisure or pleasure, and it lacked any architecture designed or intended for such purposes. Within three decades, however, Brighthelmstone had been transformed into a place for society to learn about

Sheltering from the sun: the beach at the foot of Shanklin Chine, Isle of Wight, c. 1860.

and consume seaside nature and had become the nation's most fashionable and successful resort. It subsequently became better known as Brighton and, as one of England's most emblematic resorts, the place name was reused around the English-speaking world to conjure up the fashionable seaside.

Society's new-found and evolving desires and pleasures of the sea, beach and shore led to an innovative and revolutionary architecture designed to facilitate the consumption of seaside nature. At first slowly, then with gathering pace in the nineteenth and twentieth centuries, an inventive and novel architecture of the seaside was created.

Changes in how seaside nature has been used have been partly the consequence of the evolution of popularly held definitions and understandings of health and pleasure, sometimes conflated together, sometimes stringently separated. This underlying sweep of shifting popular social movements and fashions shaping the seaside has worked alongside and sometimes collided with the persistent attempt of seaside authorities – including central and local government and varied experts and official bodies – to guide and regulate the consumption of seaside nature. Although it is difficult to untangle cause and effect and the

initial and underlying impulses leading to a particular change in how the seaside has been used, the power of authorities to impose a particular design on the seaside has been uneven, and most likely to be successful when it is in sympathy with what people want to do.

This engagement between popular demands and the forces of regulation had architectural consequences. A prime example is the role of the medical profession in codifying the use of the seaside and its resultant built form. Doctors frequently had a promiscuous attitude to seaside nature, happy to proclaim its varied benefits. By the end of the eighteenth century, for example, they had variously asserted the attractions of sea water, sea air, the coastal climate and seaside sunshine. Dr Lettsom's Royal Sea Bathing Hospital, for instance, which opened in Margate in 1796, included a solarium designed to use sea air and sunlight in the treatment of tuberculosis.[5] Yet it was not until the 1920s and '30s, when sunshine seized the popular imagination and dominated what people wanted of the seaside, that the open floodgates released a torrent of new architectural responses to the seaside sun.

Holidaymakers at times resisted the architecture of the commodified and regulated seaside and instead created

Margate's Royal Sea Bathing Hospital, founded in 1791, pioneered sea-bathing treatments. It closed in 1991. Photographed in 2003.

A self-built cliff-side cabin, Branscombe, Devon, 1991.

The terror of the sea. Thomas Rowlandson, *Salt Water*, *c.* 1800, pen and watercolour.

their own architectural responses, some temporary, some more permanent, to being by the sea. Marginal locations away from the dominant resorts were sought out and used to build a people's architecture for staying and playing by the sea and to consume nature in alternative ways. One of the most revealing – literally – themes in the resistance to seaside authority is the still-unfinished story of how people have fought against prescriptions on how they should use the sea and beach – when, where, how, with whom, in what dress and using what architecture.

SEA WATER, SEA AIR AND SEA VIEWS

The emergence of seaside resorts in the eighteenth century allowed the sea, newly discovered by the leisured classes as a site of pleasure and health, to be consumed. Central to this new form of consumption were the assumed therapeutic and health-enhancing qualities of

sea water. Alain Corbin's path-breaking history of the discovery of the Western seaside between 1750 and 1840 roots the emergence of seaside resorts in the Enlightenment and profound changes in people's attitudes to and perceptions of the sea.[6] He details the 'revolution' that occurred in how people understood and appreciated nature and their own bodily consciousness. Gradually the seaside became an attractive, 'sublime' place that was perceived to offer therapeutic remedies for the excesses and ailments of the ruling classes. In contrast to the malevolence of the cities and the overcrowded, dissolute inland spas, the seashore resorts offered a new closeness to nature, because, as Corbin argues:

> The ocean represented indisputable nature which was more than just scenery, and which remained unaffected by falsehood . . . the sea became a refuge and a source of hope because it inspired fear. The new strategy for

Bathing machines at Bognor Regis in an early 20th-century postcard.

seaside holidays was to enjoy the sea and experience the terror it inspired, while overcoming one's personal perils. . . . The sea was expected to cure the evil of urban civilization and correct the ill effects of easy living, while respecting the demands of privacy.[7]

As the untamed, natural sea came to be seen as a source of society's salvation, medical opinion galloped to aid and abet the discovery of the seaside, doctors proclaiming the extraordinary additional virtues of sea water over ordinary cold-water medicinal bathing and drinking. Writing in the mid-eighteenth century and developing the work of other physicians, the Brighton-based Dr Richard Russell was the most important publicist for the therapeutic benefits of consuming sea water. Published in Latin in 1750 (fourteen years after the Clarkes' visit to the town) and English in 1752, his *Dissertation on the Uses of Sea Water in the Diseases of the Glands*, appeared in various editions, some pirated, and the last published in 1769. A century after publication it continued to be quoted throughout the Western world as a standard reference.

For Russell and many other physicians, the sea had mystical qualities, 'which the omnificent Creator of all Things, seems to have designed to be a kind of common Defence against the Corruption and Putrefaction of Bodies.[8]' Russell's starting-point was that 'Nature is the Healer of diseases'. Believing sea water was superior to the cures provided by the inland spas, he argued that its impact could be miraculous, promising cures for everything from gonorrhea to glandular consumption, 'of which none ever did recover'. His casebook approach, a popular and long-lasting genre for doctors and other experts writing about the medicinal benefits of seaside nature,[9] offered different sea-water prescriptions according to the disease being treated. In one treatment, for example, 'the Cure is to be finished by cold bathing in the Sea, drinking every Morning enough Sea Water to procure two or three Stools a Day, immediately upon coming out of the Sea'.[10]

Although he was working in Brighton, Russell's ideas were both adopted and adapted nationally and internationally. Despite arguments among physicians about how best to use sea water, few disputed its value. For example,

John Fraser, *The Chain Pier, Brighton*, 1883, oil on canvas. Low tide reveals the idiosyncratic yet innovative structure of this 1823 pier.

Margate's Dr John Anderson in the mid-1790s enthused about the practice of sea-bathing in 'nature's richly saturated compound'.[11]

The sea as saviour was realized and mediated by the development of a small piece of architecture, the bathing machine, that was intricately entwined with the therapeutic consumption of the sea and for many decades enabled the medical profession and other powerful groups to control the sea-bathing process and the use of the seaside. Despite its seeming insignificance, the bathing machine became the first purpose-designed form of seaside architecture, performing the extraordinary function of taking society to nature, allowing the private individual to consume nature and a profit to be made in the process. Two other pieces of distinctive seaside architecture developed at the same time: bathing rooms, where people waited for machines and drank sea water, and sea-water artificial baths, which provided an alternative to the bathing machine experience.

Doctors detailed the features of the ideal seaside resort. For Russell the model resort should be 'neat and tidy',

distant from any river mouth to ensure high waves and a sufficiently salty sea; the beach should be sandy and flat – making for the easy use of bathing machines – and the shore surrounded by cliffs and dunes suitable for exercise on foot or horse. These characteristics were, perhaps unsurprisingly, reminiscent of the coast where Russell practised, although other resorts were quick to claim that they perfectly fitted his preferred topography. Other physicians subsequently defined other necessary qualities, including the ideal character of the climate and air, landscape and relief, and soil and vegetation.

The bathing machine, the associated bathing rooms and sea-water artificial baths became the chief distinctive architectural manifestations of the eighteenth-century seaside resort. Apart from a very few innovative original purpose-built resort buildings where a front of the sea location and sea view was prioritized, in the initial phase of resort development there was no great clamour to build as close to the sea as possible.[12] The concern appears more to have been in sight of polite society than with views of

The Brighton Aquarium, on the formal opening day, *Illustrated London News*, 10 August 1872.

The ornate entrance to the multi-purpose Brighton Aquarium, late 19th century.

Fountain in the Winter Garden of the Aquarium, Brighton, *c.* 1910.

watery nature and with the provision of all the attractions of an inland spa, from the spa building themselves to promenades and parades, assembly rooms and libraries.

From the late eighteenth century, however, and at a critical turning point in elite society's perceptions of the sea and shore, the seaside began to be valued for other than the assumed medicinal benefits. Crucially, there was a growing acceptance that the seaside should be appreciated for its beauty, for the visual delights it offered, for the nature it revealed, for the exercise and relaxation it could provide, and for the quality and purity of its air. These new ways of experiencing the seaside produced a remarkable new array of architecture and open spaces.[13] Promenades, parades and piers, for example, functioned as platforms from which to take in sea views and breath sea air, and the winter garden, floral hall and aquaria demonstrated the subjection of nature by society.

A growing interest in marine aesthetics and a developing importance of the sea in the visual imagination, both prioritizing views, panoramas and perspectives of the sea and coast, were radically to change the design of the seaside. By the mid-nineteenth century esteem for the glories of the sea view was deeply embedded in wider society's consciousness, leading to varied artistic and literary representations. The horizon, for example, became a particularly important part of the Victorian visual

imagination, suggesting, 'futurity, the space into which the imagination and inner vision may travel: it connotes expansiveness'.[14]

Seaside architecture increasingly sought to capitalize on the sea view and panorama. The sea view became an enduring attraction of the seaside, sustained to the present day, and with major consequences for resort architecture. The grand Regency terraces of the Brighton and Hove seafront gloried in the sight of the sea.[15] On the rolling heathland of the south

'Nelson Crescent, Ramsgate', from *Twelve Views of Ramsgate* (London, *c.* 1850s).

coast, Bournemouth's first purpose-built resort house, constructed in 1812, was designed to have 'magnificent seaward prospects',[16] while by 1830 in north-west England, across the Mersey from Liverpool, in the new development of New Brighton 'every house should have an uninterrupted view of the sea'.[17] Over the following decades and into the subsequent century, promenades and piers,

Sea views and sea-bathing in mid-19th-century Brighton. John Wilson Carmichael, *Kemp Town from the Sea*, 1840, oil on canvas.

Seafront shelter, Ramsgate, Kent, 2002.

The view from a bench in memory of 'Caroline Bartlett, 1864–1942', Sidmouth, Devon, 2002.

The sea view remains a critical design element in the architecture of modern Mediterranean hotels; Mallorca, 1995.

towers and pavilions, seafront shelters and beach huts, all offered the attraction of views of the sea. In Britain, 'Sea View' became the archetypal name for a seaside guesthouse or bungalow. For holidaymakers there was and still is an additional price to be paid for the hotel room with the finest view. The fixation with the view continues unabated today and is evidenced, for example, in the positioning and design of balconied hotels around the Mediterranean and many other coastlines.

Philip Gosse, a famous mid-nineteenth-century popularizer of seaside nature, was passionate about the delights of the sea view and gazing on both nature and society. Writing of a seaside holiday in Tenby in Wales, he describes 'taking a satiating look at the noble promontory' of Tenby Head and evening walks around it as a favourite promenade 'thronged with gay visitors'. There were other visual pleasures to be enjoyed, including cliff-top walks that allowed 'the gaze to go out freely upon the sparkling sea',[18] and a carriage drive along the coast that with its 'constant panoramic change of scene, as the various points of the landscape altered their relative positions – afforded us endless occasions of admiration, and sources of delight'.[19] For Gosse, writing or talking about a view was 'a poor substitute for the gratification of which the visual organ is the seat, when we look upon that which is grand or beautiful, and, as it were, drink in its grandeur or beauty without an effort.'[20] To consume an outstanding view was a mystical experience 'exhilarating to the spirits'.[21]

Apart from gazing at nature from a distance, Victorian holidaymakers also peered at nature close-up. By the mid-

William Dyce, *Pegwell Bay, Kent – A Recollection of October 5th, 1858*, oil on canvas.

nineteenth century, and reflecting middle-class interest in new scientific theories about evolution and the natural world, many seaside holidaymakers became amateur naturalists, classifying shells and pebbles and hunting marine life in tidal rock pools. This consumption of nature was supported by the publication of many guides to seashore natural history, often written by clergymen, and cut through by revealing tensions between, on one hand,

notions of scientific observation, classification and understanding, and, on the other hand, the role of the 'Creatorial Power' and the 'Deity Himself' in producing a mysterious nature.[22] Many of these guides also expressed Victorian sentiments about self-improvement and the strengthening of 'our corporeal and mental faculties'.[23]

The most famous Victorian visual representation of natural history at the seaside is William Dyce's *Pegwell*

John Leech, 'Common Objects at the Sea-Side – Generally Found upon the Rocks at Low Water', *Punch*, c. 1857.

Bay, Kent – A Recollection of October 5th, 1858. In one view, Dyce captured contemporary anxieties, his amateur naturalists appearing overwhelmed and anxious yet dignified;[24] from another perspective, the painting is redolent with religious symbolism and solemnity.[25] Yet the nature-seekers could also be satirized, as in John Leech's *Punch* cartoon of 1859, 'Common Objects at the Sea-Side – Generally Found upon the Rocks at Low Water', a parody on the impact of a recently published natural-history guidebook of the same title.[26] Despite the contrast in medium and intent, Dyce's and Leech's images are remarkably analogous.

Gosse himself was the author of a string of books on seaside natural-history, including the popular *A Naturalist's Rambles on the Devonshire Coast*.[27] His Tenby work, designed as lessons in the 'important art' of 'How and What to Observe',[28] included directions to the most remote and inaccessible shoreline locations. When not collecting nature

on the inter-tidal zone, Victorian holidaymakers were able to observe it either alive – in purpose-built aquaria – or dead – in natural history museums.

The vast and evolving literature about the medicinal value of the seaside became an international trade. Medical opinion and advice was not only exported from Britain but American and French guides to using the seaside were re-published for the English market. Increasingly during the nineteenth century, rather than just proclaim the virtues of bathing, the medical profession and the published guides and manuals also emphasized the value of sea air, coastal climate and the benefits of swimming.

One such early transitional guidebook was John Bigsby's *Sea-side Manual for Invalids and Bathers*, published in 1841 and a reworking of an 'elegant treatise' from France.[29] Respecting Russell's legacy from nine decades earlier, the author argued that the important choice of a sea-bathing place should be 'left to the discernment of the professional adviser, who will be guided by the end he has in view'. Unlike Russell, however, Bigsby was clear that sea-bathing was not a universal remedy and instead recognized the alternative advantages of sea air: 'There are many complaints which may be benefited by sea air alone, but in which sea bathing is manifestly injurious.'[30]

Doctors took to pronouncing on the advantages of one region or resort compared to another and even on the best location within a resort for invalids suffering particular complaints. Writing in the early 1880s, George Moseley, for example, extolled the medicinal virtues of the 'empress of resorts', Eastbourne: 'In the matter of softness of climate Eastbourne is almost unapproachable, certainly within the British Isles. Its nearest competitor, Bournemouth . . . enjoys a reputation that in time must give way before the immense superiority of Eastbourne.'[31]

The cult of sea air. A postcard of c. 1919.

'A Swimming-Lesson at Brighton' (detail), originally from *The Graphic*, 23 September 1871, subsequently coloured.

In the last quarter of the nineteenth century the cult of sea air became dominant. In the USA one formative guide, *Sea-Air and Sea-Bathing*, subsequently re-published in Britain without the American place-specific references, emphasized at 'the sea-shore we have not merely a pure atmosphere, but one saturated with sea-salts'.[32] The combination of pure air 'containing oxygen in the form of ozone, besides finely divided sea-salts' and the same salts in sea water made for the miraculous transformation of people:

Upon most persons the effect of breathing this air is tonic and invigorating, producing an immediate sense of exhilaration, improving the appetite, and promoting digestion. In like manner, the bathing in salt-water stimulates the skin, and renders the circulation more active. Compare the pale, bleached, puny children, who are taken down to the sea-shore in the nearly summer, with the same children returning to town in September – tanned, ruddy, and hearty.[33]

It was sea air and sea-bathing – not spending time in the sun – that was thought to restore and transform. Ozone as an element of sea air became a powerful recommendation of the coast, repeatedly analysed by doctors, vigorously promoted by the seaside authorities and endlessly debated in respectable society. Ultimately, though, its use and value were imagined rather than real and it was vainly hunted for invalids in search of health.[34] The restorative value of sea air and its role in blowing away the malaise of work and the city continued to be acclaimed for much of the twentieth century, although it was to be rivalled and ultimately vanquished by the cult of the sun.

Although present-day histories of the seaside usually conflate the two, bathing was not the same as swimming.

Few people visiting eighteenth- and early nineteenth-century resorts could swim, and it was strongly believed that swimming or floating in the sea was an unnatural, if not impossible, human activity.[35] Set against the persistent fear of death by drowning, this unusual and extraordinary activity had to be learnt.[36] Initially those who did swim – usually men – engaged in a very different practice from what became commonplace in the twentieth century. The resulting strenuous, almost desperate, frog-like swimming style was designed to keep the body on the surface of the water and the head above it. Almost as an addendum, Bigsby's 1841 manual provided a series of instructions on how to swim:

The common way of swimming is with the face toward the water. In this situation the body lies extended, prone, upon the fluid – with the mass of muscles on the back in a state of powerful and permanent contraction, so as to fix the hips and spine, and keep back the head. The muscles of the limbs are in somewhat rapid action, propelling the body through the water. The first mentioned set of muscles are most called upon, because their state of contraction has no respite, and therefore these are the muscles most benefited . . . In the graceful kind of natation, called walking in the water, the muscles of the chest are principally called into exercise; and the organs which it contains thereby acquire volume and force; but requiring considerable effort, it cannot be kept up long.[37]

Unsurprisingly, swimming did not become a popular seaside activity until other user-friendly strokes were invented and accepted. One version of the development of swimming includes a heady brew of the heroic feats of the

MISS. G. POWSEY. WEST PIER. B'TON.

Romantics, the impact of the British public schools and growing awareness of practices elsewhere in the world: one impulse was a visit of Native Americans to England, using innovative, although for them traditional, strokes to race against and beat English swimming champions.[38] An alternative history stresses that the flowering of swimming at the British seaside, away from the early-to-mid-nineteenth-century swimming baths designed for the affluent and into the sea itself, where it was increasingly enjoyed by a broad range of holidaymakers, owed much to amateur swimming clubs and professional seaside entertainers. In Brighton, for example, the amateur club had a membership of local working people who, as part of a voyage of self-discovery and heightened consciousness, were eager to push at the boundaries of how nature might be enjoyed. From the 1860s the club provided what for the times were remarkable swimming displays and competitions in the sea for holidaymakers to view from the pier. Professional entertainers also seized on swimming, and associated skills such as diving into the sea and staying underwater for seemingly superhuman lengths of time, as a spectacular attraction for seaside holidaymakers to wonder at.[39]

top: Gladys Powsey, aquatic entertainer and diver, performing in Brighton, c. 1930.

middle: Portsmouth Swimming Club, Ladies Branch, diving platform and changing rooms, c. 1905.

left: The joy of swimming races. The Venetian Pool, Coral Gables, Florida, late 1920s.

IT'S VERY HOT IN THE SHADE HERE.

The lure of the sun portrayed in a postcard.

Although it took decades to achieve, eventually holidaymakers were able to swim away from the clutches of the medical profession and the restrictions of bathing machines and instead enjoy the sea as independent individuals and family members. The bather as a passive recipient of a medical prescription was transformed into the swimmer as an active participant enjoying nature. Gradually, swimming became a popular and widespread seaside activity, architecturally expressed with new buildings on the beach and pier, and indoor and outdoor pools of fresh or salt water designed for swimming rather than bathing.[40] From the late nineteenth century and in response to changing attitudes to nature, there were also significant changes in how holidaymakers dressed and behaved on the beach. Although there

were local and national, and indeed international, differences in the speed of change, over the following decades costumes became ever briefer and the use of the beach ever more liberated.[41]

THE SUNNY SEASIDE

Such manoeuvrings were a prelude to other significant developments. From the late nineteenth century the sun emerged first as an accompaniment to sea air and then, by the 1930s, as the dominant natural force shaping what people searched for, did and built at the seaside. As with other uses of seaside nature, it is difficult to untangle popular movement from expert prescription in the developing interest in the sun. The Russells sunning themselves on Brighton beach in the 1730s and Margate's 1790s solarium suggest that the seeds of interest in the sun, although laying mostly dormant during Victorian society's preference for other aspects of nature, had been sown many decades before.[42] But by the end of the nineteenth century the latent potential at last began to be realized. In Germany, for example, in the context of an increasing interest in a return to nature, the 'air- and sun-bath cult' established by Adolf Just in 1896 subsequently developed into a nationwide movement.[43]

In the early part of the twentieth century the medical profession, too, promoted the therapeutic use of the sun, particularly in combating tuberculosis (consumption), then still a scourge of many parts of the Western world, despite earlier beliefs that it was preventable or curable through the use of sea water or sea air. Heliotherapy, the direct exposure to sunlight combined with fresh air and relaxation out of doors, became an accepted medical treatment for tuberculosis and other illnesses. By the 1930s the medical benefits

HASTINGS & ST. LEONARDS

SUNSHINE AND HEALTH

OFFICIAL HANDBOOK

The public promotion of 'Sunshine and Health', the cover of one 1935 guidebook.

ness. The coming of the sun, however, inverted these existing values: a suntan became a 'distinguishing trait' for the elite and 'a new symbol of modern times, an external manifestation of prosperity'.[47] But the value placed on the sun extended to other parts of society. For social reformers, architects and town planners of the period, a 'dream of health, sunlight and the body reformed'[48] was bound up with a quest to transform existing society into a new and modern social order. But the upper class and social reformers apart, there was also a more broadly based popular appreciation of health, physical activity and pleasure in the sun and open air. All these impulses led to new ways for holidaymakers to use the seaside, and new responses to these demands from the seaside builders.

At the leading edge of the cult of the sun in Britain and other Western countries was the nudist or naturist movement. Sunbathing was the heart of the naturism, although it also almost invariably involved bathing, swimming and playing in water. In Britain, *Health and Efficiency* – using the

of the sun were widely acknowledged: on one side of the Atlantic, for example, New York's health commissioner announced: 'The sun is the greatest bottle of medicine in the world',[44] while on the other side of the ocean, a British commentator described the 'profundity and prodigality' of the sun's ultra-violet radiation.[45]

The sun, though, seized more than the medical imagination. It had class and gender dimensions. Previously, the social and economic elite privileged white skins for the indication of both status and health. The suntan, in contrast, was distasteful because of its connotations with degrading physical activity.[46] Similarly, until the 1920s, the feminine ideal of wealthy women stressed pallor, fragility and white-

Sheltering from the sun: weather screens and parasols in use on Brighton's West Pier, late 19th century. Postcard.

Modernizing a 19th-century resort with a new architecture for the sun: 1930s St Leonards on Sea.

strapline 'the national sunbathing and health magazine' – became an influential publicity vehicle for the movement. The magazine proudly proclaimed itself the pioneer of 'Sane Nudism', and subscribed to a manifesto that included the beliefs that 'sunlight is the greatest factor in promoting and retaining Radiant Health', 'complete exposure of the body to the sun under particular circumstances, and with respect to propriety, is essential for the full benefits to be gained', and that 'many persons to-day are ashamed of their bodies, and we desire to inculcate in them a will to improve and perfect the human body by the life-giving rays of the sun'.[49] Although separated by almost two centuries, there are remarkable similarities in the claims being made for the life-giving sunrays when set alongside those made by Dr Russell for the sea.

Naturism was a minority but influential activity. Its attraction could be argued in contrasting ways. For George Ryley Scott, writing in the late 1930s, nudism's rise was partly due to 'increasing penchant for notoriety' and 'sex curiosity'.[50] Many naturists, however, argued that it did away with the prudery and shame previously associated with being naked, with the body viewed, at least for most of the time, as an asexual object, 'yet another machine for living in'.[51] Scott, though, was correct in arguing that as practised in the late 1930s 'by the majority of its devotees',

sunbathing did 'not represent nudity in any complete sense. Usually it refers to the practice . . . of sprawling about on the beaches with the main portion of the skin exposed to the sun and air.'[52]

The cult of the sun had concrete results for the design of the seaside in Britain and elsewhere in Europe. A new seaside architecture developed that included sun terraces,

The distractions of the beach. c. 1930.

communal beach bathing stations, solariums, holiday camps and beach huts. Seafronts were remade with new parks and gardens designed for pleasure, sport and children in mind. Most iconic of all, the inter-war open-air lido reflected both the coming of the sun and the flowering of swimming. The relationship between the architecture and clothing of the seaside moved into close alignment: the stripped-down, clean-lined, modernist lidos of the 1930s went hand-in-hand in the development of minimal, figure-hugging costumes for swimming and sunbathing. The tumultuous wave of lido and swimming-pool building dissipated with the beginning of the Second World War.

Naturism stripped away the remaining architectural and clothing interventions between people and nature with, by the 1990s, high-factor protective sun lotion, Ray Ban shades and perhaps a hat being the only products – a minimal personal architecture – separating one from the other. Most beach users, though, continued to use costumes, however brief. In France and Spain by the early twenty-first century, naturism was a major summer seaside movement, dedicated to 'totale communion avec la nature' [53] and architecturally expressed in pine-forest-located specialist campsites in the south-west of France and in naturist resorts such as Costa Natura in Spain and the Cap d'Agde in France.

The contemporary holidaymaker's continuing love of the sun provides the key to understanding the fate, over the last four decades, of resorts and seaside architecture in different parts of the Western world. Facilitated by cheap, fast and relatively comfortable air travel, northern holidaymakers headed south in the search for the sun, leading to the decline of many colder and older resorts and the increasing dereliction and often the destruction of earlier forms of seaside architecture. In contrast, the development of new and more distant seaside places on

The summertime resort: Sidmouth Esplanade, Devon, 1923.

The paraphernalia and furniture of the French 1930s beach and promenade at Juan-les-Pins.

top: A 1934 advertisement for Branksome Chine Solarium and Caf , Poole, Dorset. The Solarium replaced the winter garden as an English seaside attraction.

above: Butlins Holiday Camp, Clacton-on-Sea, Essex, on a postcard.

top right: The modern marina is often as much a site of property development as a safe haven for pleasure boats. Brighton Marina, 2005.

warmer and sunnier coasts has been bound up with a seaside architecture of balconied tower hotels, holiday villages and villas reflecting the contemporary consumption of seaside nature.

But apart from the sun, twentieth-century Western seaside holidaymakers found an increasing diversity of other ways to use nature. Sailing and surfing (the latter a long-established indigenous Hawai'ian pastime almost destroyed by the coming of the West to the Pacific and then reborn in the twentieth century),[54] the two seaside sports to become firmly established during the century, each contributed new and original dimensions to the architecture of the seaside, including the marina, sailing club, surf shop and surfing school. The intriguing question is whether and how contemporary new ways of experiencing seaside nature, including extreme coastal sports such as wind surfing, kite surfing and coasteering, will produce new forms of seaside architecture or, alternatively, new uses for existing coastal buildings.

Surf boat, Bondi Beach, Sydney, Australia, 1988.

GAZING AT THE SEASIDE

This discussion of the use of seaside nature and its architectural consequences nestles amid contemporary debates about nature and society and the schisms and relationships between the natural world and the human environment.[55] There are arguments about what nature is, with one persistent theme from the eighteenth century to the present being that nature is mysterious and unknowable; whether or not people are part of nature; whether nature can be consumed and, if not consumed, how it is used, experienced, perceived and represented; and how nature has been commodified, replicated and themed.

This evolving debate, however, has rarely turned attention to nature and society at the seaside or provided any purchase on the significance of seaside architecture. An influential exception is John Urry's account of the tourist gaze.[56] From the mid-nineteenth century, Urry argues, the visual sense was increasingly hegemonic in the sensing of the natural world, and nature, including the sea, was transformed into an overridingly visual spectacle.[57] In turn, the fundamental process of tourist consumption became capturing the gaze, each one of which could 'literally take a split second'.[58] Everything else in the tourist experience and tourist services was relegated as subsidiary.

The sea, during the nineteenth century, was tamed and domesticated, and seaside architecture including piers and promenades, the use of the beach and development of swimming all 'exerted the mastery of nature on the margins of society.'[59] Seaside resorts, particularly through their architecture, provided concentrations of services 'designed to provide novel, and what were at the time utterly amazing, objects of the tourist gaze'.[60]

Then, in the mid-twentieth century, a fundamental refocusing of the tourist gaze occurred away from resorts. A critical role is given to those social groups 'structuring taste communities' – whose values and practices exert a significant impact on those of other social classes.[61] On the one hand, according to Urry, British resorts and their architecture were deemed tasteless and unfashionable; on the other, there was a new search for 'real holidays', and distinctive and out-of-the-ordinary leisure locations in places where

Sunbathing at Praia da Luz, Portugal, 2001.

nature appears to dominate over culture. As tourists went elsewhere, many older and established seaside towns and their architecture spiralled into decline and decay.

Although appealing and influential,[62] the approach may be criticized. There is an inevitability of consequences with the tourist gaze so piercing that there is little or no room for exceptions, counter processes or conflicting outcomes. Resorts, their builders, users and architecture are powerless and passive, swept along (and sometimes away) by overwhelming processes of change determined by the gaze. Tourism and travel are also conflated with holidays and vacations. Not all holidaymakers and vacationers are tourists in the sense of structuring a holiday around a tour of visual sights, and the coach tour, identified by Urry as the

archetypal vehicle of the collective tourist gaze, is not a dominant seaside holiday form. At least as far as British holidaymakers are concerned, and the point seems also to apply to many other Western vacationers, most seaside visits are relatively sedentary affairs, involving a stay in just one or two resorts or coastal locations.[63]

The visual sense is fetishized. An alternative perspective proposes that the experience and consumption of nature relies on 'multiple sensing', with the natural world 'apprehended through its sounds, its smells, its tastes, its textures and its colours and shapes'.[64] This, indeed, was the experience of seaside nature recorded by William Clarke in 1736. People today continue to take seaside holidays in the anticipation and expectation of varied experiences and activities, with the

Funland amusement arcade on Blackpool's Golden Mile, 2002.

pleasures of the sun – not the search for objects to gaze at – often dominant. Nature is not simply watched or observed, but experienced in a variety of ways. Sunbathing, building sandcastles or rock-pooling, playing in breakers and swimming, surfing and other sporting activities in the sea and along the seashore all involve alternative ways of consuming and sensing nature. And the contemporary resort experience includes other synthetic attractions, from funfairs to clubs assailing the senses. Indeed, most of the architecture of the seaside past and present has been designed not simply with the visual sense in mind – although at best it also provides a spectacular visual feast – but to generate heightened and often extreme experiences across all the senses.

AN UNEASY BALANCE

A common pretence is that society and nature are in harmony at the seaside. There is, though, an alternative story in which seaside nature is repeatedly exploited and destroyed by society and, in turn, society and its individuals are harmed through misunderstanding or mistreating nature.

Even the mid-nineteenth-century amateur naturalists, for instance, according to Gosse's son Edmund, had a profoundly damaging impact:

These rock-basins, fringed by corallines, filled with still water almost as pellucid as the upper air itself, thronged with beautiful sensitive form of life – they exist no longer, they are all profaned, and emptied, and vulgarized. An army of 'collectors' has passed over them, and ravaged every corner of them. The fairy paradise has been violated, the exquisite product of centuries of natural selection has been crushed under the rough paw of well-meaning, idle-minded curiosity.[65]

Young Gosse also bewailed the taming and artificial remodelling of the natural environment of the coast. Reflecting on his first childhood experience of the 'uncouth majesty' of the Devonshire sea and coast at Oddicombe, Torquay, in 1857, he commented how

In these twentieth-century days, a careful munici-
pality has studded the down with rustic seats and
has shut out its dangers with railings, has cut a
winding carriage-drive round the curves of the cove
down to the shore, and has planted sausage-laurels
at intervals in clearings made for that aesthetic
purpose. When I last saw the place, thus smartened
and secured . . . I turned from it in anger and
disgust, and could almost have wept.[66]

A similar outrage was expressed a few decades later
over the rash of suburban expansion covering the previously undeveloped coastline. R. M. Lockley, writing in the
propagandizing *Britain and the Beast* (1937), argued the need
for radical solutions:

Nothing but a dictatorship will save the English coast in
our time . . . When the millennium arrives, when the
battleships are turned into floating world-cruise universi-
ties, perhaps their guns, as a last act before being spiked,
will be allowed to blow to dust the hideous, continuous,
and disfiguring chain of hotels, houses and huts which by
then will completely encircle these islands.[67]

Yet municipal authorities offered alternative representations, especially in their guidebooks, stressing instead
progress, modernity and the transformation of previously
valueless places into new landscapes of leisure. The 1939
official guide to Poole, a rapidly developing and modern
resort and residential area in Dorset, described the
remodelling of the Sandbanks neighbourhood:

Surely nowhere else in this land is found such an idyllic
pleasaunce as the Sandbanks Peninsula . . . entirely

surrounded by sea, and permeate with ozone. Fifty
years ago a wilderness of sand-dune and tussock-grass,
populated only by the gulls, it is now a modern Lido:
its sun-trap residences, hotels and beautiful marine
promenade giving it an exotic charm.[68]

The transformation of Oddicombe and Sandbanks are local
and historical examples of what by the twenty-first century
was presented by the United Nations as an international
issue. A 2001 UN report identified the building of new
resorts as a particular cause for worldwide concern:

There are strong economic incentives to site hotels and
other tourist facilities as near to attractive spots as
possible, regardless of the aesthetic and environmental
damage that may result. Building hotels, marinas and
their supporting infrastructure . . . often greatly changes
natural coastlines and their habitats. In extreme cases,
whole ecosystems – such as wetlands, estuaries,
mangroves and coral reefs – are destroyed or reduced to
insignificance and, as a result, the very survival of key
economic or ecological species is thrown into doubt.[69]

'Sandbanks Road, near Poole', Dorset, before the 1920s and
'30s resort and residential development of the area.

But once a resort is built the environmental impact continues with, for example, the tourist demand for local seafood and souvenirs leading to the over-exploitation of indigenous species and the destruction of habitats by people walking on reefs, diving and snorkelling – there are echoes here of Gosse's description of the environmental impact of the Victorian amateur naturalists – and by the anchors and propellers of boats. Within Britain, a peculiar recent example of environmental degradation was the plundering of shingle and pebble from beaches to create 'natural' domestic garden designs, with the danger that coastal defences would be weakened and magnificent natural features such as the long shingle beach of Chesil Bank in Dorset put at risk.[70]

The exploitation of seaside nature had other unintended consequences for society itself. The poor quality of sea water around British resorts has remained an enduring issue for two centuries. Mostly caused by sewerage effluents flowing into the sea, the pollution of sea water was partly the product of holidaymakers themselves: what they had evacuated in the morning they might be swimming in a few hours later. As John Hassan points out, until the 1990s public authorities in Britain had a profound belief in 'the sea's infinity and unlimited capacity to purify'.[71] The pollution of beach waters, although perhaps glimpsed, touched or sniffed by holidaymakers, was mostly out of sight and out of mind in the sense that dominant opinion held it was not a public-health risk.

The unhealthy and unattractive sea-waters could, though, have spectacular consequences, damming particular resorts and leading to sometimes half-hearted ameliorative measures. There were repeated problems, for example, in the small resort of Worthing in Sussex. In the 1840s the value of the houses on the resort's esplanade was

A DELICIOUS DIP

Bathing Attendant. " Here, Bill ! The gent wants to be took out deep—take 'im *into the drain ! !* "

Bathing and health explored in a 19th-century *Punch* cartoon.

greatly reduced because of the unpleasant smell of the sewerage languishing on the beach; five decades later a disastrous typhoid outbreak caused by a contaminated water supply killed 155 people and led visitors to flee the town.[72] Along the coast at Brighton, one commentator in 1841 described the sewers discharging onto the beach and 'the meandering streams of pollution issuing from those pipes, not far from where bathing takes place, and in hot weather not only smelling abominably, but penetrating into the cellars of some of the houses'.[73] The partial solution, three decades later, was the construction of an Intercepting Sewer, 'a masterpiece of later Victorian civil engineering, culminating in the great barrel-vaulted brick junction chambers'[74] underneath the centre of seaside Brighton and today a popular public tour. The debate about how to handle Brighton's sewerage continued into the twenty-first century.

There was a long, slow struggle to improve British resort seawaters. Into the early post-war period children continued to play on a usually unnoticed architectural feature of the beach, the sewer pipe, sometimes with tragic and fatal results.[75] More recently, in the 1980s and '90s, many British resorts failed to meet European Union bathing-water quality directives. Negative comparisons were made with the seaside elsewhere in Europe and contributed to the erosion of the previously unassailable

'TWIXT SEA & DOWNS

Sunny

WORTHING

BRITAINS SUNSHINE RECORD TOWN

Nature and architecture presented in harmony: mid-20th-century guide to Worthing, Sussex.

To shelter from the sun or not? Marina di Cécina, Italy, 2005.

belief that the seaside was necessarily a place of health. Public repulsion, media interest, growing ecological awareness and concomitant political concern provided a context for environmental campaigning and pressure groups, some local and others national, to assert the need for radical improvement.[76] By the early years of the twenty-first century, organizations such as the Marine Conservation Society and Surfers Against Sewerage painted an improving, although still far from ideal, picture of the English seaside.[77]

Although Britain is often presented as a major culprit in the pollution of resort sea water, the 2001 UN report suggests the problem is worldwide. The UN study estimates that tourists bathing in polluted seas causes 'some 250 million cases of gastroenteritis and upper respiratory disease every year',[78] in turn leading to the loss through disease, disability and death of an estimated 400,000 years of healthy life annually with a cost to worldwide society of $1.6 billion. For all of Dr Russell's prescriptive guidance two-and-a-half centuries before, contemporary bathing in the sea is a hazardous and sometimes fatal activity.

The sun as well as the sea put society at risk. Just as expert opinion had endlessly warned and advised about, and therefore been able to control, bathing in the sea, so there were growing cautions about how to sunbathe. Writing in the late-1930s, Scott warned against the too-rapid and intense use of the sun because 'in the case of anyone who is not robust and amazingly healthy it will almost inevitably have dangerous consequences', and recommended the use of olive oil or coconut oil as 'an effectual preventive of sunburn'.[79] Apart from sunburn and sunstroke, his detailing of the dangers connected with bathing – both in the sun and sea – have a contemporary ring, including the hazards of polluted water and the early degeneration of the skin caused by the sun.

After the Second World War, the range of tanning and sun-protection products multiplied, each associated with a particular image of the seaside. By the 1980s, however, protection from sunburn and the deterioration of the skin became more important than the tan itself.[80] Within just a few years the dread of skin cancer was an added fear. The potentially fatal dangers of the sun were first recognized in

Australia in the 1980s and, despite an extensive public-health campaign, by the early twenty-first century half the Australian population was predicted to develop melanoma at some point in their lives.[81] Despite increasingly dire warnings to young British people, in 2004 about 70 per cent of young Britons still wanted to get a tan while on holiday.[82] The underlying problem was the difficulty in severing the deeply inculcated link between the sun and a tan on one hand and, on the other, health, leisure and pleasure by the sea.

The fear of the sun led to a variety of reactions. A minority of people eschewed the sun, breaking free of the belief in its positive benefits. For many beach-goers, however, a bottle of sun lotion became both a container for a protective liquid and a fashion accessory. There were pharmaceutical responses, including the development of the 'Barbie drug' that promised prevention of skin cancer and an artificial tan with the added benefits of increased libido and weight loss.[83] There was also a growing use of self-tanning products, one of the most popular – St Tropez – named after a fashionable French seaside resort and another – Fiji – after an exotic seaside island. The fake tan as an alternative to sunbathing was a remarkable statement of the continuing allure of the sun and the value many white Western people place on a bronzed body. There were also concerns that the potential flight from the sun would have devastating consequences for the Western seaside holiday industry in warm sunny climes and, perhaps, a new value placed on the traditional cloudy and wet British summer days.[84] The tantalizing implication is that declining resorts and their abandoned architecture will be rejuvenated because of the weather and that a new seaside architecture may emerge designed for the overcast beach and stormy seas. Such a development would be consistent with the previous transformations in the relationships between nature, society and seaside architecture.

The seaside as a place for holidaymakers to fear nature has other dimensions. The terror of the mysterious sea revelled in by eighteenth-century aristocratic society subsequently developed and evolved, although remaining a consistent if subsidiary theme in how the seaside was perceived and experienced. Closeness to nature is a primary attraction of the seaside as a place of recreation, but the natural world is also mysterious and unknowable, and therefore sometimes unreliable and frighteningly dangerous.

Today, many of the most popular literary and filmic representations of the seaside counterbalance people enjoying the beach, sea and resort architecture with sudden, unexpected and fearful natural interventions that destroy a society and nature in harmony. These fears of seaside nature's terrifying characteristics were wonderfully exploited in Peter Benchley's 1974 novel *Jaws* and transformed by Steven Spielberg into the 1975 film of the same name and the first modern movie blockbuster. Nature, in the form of a great white shark, threatens not merely to take a bite out of holidaymakers enjoying the beach pleasures of a small American seaside town, but also destroy the resort itself, dependent on the summer tourist season. The cinematic technique interposes the beach and resort at play with the natural menace from the deep. Alex Garland's novel *The Beach*, also translated into a film, and Chris Kentis's 2004 movie *Open Water*, mercilessly utilize the interplay between society and an unpredictable and destructive nature.

Similarly, one of the attractions of present-day extreme coastal sports, particularly in the context of mundane everyday lives, is meeting and beating the challenge of nature and the apprehension it induces. Even the pleasure of a walk along a pier out over the sea may be enhanced because it is tinged with a sense, however slight, of unease and doubt.

Designing the seaside also involved considerable engineering feats intended to make safe the margin between land and sea. At the turn of the nineteenth into the twentieth century, when for most of the time society appeared to dominate nature, people took great pleasure in watching storms battering piers and promenades. Ultimately, and one of the reasons why society is fascinated by the seaside, nature on the coast cannot be controlled or tamed. Nature has frequently inundated the Western seaside resort or wrecked its architecture, including piers, promenades and seafront buildings, through storm, flood or erosion. Mostly these were local events of local significance. Occasionally, though, the tragic consequences of the natural destruction of the seaside, in terms of the loss of life, had a national or international impact. In south-west England the Lynmouth flood disaster of 1952 killed 34 people;[85] a year later storm surges on the east coast of England led to the destruction of hundreds of holiday homes built on marginal land and the death of dozens of people.[86]

At an altogether different and previously unimagined scale, the Asian tsunami of 2004 wreaked havoc on the recently developed exotic coastal holiday industry that ringed the shores of the Indian Ocean, which was patronized by many thousands of Western holidaymakers. This extreme and seemingly 'freak' – at least in terms of the human lifespan – event destroyed hundreds of thousands of lives and devastated much of the architecture of relatively new seaside resorts. A much longer-term process, global warming, also threatens to destroy the seaside, its beaches and architecture.[87] Whether such events and processes will lead to a fundamental reappraisal of the relationships between society and nature at the seaside, undermining the existing balance between the two, will be resolved over time.

CHAPTER 2
BUILDING THE SEASIDE

In 1885 one perceptive commentator on proposals for a new promenade in Margate, one of London's great seaside leisure sites, described the resort as 'a great business, the gross receipts of which total about a million a year received from visitors'.[1] But resorts were and are peculiar businesses, not least as enterprises that directly or indirectly attempt to profit from nature. However, nature in the raw is free: as we saw in the last chapter, the Revd Clarke paid nothing to sun himself, bathe in the sea or enjoy the views from the cliffs. Resorts and their architecture became an important mechanism for society to consume and commodify seaside nature.

Some seaside architecture – the bathing machine, the pier and the lido, the seafront hotel offering sea views, for example – enhanced the experience of seaside nature and in turn involved a direct monetary transaction. Although rarely in Britain, elsewhere in the West even the use of the beach may be commodified, with the most exclusive zones architecturally embellished and fenced off from people unwilling or unable to pay for the experience. Other forms of resort architecture directly relating to nature – for instance, the promenade or boardwalk, the seafront shelter and seaside parks and gardens – were provided by the state or private companies as communal public attractions designed to lure and keep people in particular seaside places.

Seaside resorts needed to do more than make money from nature, and offered an evolving range of leisure, entertainment and health services for holidaymakers to consume, with the resorts themselves becoming spectacular sites of consumption that needed to be both produced and reproduced.[2] Seaside architecture became a critical part of the process, attracting and enticing visitors, both to a resort overall and to individual seaside buildings, reflecting and helping determine the fortunes of a resort, and defining its character as a site of seaside holidaymaking consumption. Some crucial characteristics of seaside architecture – its eclecticism, the uniqueness of the design challenge, the lack of a coherent architectural symbolism, the frequent emphasis on the showy façade – allowed for a variety of architectural visions. Not simply a physical and material product, seaside architecture became culturally embedded. As a crucial component in the resort environment, it became an integral part of the process through which people as individuals and members of social groups create and develop their identities as seaside holidaymakers.

Cast-iron seat back on the North Pier, Blackpool, 2004.

I've forgotten all about Work at Clacton-on-Sea.

Generic postcard, *c.* 1929, overprinted with the resort name.

right: Postcard, *c.* 1924.

At times, too, the production of the seaside has been explained away in a simplified and partial manner, by concentrating on the role of one individual or family – in Britain, royalty and members of the aristocracy and gentry have, historically, been those most often identified with the making of specific seaside places. An extreme form of fetishizing individuals in seaside history is the treatment frequently given to Brighton's influential eighteenth-century doctor and sea-water promoter, Richard Russell, whose work was mentioned in the previous chapter. The privileging of Russell includes the wall plaque in Brighton's contemporary seafront, commemorating him with the phrase 'if you seek his monument, look around'; through the nineteenth-century French historian Jules Michelet's view that he was 'the inventor of the sea';[3] to recent popularizing seaside historians presenting Russell as 'the man most responsible for . . . the seaside mania of the second half of the eighteenth century',[4] and his medical treatise as 'a permission slip to experiment with a new elixir

For most visitors the seaside resort was an anticipated escape from the everyday, humdrum, ordinary and, perhaps, the present day. Being at the seaside was to be on the edge of the normal environment and, at times, society. Resorts proffered an utopian world combining in various measures leisure, pleasure, health and nature separated from work and sometimes from family and community. This cultural landscape of consumption was subject to various representations and imaginings, and as such was illusionary and reductive.

of health'.[5] In such perspectives Dr Russell not only made Brighton but was also the creator of the Western seaside, and in this sense its original architect and designer. Alternative explanations, however, emphasize that the growing popularity with the therapeutic uses of the sea and the development of seaside resorts had their roots in the changing attitudes to nature and society described in chapter One, privileged, moneyed and professional groups (including doctors) willing to turn their backs on the inland spa towns, the beginnings of the Industrial Revolution, the rapid urbanization of Britain and the rise of the British empire. The most influential of a host of eighteenth-century doctors pronouncing on the benefits of the sea, Russell's success was to be at the right place and at the right time to capitalize on the recently discovered seaside.

TECHNOLOGY AND SOCIETY AT THE SEASIDE

The reality of the make-believe world of the seaside and its architecture was consistently structured around and worked to existing social divisions. Class was the most important, and a determining force on what was built at the seaside. On the Sussex coast south of London, for example, there was a series of attempts by controlling landowners to build exclusive complete resorts for elite and subsequently respectable middle-class visitors. Illustrations range through the late-eighteenth-century plans, largely unfulfilled, of Sir Richard Hotham to develop a seaside resort bearing his own name;[6] the more fully realized proposals, in the 1820s and '30s, of the architects and developers James Burton and his son Decimus, for the planned seaside town of St Leonards;[7] the 1820s development by Thomas Read Kemp of Kemp Town to the east of the established and

The centrepiece of Hothamton Crescent, now the front façade of The Dome, Bognor Regis, Sussex.

The core public buildings of the planned resort at St Leonards; a print, c. 1835, with a 'View of West Ascent, Edlin's Royal Hotel & the Assembly Rooms'.

immensely fashionable Brighton;[8] the role in the mid-nineteenth century of the Duke of Devonshire, the locality's aristocratic and powerful dominant landowner, in determining the shape and style of Eastbourne, for many decades one of Britain's most fashionable and elitist resorts;[9] to the similar part played in the late nineteenth century by the De La

Kemp Town, Brighton, in 2005.

Warr family in the creation of Bexhill-on-Sea.[10] Jane Austen, in her unfinished novel *Sanditon*, satirising the attempted development of a fashionable resort in the early nineteenth century, describes the importance of both landscape and architecture to designing the seaside.[11] These developments drew on established traditions and architectural styles from inland. The designs for Hothamton and St Leonards, for example, copied the main elements, such as assembly room and baths, of the most successful inland spa towns. Stylistically, the early classical and the later heavy Victorian architecture developed in the most fashionable residential areas of London were both transferred to the seaside. But being by the sea could make an essential difference, with architects and designers laying out towns and estates in full view of the sea and shore: unlike more ordinary inland developments, at the seaside the built form of respectable society butted up against raw, untamed nature.

Planned complete resorts with hegemonic landowners

Pelham Crescent, Hastings, 1824, built on land secured after the cliff face had been cut back.

were at one extreme. At the other were unplanned resorts, developing gradually over time and with a diversity of landowners; but even these seaside places could accrue a particular style and feel in response to evolving social structures and technological possibilities. In the late 1950s Ivor Brown captured how each successive wave of holiday-making and its resultant seaside building was imprinted on the small English resort, to become 'a social chronicle as well as a decoration of our shores. It wears its history on its sleeve – in stripes.'[12]

Developing economic and class structures in Western countries, together with political struggle and emancipation in evolving parliamentary democracies, lay behind the rising standards of living and improved holiday entitlements that allowed an ever-broader range of people to holiday by the sea.[13] The broadening of the potential class make-up of resorts, facilitated by significant technological changes in transportation, had major implications for seaside towns and their architecture, resonating in different guises to the present day.[14]

Before the introduction of the steam engine and rail transport technologies, few resorts were within reach of other than 'persons of high rank and fashion': in Britain, Gravesend and Margate on the Thames estuary, with cheaper and comparatively easy access by water from London, were among the exceptions.[15] In the mid-nineteenth century, however, the coming of the railway permitted faster, easier and cheaper trips to the coast, eventually undermining the previous class basis of many European resorts. As the cost of using the technology fell, an ever-increasing number of middle- and working-class visitors were carried by train to the expanding resorts, as day-trippers or to holiday by the sea for a week or more.[16] The consequences included radical changes to the urban morphology of many resorts, as the new entrepôt stations – often architectural spectacles in their own right – became magnets, sucking development to them, and usually linked to the seafront by prosperous thoroughfares. Occasionally, as at Ramsgate, Kent, a station was located on the beach itself, disgorging excited visitors directly into their seaside experience.

Building and designing seaside resorts took place in the context of evolving construction and building technologies and their design and social uses. To cope with the influx of new visitors in the second half of the nineteenth century, innovative, modern, seaside architecture emerged. Iron and subsequently steel, combined with concrete and plate glass, became the main building materials of seaside entertainment buildings. The cast-iron manufacturing process, for example, ideal for the cheap production of prefabricated identical elements, was used to create the core elements of the range of seaside buildings from piers to pavilions and concert halls to winter gardens that clothed the expanding resorts and provided for a large and often diverse holidaymaking population rather than the small and elite clientele of the past. Iron featured again in the railings, shelters and bandstands on new seafront promenades. Not simply a functional structural building material, cast iron allowed architecture to be embroidered with symbolic decoration.[17] Apart from lamp-posts and railings marked by the obligatory resort crest or shield, cast-iron seaside decoration used an eclectic blend of

A Blackpool postcard, c. 1918.

elements, sometimes drawing on standard pattern-books from iron foundries, but determinedly ornamental and often Oriental in its design and purpose.

The invention of new piling and bracing techniques and advances in constructing metal-framed buildings enabled the quick construction of pleasure piers over the sea.[18] Of all seaside pleasure buildings, piers, so often broken by storms and swept away by tides, reveal the design and construction challenges inherent in building in an extreme environment between land and sea; the challenge was, though, compounded because in developing new and spectacular pleasure architecture the builders often pushed existing design and construction knowledge beyond its limits.

Society and architecture on display. George Cruikshank, *Beauties of Brighton*, 1826.

'Shocking savages' invading a select resort: the anticipated consequences and partially accurate observations on the coming of the railway to Brighton, late 1830s.

LIFE WOULD BE PLEASANT, BUT FOR ITS
"PLEASURES."—*Sir Cornewall Lewis*

In consequence of the English watering-places being
crowded, people are glad to find sleeping accommodation in
the bathing-machines.

Boots (from Jones's Hotel). "I've brought your shaving
water, sir; and you'll please to take care of your boots on
the steps, gents: the tide's just a comin' in!"

The overcrowded seaside viewed by a 19th-century *Punch* cartoonist.

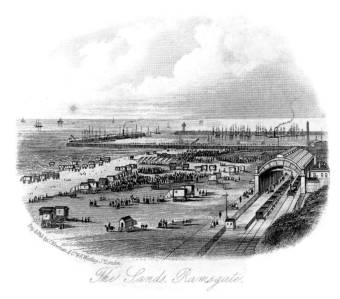

'The Sands, Ramsgate', from *Twelve Views of Ramsgate* (London, *c.* 1850s), showing the railway station situated by the beach.

The invasion of the seaside by working-class people also took place in North America. One disapproving commentator, writing in the last quarter of the nineteenth century about excursions from New York to Coney Island and Manhattan Beach, noted: 'The people who participate in these excursions belong mainly to the working-classes; among them are a great many rough characters, and there is occasionally a good deal of drunkenness and rowdyism manifested in their behavior.'[19] Coney Island became the iconic early twentieth-century amusement resort and the site of a new built form for pleasure and entertainment, the fixed amusement fair. Copied in many large working-class resorts on both sides of the Atlantic, amusement fairs were usually on or close to the seafront and, in the case of the American and British amusement piers, even built above the sea.

Apart from class, in the United States significant social schisms around ethnicity also had conse-quences for the use and design of seaside resorts. In a white-dominated resort such as Atlantic City, African Americans as vacationers (although not as resort workers) were excluded from much of the town and from all but limited areas of the beach and hotels run by other African Americans.[20]

Responding to the expansion of the seaside and new demands from new holidaymakers, the designers of the seaside were enormously imaginative – and sometimes derivative – both in the architecture of seaside pleasure buildings and in their response to new technologies.[21] Apart from seaside pleasure piers, the most iconic

Blackpool's North Pier, Tower and Big Wheel, *c.* 1925.

The promotion of the English select resort in the late-1930s – theatre-goers leaving Southport's Garrick Theatre, with the resort's 'Fairyland' illuminations glimpsed to the left. From a painting by Fortunino Matania reproduced in *Sunny Southport, Official Guide, 1938–39*.

entertainment building at the British seaside was the Eiffel Tower-inspired tower of 1894 designed by Maxwell and Tukes of Manchester for the booming and hugely successful northern resort of Blackpool. Sustained for more than a century as the centrepiece of England's most popular seaside resort, the Blackpool Tower is Britain's single most famous seaside building.

In the twentieth century the char-à-banc and then motor coach, travelling along a developing road system and parked in new resort coach stations, became a favoured more flexible route to the sea. The automobile also emerged as an adaptable private form of transport, allowing independent access to a huge range of seaside places, made more accommodating still by towing a portable home – the caravan – or replaced in North America by RVs. The hegemony of the car had various consequences for the seaside. From the 1930s the older resorts struggled to react to the demands for parking spaces. In Hastings, for example, one early 1930s response was the construction of England's first 'under-

ground municipal car park', using the enclosed empty space between an old and a new sea wall, and also allowing the building of a wide new road along the seafront.

Other materials came to the fore, especially steel and reinforced concrete, used, in the 1920s and '30s, to construct a new architecture for the sun, including massive sea defences embroidered with walks and sun terraces, modernist lidos, and minimalist Art Deco pavilions and hotels. Buildings included modernist structures such as the De La Warr Pavilion of 1935 designed by Erich Mendelsohn and Serge Chermayeff and sited incongruously on Bexhill's otherwise sedately suburban seafront, and the equally out-of-place Midland Hotel, constructed two years earlier to the designs of Oliver Hill with decorative ornamentation added by contemporary artists, on Morecambe's decidedly Victorian coastal fringe. Concrete was the making of a number of individual seaside builders: for example, the borough engineer for Hastings, Sidney Little, became known as the Concrete King for his 'essays in reinforced concrete' that

resulted in the wholesale redevelopment of the resort's seafront.[22]

Once the middle and working classes were able to holiday by the sea, one persistent conflict revolved around whether resorts were select and respectable or popular and open to all-comers. At times the controlling seaside authorities, including landowners and municipal authorities in Britain, deliberately marketed their resorts to the wealthy exclusive market. The use of the seaside and its architecture by holidaymakers and the social tone of a resort were regulated through a range of mechanisms, albeit sometimes unsuccessfully. A higher social tone could be attempted, for example, by resisting the freeing of restrictions on bathing, entertainment and transport that might lure working-class visitors and opposing the development of facilities, including piers in the second half of the nineteenth century and holiday camps in the inter-war period of the next century, thought to endanger a resort's reputation by making it more popular.[23]

One response in exclusive resorts to the potential threat of the new visitors mingling with the status quo was to use architecture to segregate the fashionable and respectable from the unsavoury and the rough. At an extreme, and particularly in prim and respectable towns such as Bexhill and Folkestone, this was achieved through commanding entrances and gates guarded by police and gatekeepers protecting select piers, promenades and parks

top: A day trip to the beach, Margate, Kent, c. 1930s.

middle: A complete resort: Scarborough, c. 1890s, with the Spa entertainment complex, Grand Hotel and bathing machines using the sands.

right: English working-class seaside catering in the mid-20th century: Garden Café, Dreamland, Margate, Kent, 1957.

The complete resort: Butlins Holiday Camp, Clacton, late 1960s. Cover of the camp guide.

The fashionable Leas in Folkestone, early 20th century.

from invasion by hoi polloi.[24] A new breed of 'grand' luxury seaside hotel was also developed with imposing architecture, too daunting for most working-class holidaymakers to venture across the threshold or risk the wrath of the uniformed doorman. Through such architectural and design devices, which in the following century developed across the

Western world to include gated and private residential estates, golf courses, health clubs and private resorts all hidden from public gaze, the upper classes were able to maintain some semblance of exclusivity at the seaside. Although the language has changed, the contrast between mass-market and exclusive resorts – and sometimes between working-class and middle- and upper-class zones within a resort – continues into the present century.

Even though hegemonic landowners continued to have a formidable influence in some British resorts into the twentieth century, from the middle of the nineteenth seaside town councils became progressively more critical.[25] The municipal authorities increasingly judged and determined the architecture of the seaside and what should be built. This eventually extended to funding and designing individual seaside buildings and producing the design and architecture of the principal open spaces, particularly the important mood-creating and tone-setting seafront promenade and public gardens. The resort and its architecture was then vigorously promoted through official guides and other advertising mechanisms.

Seaside architecture, particularly in the principal entertainment buildings and public open spaces, was designed as a visual spectacle. But it also performed other functions, both allowing the seaside to be commodified and helping create the resort experience consumed by holidaymakers. As such, resort architecture had a wider sensory

role than merely the visual. For example, it was bound up with the evolving sounds of the seaside, both natural and artificial. In Britain, most apparent was seaside architecture, in the form of concert halls, winter gardens, pavilions and seafront bandstands, as a vehicle for listening to music. Architecture combined with music – and especially from the mid-nineteenth century as specific seaside music developed – was an important part of designing the seaside. One early twentieth-century guidebook to the deeply staid and respectable Folkestone described how architecture and music were related:

> But the sociable will prefer the Leas, the fashionable rendezvous of the town, where excellent bands play morning, afternoon and evening. On wet mornings you can sit in the Leas Shelter, a spacious concert hall formed in the face of the cliff and while listening to the Red Band discourse sweet music, you have the panorama of the English Channel and the Straits of Dover. In the afternoon you can visit the Leas Pavilion, and have a delightful afternoon tea to the music of a very good string band composed of lady performers. They also cater for you in the same way on the Victoria Pier.[26]

This was the musical architecture of the respectable European resort in the past;[27] vestiges of both the music and the buildings remain in the early twenty-first century, usually promoted as nostalgia or heritage. But the musical sounds of the seaside evolved in other ways. During the twentieth century, Hawai'i, for example, became a seaside

The informal seaside, 'The Camp, St Osyth Beach' near Clacton, Essex. Posted in July 1938, Dick writes: 'We are having a week here, and so far have had grand weather. Our shack is marked with the arrow'.

Bandstand music in Folkestone, early 20th century.

'set to music',[28] which then developed into the popular music of surfing and an associated youth beach culture, while by the end of the century a number of reinvented British resorts, including Brighton and Bournemouth, and Mediterranean resorts marketed to young people, developed a contemporary music and architecture of clubbing. The example of the evolving relationship between resort architecture and the music of the seaside is also one

Redundant railway carriages converted into seafront bunga-lows at 'Patsy Woo', c. 1930.

The exotic architectural splendour of a French Riviera villa, photographed in 2003.

illustration of how age, as well as class, as a social division could impact on different seaside places and the production and use of resort architecture.

But away from the established resorts, there were always new seaside places to be discovered and new resorts to be designed and built. Towards the end of the nineteenth century, for example, John Packard described an uneven process of resort development on the north-eastern seaboard of the United States:

The number of sea-side resorts has been greatly multiplied within the last few years . . . From Maine to the lower end of New Jersey, the Atlantic coast is fringed

with watering-places. Some of these, long established, have been greatly enlarged and improved; others are still struggling to obtain popular favor . . . On the coast farther south, there are very probably other very suit-able beaches for health-resorts, but they are not widely known or largely patronized.[29]

Often these new holiday locations were discovered and exploited first by people eager to distance themselves from the established resorts and searching for a coastal idyll. From the later decades of the nineteenth century, artists and others able and willing to separate themselves from the confines of contemporary society and instead attracted by what appeared as unsullied nature or an undisturbed and authentic indigenous culture were partic-ularly important in the process of discovery.[30] In Europe and in the context of the democratization and enlarge-ment of established resorts, a search for new seaside places and changes in attitudes to seaside nature, artists retreated from the colder northern overcast landscapes they had previously painted, turning instead to the sunshine, warmth and brighter colours of the Mediter-ranean; those that stayed 'southernized' northern beaches.[31] Progressively the human figures portrayed by many artists moved away from dignified local working people to leisure-enjoying seaside visitors.[32]

There were also other processes of discovery and trans-formation at work in reaction to existing resorts. One was a get-away-from-it-all search for personal freedom by the sea, seen most clearly in the plotland shacks of the inter-war years, but still visible in the use of beach huts today. In the United States racial exclusion and discrimination in estab-lished resorts led to the separate development of both African American and Jewish resorts.[33]

Bandstand, Eastbourne, 1997.

Bandstand, Ahlbeck, Baltic coast of Germany, 2000.

The fantastic architecture of seaside Nice, *c.* 1910.

The new delights of the summertime Riviera, with the architectural expressions of an earlier seaside experience in the background, *c.* 1935.

At another extreme, for the most privileged visitors to the seaside one option was to fashion their own exclusive seaside places. Most famously, in the second half of the nineteenth century, European aristocracy created the French Riviera. It involved a remarkable transformation of the locality into a *belle époque*-inspired winter playground by the sea. The architectural components included luxury hotels, private villas, exotic gardens, casinos, opera houses and the Oriental pier at Nice. Subsequently out-of-doors sports –

sailing, tennis and golf – became a significant part of the Côte d'Azur elitist seaside, with an architectural manifestation of country clubs and yacht clubs. Often there were references back to other places. The oldest Riviera golf course founded in Cannes in 1891 was modelled on a course at the home of golf, St Andrews in Scotland, and included a half-timbered clubhouse, part colonial Indian bungalow and part Tudorbethan manor house.[34] But the coming of the sun subsequently transformed the Riviera into a summertime seaside place, with the summer beach replacing the winter promenade as the critical seaside site.[35] After the Second World War, the region's exclusive reputation was increasingly eroded and nostalgically mourned through books celebrating its past elite holidaymakers and architecture.[36] Meanwhile, although still partly promoted as stylish and exclusive, the Riviera was remade into a more democratic holiday place and, perhaps more significantly, a new postmodern workplace.[37]

The continued evolution of transport technologies had considerable significance for resorts and their holidaymakers. The coming of the car changed the nature of the older resorts, either ignored as people found new places to make their holidays or, if their popularity was sustained, swamped by waves of motor vehicles. In many successful European resorts, the old promenades and parades became traffic-laden thoroughfares, separating seafront from town, while in North America the response was often more automobile-friendly still and, in resorts such as Atlantic City, combined with a characteristic continual reinvention and replacement of seaside architecture.[38] The car also opened up previously remote and inaccessible seaside places and once more left its physical mark on seaside villages visually dominated by parking places and car parks.

In the second half of the twentieth century, another transport revolution took Europeans and North Americans into the air and away to holidays far from the northern cities and their accompanying resorts. Air travel has allowed the thirst for sun, warmth, the exotic and 'foreign' to be quenched, ensuring the burgeoning of new southern resorts. Governments, local politicians and business people, and multinational holiday companies, were often quick to realize the potential of the undeveloped seaside.[39] Concrete and steel became the defining building materials of the resultant new sunny, warm and southern resorts. Seaside places initially visited by travellers subsequently became the habitat of tourists and holidaymakers. In the process the 'authentic' was transformed and remade into the artificial.[40] Air travel and holidays in the sun also contributed to the decline and dereliction of the least fashionable northern resorts, with often-ruinous consequences for once proud architectural spectacles. Examples are invidious, but they include Margate and Morecambe in England and Coney Island and Atlantic City in the United States. Atlantic City has subsequently been remarkably regenerated through a new casino economy; elsewhere plans for rejuvenation often centre on restoring existing architecture and resort open spaces or proposals for new seaside buildings.

We began with some examples of late-eighteenth- and nineteenth-century planned resorts on the south coast of England. The envisaging and making of complete resorts designed to a grand plan, and reflecting the society and

Promoting the summertime Côte d'Azur in a French railway poster of 1955: sun, sea and sand, tropical vegetation, architecture and, in the foreground, the promise of sex.

technology of the times, have continued. Recent iconic examples include La Grande Motte in France, Seaside in the United States and The Palms in the Arab emirate of Dubai. The powerfully modernist French Mediterranean resort, La Grande Motte, was designed in the 1960s by Jean Balladur

One of the iconic buildings, designed in the 1960s, to reflect natural shapes at La Grande Motte, a planned resort on the French Mediterranean coast.

left: A Menorca seaside hotel, 1995.

as part of a government initiative to modernize the French seaside in reaction to increasing competition from Spain.[41] In complete architectural contrast, in the 1980s one landowner, Robert Davies, and two architects, Andrés Duany and Elizabeth Plater-Zyberk, fashioned Seaside, a much-debated 'neo-traditional' new town beside the sea on the Gulf coast of Florida, looking to the past in building for the present.[42] Most ambitious of all, The Palms artificial island resorts on the shores of Dubai are promoted in the early twenty-first century as the biggest construction projects in the world and as the creation of the ruler of Dubai.[43]

RESPONDING TO THE CHANGING SEASIDE

Resorts and their architecture are not simply made but continually remade, adapting to new ways of using nature, responding to changing social structures and processes, fashions in leisure and entertainment, and developing ideas about the seaside and its use.

Between the two twentieth-century world wars, a theme repeatedly explored by British architectural and planning commentators was how to modernize seaside resorts and their architecture. In the context of the inadequacies of existing resorts and the growing number of working-class people visiting the seaside, the concern was with the production of a modern architecture of leisure responding to the widespread interest in health and fitness in the open air and sunshine. Edmund Vale, rehearsing a commonly held view, believed 'A bombardment is the very thing that most of our seaside towns need; it is the only way out of a horrible architectural impasse.'[44] Wesley Dougill used the influential professional journal *Town Planning Review* to urge a new planning and architecture for the British holiday resorts in response to the 'great movement seawards' that had 'popularised' former select seaside towns, 'artificialised' natural ones and changed and enlarged previously small resorts.[45] Dougill was ambivalent about the massive coastal changes taking place, praising the 'democratisation of the coast' but fearing, as did many

The salacious attractions of the Montmartre Theatre on Blackpool s Golden Mile, c. 1950s.

The delights of the amusement park: Dreamland, Margate, Kent, 1954.

commentators, the concreting over of vast stretches of scenic coastline with private enterprise as the chief villain. Using examples of modern building planning around the coast, from the large-scale amusement fairs of Dreamland at Margate and 'Pleasure Town' at Blackpool to the smaller scale of shelters, bungalows and pavilions elsewhere, and quoting approvingly of both American coastal planning and the 'rationalisation' of the Italian seaboard with new resorts and 'large holiday establishments for children and operatives from inland towns', Dougill thought that 'beauty, economy and fitness for purpose and environment' were not irreconcilable.

Not to be outdone, the *Architectural Review* responded with a seaside theme issue in 1936 with contributions by many of the most respected commentators of the day that

set out 'the programme the architect has to follow in planning for leisure spent at the seaside'.[46] The primary virtues of the seaside, the newly appreciated ones of light and air, provided architects with the maximum opportunity of 'achieving a characteristic modern expression'. This was in contrast to a range of problems, including lack of planning and zoning, poor or inappropriate design, growing traffic congestion, the poverty of entertainments and amusements at the seaside and, for some authors, the very character of the holidaymakers themselves.

There were conservative and reactionary views, with Osbert Lancaster bemoaning the vast clutter of modern resorts, including the 'unnecessary' bathing pools, the 'hideous rash' of bungalows and the 'gim-crack' funfairs disfiguring the south coast. Lancaster believed the 'vulgarization' of the seaside was a result of the American phase of civilization and an inability to control present-day abundance. Harry Roberts, in contrast, saw the rise of 'synthetic' resorts such as Blackpool, Margate and Southend as a product of the 'half-cultivated public of the moment' being 'too tired, mentally, physically and emotionally, to entertain themselves'.[47] His proposed solution was to 'establish a habit of wise and wholesome living' and the provision of open-air gymnasia, playrooms, reading and music rooms and lounges.

There were more cautious voices, less keen simply to abandon the past for some uncertain future. Writing two years later, John Piper urged a return to 'the sound tradition of maritime building that we have begun to lose track of' and the nautical style of architecture to be found both in the 'simple functionalism' of coastal maritime objects such as harbour piers, cottages and lighthouses as well as the 'gaiety' of good coastal resort building.[48]

The debate was interrupted by war and was then largely stifled as resorts responded to the need for a post-war reconstruction project and the revitalized demands of the holidaymaking public. By the late 1960s, however, many individual resort authorities were increasingly aware that the resort business could not be taken for granted. For example, a 1969 holiday survey commissioned by Ramsgate Council to provide guidance on the future of the holiday resort, recommended that the local authority consider a host of measures to improve the physical environment of the resort including building a multi-purpose entertainment centre, the construction of 'extra shelters and toilets on promenade, piers and by main sands' and dealing with 'sewage odours on West Cliff beach area'.[49]

The incipient decline of many British resorts led, in the 1970s, to conflicting views about the most appropriate response. In the face of the threat of the overseas package holiday, for the English Tourist Board the major issues were to do with the provision of cheaper accommodation and all-weather leisure facilities.[50] There were lone voices suggesting that architecture had a role to play, with the historian, James Walvin, commenting on how over the previous twenty years 'new structures of foam, plastic and polythene' had made resorts into different places, and arguing that resorts represented 'classic examples of Victorian and Edwardian architecture and style (particularly in their theatres, piers and hotels), and it is consequently all the more important to preserve them'.[51]

In the last two decades of the twentieth century some commentators became deeply pessimistic about the future of British resorts, arguing that they were in the last stages of the product life cycle and experiencing long-term market decline. The concomitant disintegration of the 'economic and built fabric of the resorts . . . now threatens their character as places to visit, live, work and retire. Indeed, it is the very buildings and structures which once defined the character and nature of the resorts – piers, theatres, large hotels – which are now threatened or have already been lost.'[52] More recently still an alternative analysis has argued that reports of the death of the British seaside 'have been greatly exaggerated'[53] and provides new material indicating 'The common assumption that the British seaside tourist business is in terminal decline is profoundly wrong' and that 'The seaside tourist industry is one that should be nurtured, not written-off as a lost cause.'[54]

Nonetheless, from the 1960s there was a remarkable neglect of much of Britain's seaside architecture. The eclecticism and diversity of seaside architecture were part of the problem, allowing declining resorts searching for new roles to use architecture designed for other cultural purposes – numerous British seafronts were redeveloped with plain boxes of conference and entertainment centres or with nondescript apartment blocks seeming to shun the seaside location. On the other side of the Atlantic the decline of seaside places such as Coney Island saw the sites of former amusement parks refilled with ordinary urban apartment developments.

There was growing media recognition of the decline of the British seaside. The decay of seaside architecture in 'the last resort' was increasingly related to social changes, Britain's seaside towns becoming 'the haunts not of the holidaymakers but of the drifter, the jobless youngster, the psychiatric patient and the lone mum'.[55]

Artist's impression of the proposed Turner Contemporary Art Gallery, intended by Kent County Council to assist in the regeneration of Margate as a resort.

The 2003 Frank Gehry proposal for residential towers on the Hove seafront, Sussex.

But a more recent string of official reports, charting the decline, over several decades, of the English seaside resort and arguing that many of the problems sprang from the age of resorts, a failure to reinvest in the product and a reliance on low cost and declining markets, also recognized that the regeneration of the seaside might be achieved through investment in the built environment and architecture. The titles of these reports using maritime analogies – *Shifting Sands*, *Sea Changes* and *Turning the Tide* – suggesting a natural process of uncontrollable movement, reflected an uncertain optimism that architecture, either through the restoration of heritage buildings or new build, could form the basis of a regenerated seaside.[56] In contrast, for example, to the confident and wholesale regeneration of architecture and resorts on the unified Germany's Baltic coast, in Britain seaside regeneration has had relatively weak economic, political and cultural foundations, and the process therefore has been often unsure, protracted and piecemeal.

The media, although more positive than a decade before, remained ambivalent in their view of the British seaside. In one perspective:

> Rumours of the death of the Great British Seaside seem greatly exaggerated . . . Britain's savviest seaside towns are reinventing themselves to cater for a new generation of pleasure seekers . . . the clued-up resorts know they have to adapt or die.[57]

Although Scarborough was awarded the title of 'Most Improved Resort in 2002', its reinvention, like that of other resorts, was uneven. One journalist could discern 'the fault lines between the old regime and the new vision of a revivified Scarborough', contrasting one beautifully restored hotel 'full of the Yorkshire *beau monde* sipping Darjeeling or revving up for a wedding with a few bottles of something sparkling', with the huge Grand Hotel, 'a holiday camp parcelled up in a wrecked seaside château'.[58]

By the early twenty-first century there was, nonetheless, a growing official belief that architecture could regenerate depressed resorts, and that an iconic new public building capitalizing on a natural attraction or local historical heritage would generate new flows of tourists and a revitalized economy. In the insecure and uncertain present-day Margate, for example, the proposed Turner Contemporary Art Gallery, building on the nineteenth-century painter's association with the locality, is planned as a bold architectural statement sited on the resort's ancient harbour pier. Elsewhere, in resorts that had been reinvented as fashionable twenty-first-century seaside places, the crucial issues revolved around sifting and selecting from the competing demands for new building by the sea. In Brighton and Hove, proclaimed as a successfully remade seaside city, one of the imaginative and controversial schemes was for residential towers designed by Frank Gehry and inspired by images of Edwardian female promenaders on the nearby Hove seafront lawns.

CHAPTER 3
REPRESENTING THE EDGE

Contemporary consumers buying holidays at the sea are assailed with images of the seaside and its architecture designed to sell the product to us. We know to read between the lines, that the silences and omissions may be as important as what is said and not to take promotional material for seaside places too literally. But the holiday brochure, resort website and the seaside travelogue are often still important as crucial 'guides' to the offered experience. What actual and potential seaside visitors make of the promotional materials they encounter depends on the dynamic relationship between the representation and the viewer or reader: marketing images, however carefully constructed, are always mediated by holidaymakers' own experiences, memories and imaginations and will sometimes be contested.

Marketing and promoting the seaside centres on attracting and enticing holidaymakers, allowing the seaside builders to make a success of their investment and seaside authorities to ensure the popularity of their resorts. The core of place promotion has been neatly summarized by Stephen Ward as 'Making and propagating place images that are sufficiently attractive to persuade place users . . . to part with their money. The place is packaged and sold as a commodity . . . in which any kinds of problems are played down.'[1]

Selling resorts and their architecture takes place in the context of broader social and cultural definitions of the seaside, and ideas and images of gender, class, respectability or popularity, and of nature, for example, have been inter-played with representations of resorts and seaside architecture in specific if evolving ways. Buying a room in a hotel, a ticket for a seaside attraction or simply sunbathing on a beach also involves buying into a more general idea of the seaside and a particular resort. We consume a reality and an image, and the two may not match.

SEASIDE GUIDES AND SEASIDE GIRLS

Selling the seaside has also often been by way of allusion to other places and other things. Frequently in Britain and elsewhere in the West resorts have been associated with other successful or exotic places. During the nineteenth century the name and idea of Brighton, the first great seaside resort, was relentlessly applied to other seasides in Britain and exported to emerging seaside places in the USA and Australia. Similarly, during the twentieth century, the exotic and luxurious connotations of 'Riviera' were seized upon by other, perhaps more mundane seaside places. 'Dreamland', an iconic if unsuccessful Coney Island amusement park, was imported to Britain and used at Margate. More generic concepts and ideas of leisure and pleasure were used to describe and even design seaside buildings. The outstanding early example is the use of 'Oriental' architecture to create the startlingly original and iconic Royal Pavilion in Brighton. During the mid-twentieth century, piers – their owners desperate to market them as modern and not products of the previous century – were likened to cruise liners and holiday camps, while a few decades later

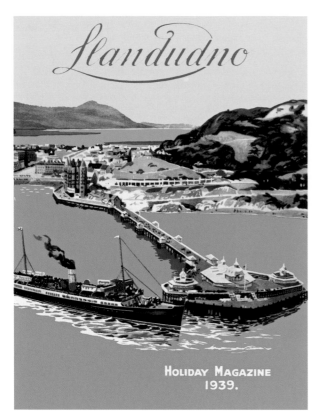

Architecture selling the Welsh seaside.

indoor swimming pools drew on the symbolism of the tropical. But the process has also been reversed with beach huts, deckchairs and the beach more generally nowadays constantly used as analogies for leisure and pleasure whether inland or on the coast.

Before the last quarter of the nineteenth century, when Blackpool became the first British resort to advertise its attractions through posters and illustrated brochures,[2] the promotion of resorts was a less secure business, outside the direct control of seaside authorities. Instead, most seaside promotional materials were commercially produced or generated by individual seaside businesses; they included guidebooks, souvenir albums of views and topographical engravings, and press advertisements for particular attractions. The problem with the commercial guidebooks was that there was no guarantee that their authors would praise the resort they were writing about. For instance, one 1860s guide to Herne Bay, a small, sedate resort on the edge of the

Thames estuary, was damning in describing a 'sort of fatality' hanging over the resort, the 'melancholy spectacle' of the pier and the swimming bath as 'a mere dry cave, from the openings in which branches of trees may actually be seen protruding'.[3] For the first half of the twentieth century the most influential of the commercially produced guides were Ward Lock's 'pictorial and descriptive guides' to groups of English resorts.[4] In part because they carried advertisements for local hotels, Ward Lock guides were rarely critical, instead flattering each resort and its natural attractions, facilities and architecture.

From the late nineteenth century the formal marketing and place promotion of and by resorts through municipal guidebooks, press advertising and pictorial railway publicity posters developed to become common throughout seaside Britain and mainland Europe and the United States.[5] In Britain, by the inter-war years, the mass market for seaside holidays, increased competition between resorts and the success of 'municipal enterprise' led to the promotion of even the most conservative resorts.[6] These 'official' promotional materials for British resorts most often explored the idealized interrelationships between holidaymakers, nature and architecture.

In selling the seaside, and promoting particular social relationships, images and ideas of social class were managed and manipulated. For much of the twentieth century, for example, even the most popular resorts resorted to representations of gentility in their guides: Blackpool's 1930s publicity, for example, suppressed the beer consumed and the flat caps worn by many male visitors to the resort at the time.[7] Respectable resorts, or those with pretensions to be so, went still further in stressing an elite and fashionable social tone and distinguished and imposing architecture. Guidebooks made it clear that some

Blackpool as a sunny, young, stylish and alluring resort.
Blackpool, original oil painting for an LMS poster, *c.* 1930s,
artwork by Fortunino Matania.

holidaymakers were unwelcome: for instance, a Torquay
guide for the mid-1920s asserted that the resort had 'no
appeal to the "cheap" tripper',[8] and a decade later a Bexhill
official guidebook described how 'Though attempting nothing on a big scale, for which, not being a popular or Bank
Holiday resort, it has no use, Bexhill is proud of its long and
well-laid-out sea walk.'[9]

The titles and slogans on the cover of guides often
summarized the intended representation. In 1938 *Sunny
Southport* was also 'England's Seaside Garden City',[10]
although by 1957 it had become 'England's Continental
Resort'.[11] Post-war, the largest popular resorts became more
blatant in advertising what they were about. In the 1980s

and '90s Blackpool was the extreme example, declaring it
was 'The Big One!', 'Costa Notta Lotta', 'Where the family
Fun Never Stops' and 'So Much Fun You Can Taste It'.

The most dominant of resort promotion images of
social relationships have been of young women, ranging
from late-nineteenth-century posters of women enjoying
the seaside to post-war photographs of bathing beauties.
These pervasive images of 'the seaside girl' represented the
development of a spectacle and a cultural ideal that were
used to sell a huge range of commodities and, once devised,
meant that the beach as a 'space of leisure had been sexual-
ized'.[12] The late Victorian advertising portrayal of the
seaside girl typically showed her alone or with one or two

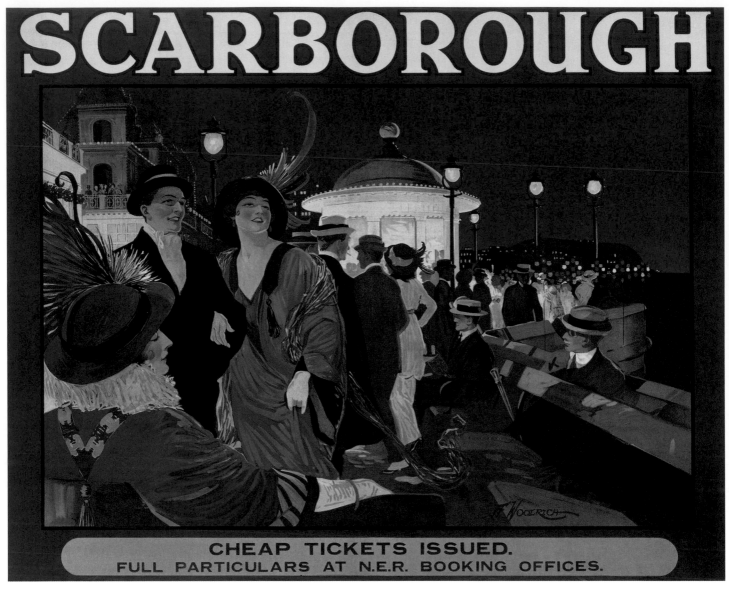

SCARBOROUGH

CHEAP TICKETS ISSUED.
FULL PARTICULARS AT N.E.R. BOOKING OFFICES.

The Spa at Scarborough with its stylish visitors, NER poster,
c. 1910, artwork by J. F. Woolrich.

other young women on the beach or in the sea – perhaps viewing a sunset or bathing – and often with a wistful or thoughtful expression. She subsequently appeared in new guises and was put to new uses across the Western world, sometimes making appearances far from the coast and being used to sell everything from holidays to automobiles with Paul Gallico, for example, arguing an 'appreciable part

of the great American real estate boom was built upon photographs of girl swimmers used in advertising'.[13]

Resorts capitalized on the iconic image in various ways. The young woman appeared in the decoration of seaside buildings. She was embodied in flesh and blood and put into an architectural context with the invention in the United States of the bathing beauty and the beauty pageant.

The seaside girl on show in a postard showing the first Atlantic City beauty pageant, 1921.

'Parade of Bathing Belles at the Colonnade', Bexhill, *c.* 1934.

Hooded beauty contest, Margate Lido, *c.* 1950s. The spectators have serious expressions, the thoughts of the participants are unknown.

Andrew Johnson, *Brighton and Hove*, inter-war publicity poster. Such promotional techniques failed to halt the decline of Brighton as a fashionable resort.

right: The English seaside goes to mainland Europe. From the *Southport Official Guide, 1957.*

between seaside architecture and sex. In Britain from the 1970s changing gender politics coincided with the waning of many resorts, and the formal beauty contest slowly declined along with the deterioration of much seaside architecture. It was replaced by new spectacles of sex at the seaside including wet T-shirt competitions, the uninhibited and celebratory displays of bodies in Mediterranean clubbing resorts and on American college

The most famous, the Miss America Beauty Pageant, began in 1921 in Atlantic City as part of the 'Fall Frolic' festivities designed to extend the summer season. An estimated 100,000 spectators watched the beachfront parade of contestants in bathing suits at the Atlantic City Yacht Club. The winner was Margaret Gorman, described in the *New York Times* as representing 'the type of womanhood America needs – strong, red blooded, able to shoulder the responsibilities of homemaking and motherhood. It is in her type that the hope of the country rests.'[14]

The beauty contest subsequently became a crucial adjunct to many Western resorts and an important ingredient in resort promotional material, helping propagate the view that young women were revealing, alluring and available, the anticipated nature of the holiday-making experience and the character of resorts. Mostly women and resort architecture were on show together, the contests occurring in the lido or seafront pavilion, creating a synthetic seaside spectacle that made explicit the link

right: The seaside girl in bas-relief, entrance to the early 1930s Branksome Chine beach pavilion, Poole, Dorset.

middle: The seaside girl etched in glass, entrance hall to the 1935 Tinside pool, Plymouth.

bottom: Maisie Trolette, Gay Pride in Brighton, 2004.

spring breaks, and the confident endorsement of diverse alternative sexualities in resorts such as Brighton, on England's south coast, and New York's Coney Island.

Apart from being embodied in the beauty contest, another architecturally related manifestation of the idealized seaside girl was in visual publicity for resorts. Often she was portrayed in sight of priapic towers, lighthouses and diving boards. In Britain, she was joined and sometimes replaced by other seaside types, including children at play, the holidaymaking family and imagined idiosyncratic local characters. The most famous of the last was the Jolly Sailor, used to publicize the delights of Skegness.

In addition to promulgating certain social relationships, selling the seaside also involved promoting particular views of nature. The twentieth century began with resorts emphasizing the quality of sea air as a crucial natural attraction; indeed, the symbolism of sea air and its relationship to health was powerful enough to survive as a subsidiary advertising theme beyond the middle of the century. Even so, the

increasing importance of the sun and all that went with it to holidaymakers meant that old ways of using the seaside faded and the summer season became pre-eminent. Initially, the promotional responses of resorts were ambivalent, not least because many were alarmed by the declining winter use of the seaside.

One reaction was the formation, in 1931, of the British Health Resorts Association (BHRA), with the objective of promoting the traditional use of resorts as places of health, particularly in winter.[15] The Association particularly trumpeted the medicinal virtues of sea air. Each of the British resorts could be distinguished, the Association argued, on the basis of their 'indications' – their climatic qualities and the invalids who would most benefit. So, in select Bournemouth, with its long-established reputation for restoring invalids to health, for example:

The winter climate is almost ideal for delicate and debilitated subjects, semi-invalids and elderly people . . . High blood pressure may be relieved and chronic rheumatic conditions assisted by hot sea baths. The aromatic emanations of the pine trees have been long considered beneficial in catarrhal and pulmonary complaints, and some cases of bronchial asthma may do well in sheltered situations.[16]

Watching a beauty contest in 'the world's finest open-air swimming pool', Blackpool, *c.* 1964.

Individual resorts took a variety of approaches to advertising their own virtues in the Association's handbook. Some stressed the traditional attractions of sea air: a visitor to Margate and Ramsgate could 'Feel the ozone doing you good at . . . the most bracing health resorts on the British Coast!' Others, though, appealed to the newer delights of the sun, and Weymouth, more in tune with the popular desires and seemingly oblivious to the BHRA intent, heralded its 'Health Sunshine Pleasure. Sea and Sun Bathing. Vitalising Sunshine'. Bexhill adopted a more subtle approach, linking sun and climate: 'It is in respect of the quality of ultra-violet rays in its sunlight that Bexhill establishes the superiority of its climate for tonic, curative and purifying properties.'[17]

The BHRA campaign was an unsuccessful rearguard action against the onslaught of the sun and the summer season. Increasing acceptance by the resorts of the sun as the most important natural attraction to be consumed by holidaymakers transformed the content and style of the municipal guidebook and railway poster in the inter-war

Southport's 'English Rose' beauty contest, 1994.

period.[18] The visual representations in resort guides reveal the story of the new seaside, resplendent with images of sunshine, blue seas, crowded deckchair-filled beaches, family fun and a proud new municipal architecture of open-air pools, sun terraces and modernist pavilions.

The enormous success, importance and symbolism of Britain's seaside were wonderfully captured and put to patriotic propaganda uses in 1940. The country had been embroiled in the Second World War for almost a year and the south-coast resorts were closed to holidaymaking. In 'Margate, 1940' John Betjeman compared the pre-war delights of Margate with the overgrown and empty wartime resort, concluding:

> And I think, as the fairy-lit sights I recall,
> It is those we are fighting for, foremost of all.[19]

In an influential radio broadcast at the same time, J. B. Priestley also used the empty wartime Margate as a symbol of why the war should be fought. He described visiting the seafront:

The seaside girl in 1947.

> The sun, with a fine irony, came bounding out. The sea, which has its own sense of humour, winked and sparkled at us. We began to walk along the front. Everything was there: bathing pools, bandstands, gardens blazing with flowers, lido, theatres, and the like; and miles of firm golden sands all spread out beneath the July sun. But no people! – not a soul. Of all those hundreds of thousands of holiday-makers, of entertainers and hawkers and boatmen – not one. And no sound – not the very ghost of an echo of all that cheerful hullabaloo – children shouting and laughing, bands playing, concert parties singing, men selling ice-cream, whelks and peppermint rock, which I'd remembered hearing along this shore. No, not even an echo. Silence.[20]

Whereas Betjeman looked back nostalgically, Priestley thought Britain was not fighting to restore the past and instead looked to the future: 'This Margate I saw was

The pleasures of Eastbourne in 1963, by day . . . and by night.

saddening and hateful; but its new silence and desolation should be thought of as a bridge leading us to a better Margate in a better England, in a nobler world.'[21]

Even the huge success of Britain's summer seaside in the middle decades of the century was, eventually, to prove unsustainable. Indeed, the ultimate paradox of Priestley's 'better England' was that half a century later it was to leave seaside Margate almost as empty as it had been in 1940. Although the sunny seaside was a dominating feature portrayed in the British municipal resort guides, from experience holidaymakers knew the reality was often different. Ironically, the continual British promotion of the sun at home helped create a demand for the almost guaranteed hot sunshine and warm seas of overseas beaches: in the last third of the century the emergence and development of the overseas package-holiday business provided devastating competition for the British seaside resorts.

By the 1980s many declining British resorts, as if embarrassed to reveal themselves publicly, became fixated with people and lifestyle; images of specific places and architecture were suppressed. The covers of many resort guides featured images of the seaside girl, young people or families at leisure and play at *a* seaside, although not obviously a specific resort and sometimes not even obviously in Britain. It was as though guide creators thought such lifestyle-focused and non-place specific promotion might lead a typical holidaymaker to be unable to distinguish between a British resort and those in Spain and Greece. On other occasions, even if real resorts were represented, they were likened to the Mediterranean or tropical seaside. Torquay had been doing this for decades, making the most of its mild climate, exotic vegetation, 'Riviera' tag and, more recently, a palm-tree advertising symbol. There were some exceptions to the trends, with respectable Sidmouth, for example, constantly highlighting the wonders of its own

Blackpool as an ice cream, 1989 —
and the idea re-worked in 2004.

rustic Regency seaside architecture and resort townscape nestling between imposing hills and dramatic cliffs. Other resorts without such advantages sometimes used alternative techniques to present a favourable face to potential visitors. Weston-super-Mare, for instance, was accused of manipulating the photographic image on the cover of its 1998 guide to show 'beautiful deep blue seas in front of the pier' rather than the real 'cold grey-green seascape'.[22]

Blackpool provides one extreme but significant illustration of how, in the last four decades of the twentieth century, resorts promoted their architecture and nature. Unlike the many resorts that turned to lifestyle above all else, Blackpool never tired of representing its iconic resort architecture, particularly the Tower, which repeatedly featured on the cover of its guides. But the town's guides went through a fascinating evolution in the promotion of sea air, the sun and the pleasures of its beaches and sea. The resort's 1964 guide proclaimed 'the crisp breezes zesty with the tang of the sea', 'calm, sun-kissed Blackpool' and the 'safe, clean, golden sand. Washed and made new again twice a day': all contributed to a prescription for 'the happiest and healthiest holiday in the world'.[23] The guide was dominated by images of people at play or rest on the seafront, the beach and promenade packed with deckchairs and the sea full of bathers. Two decades later, sea air as an attraction had disappeared from the delights of the resort, the 1982 guide making one brief mention of 'wonderful air'.[24] Even the sun was missing from the text of the guide, although not from the photographs of the still-sunny and still-crowded summer beaches. Within three years, the guide began to celebrate Blackpool's 'spectacular sunsets',[25] an increasingly dominant feature in the visual promotion of the resort's natural attractions over the following years. The council subsequently came clean on the quality of the beaches and bathing water, announcing a 'Major Cleanup' operation to tackle the problems of pollution.[26] By 2004 seaside Blackpool, if the guide is to be believed, had been largely transformed into a place of romantic sunsets and night-times spent enjoying artificial attractions and entertainments. Although some images – including the front cover – suggest that during the day the sun continued to shine on the town, the crowded sunny summer beaches and people playing in the sea appeared no more, having been vanquished from the resort's publicity.[27]

Selling package holidays abroad involved the development of a new form of seaside place promotion centred on the overseas holiday brochure. The package-holiday companies tailored their publicity to the perceived demands of seaside holidaymakers. Depending on the circumstances, holiday brochures in the 1960s might stress indigenous and therefore 'authentic' culture and architecture, the comforts and lifestyles from home, modernity or natural attractions. For example, in the case of the Spanish island of Mallorca, British brochures and guides emphasized attractions ranging from 'beautiful beaches for those whose principal requirement is to lie in the sun', 'a holiday village, which supplies ample facilities and amusements', 'hot sun, sea breeze, golden sands, comfortable chalets, homely food . . . an atmosphere of good fellowship, humour and romance', to 'life with foreign people in a foreign land'.[28]

By the 1990s, descriptions, images and prices of hotels dominated package-holiday brochures, to be scrutinized and compared by the prospective purchasers. Whatever country or resort it was located in, and whatever the other facilities it offered, the ideal package hotel came to include magnificent sea views and closeness to an idyllic beach, both to be enjoyed from the essential private balcony, and the landscaped hotel pool ringed by sun loungers and sun

umbrellas.[29] Holidaymakers sometimes despaired that the reality of the package experience fell short of the brochure promise and the British media provided counter-representations of 'holidays from hell', viewers and readers adopting a horrified but enthralled 'there but the grace of God' stance to the accounts of holidaymakers enduring cockroach-infested kitchens, filthy and dangerous pools, half-built hotels and locations next to red-light districts, motorways and airport runways. And yet to denigrate the package holiday and its architecture is to disregard its significance and the undoubted pleasure it provides millions of holidaymakers. More than this, to belittle package holidays as mass tourism ignores the role of holidaymakers in making their own holidays to their own wishes and designs with a multiplicity of meanings and enjoyments.[30]

GLORIOUS DEVON AND THE CORNISH RIVIERA

The marketing and place promotion of the seaside takes place in the context of a jostling of other representations that may endure over a long period and either affirm or refute the advertised message. This engagement between contrasting representations can be illustrated by looking at one holiday region, the English West Country.

Most strongly from the inter-war years, the West Country was marketed as a newly discovered or rediscovered wild, romantic and historical landscape. The promotional spearhead was the Great Western Railway, which published a series of guides, the most famous called *Holiday Haunts*, and evocative railway posters proclaiming the delights of the region and its seasides.[31] The titles of subsequent GWR publications, *Glorious Devon* and *The Cornish Riviera*, gained extraordinary descriptive currency that survived into the

Torquay as romantic idyll in a postcard.

right: Clovelly in Devon — the seaside as rustic in a postcard of c. 1955.

twenty-first century. S.P.B. Mais, the author of *Glorious Devon*, contrasted the monotony and sameness and 'dismal and illiberal surroundings'[32] of resorts elsewhere in England with the attractions of the West Country, likened by Mais to a bashful maiden who 'has to be wooed to be won, won to be understood, understood to be loved'.[33]

Such marketing campaigns tilled fertile ground, since from the mid-nineteenth century a stream of novelists – among the most popular were Charles Kingsley with *Westward Ho!*, R. D. Blackmore with *Lorna Doone*, Sir Arthur Quiller-Couch with his *Troy Town* novels, Daphne Du Maurier with books such as *Frenchman's Creek, Rebecca* and *Jamaica Inn* – represented the West Country as romantic, picturesque and historical. Visual artists, too, celebrating the locality's natural attractions and the quality of light, established colonies on the Cornish coast from the late

top left: The contemporary English seaside and an idyllic nature: Oddicombe, Torquay, Devon, *c.* 2001.

top right: The Tate Gallery, St Ives, Cornwall, designed by Evans and Shalev, 1993. Although applauded as an example of new architecture leading to the regeneration of a seaside economy, there was opposition to proposals in 2005 for an extension to the building on the grounds that both the structure and the activity it generated were too dominant. Photographed in 2005.

above: The Eden Project, Bodelva, Cornwall, in 2004.

nineteenth century, unintentionally helping to found the locality's fashionabilty.[34] As a holiday region the West Country and its seaside was presented as exotic, tasteful and at least a little remote, in contrast to the familiarity and sameness and even coarseness of being beside the sea elsewhere in Britain. Represented as the antithesis of the traditional resort and its architecture, people visited the West Country in the anticipation of another type of seaside. Crucial elements of this maritime holiday identity continue to be reproduced today. Many of the most recent in the stream of historical or romantic locality-based novels, including Winston Graham's *Poldark* saga and Mary Wesley's *The Camomile Lawn*, have been translated into film or television series.

The success of depicting the West Country as an alternative and different type of seaside led to a backlash of concern and criticism and an alternative representation of the destruction of beloved vernacular architecture and the historical environment, the displacement of local people and the influx of unwelcome visitors. One of the most strident critics was Daphne Du Maurier, whose own novels had contributed to the romance and popularity of the region. Writing in the mid-1960s of 'Vanishing Cornwall' and fearing that the fishing villages of Cornwall would suffer a similar fate as those of Spain's Costa Brava, with 'every widened street, in every quayside cleared to allow more cars, more amusement arcades, more bingo-halls, bowling-alleys, dance-clubs, set upon sites where terraces or cottages once stood', she thought one hope lay in the weather – 'playgrounds do not thrive under the rain'. Du Maurier lamented that 'Those visitors who came to Cornwall in the past, year after year, because it offered a different sort of holiday, remote from the crowded seaside places . . . are forced, through disenchantment, to stay away.'[35]

Rosamunde Pilcher in her 1987 novel *The Shell Seekers* also develops the theme of the modern world and modern holidaymaker harming an older and superior Cornish landscape and architecture. Returning to the fictional Porthkerris after an absence of 40 years, the heroine discovers that the coastal village has been transformed:

> Carn Cottage was not the only house with a bulldozed garden, an hotel sign over the gate, and striped umbrellas set up on the newly constructed terrace. The old White Caps Hotel had been hideously enlarged and converted into holiday flats, and the harbour road, where once the artists had lived and worked, had become a fairground of amusement arcades, discos, fast-food restaurants, and souvenir shops.[36]

There is ambiguity here, though. Some of the architectural changes were to be welcomed, removing the physical evidence of an anguished wartime romance, and yet the essence of the place seemed to have survived, and 'nothing could ever alter' Porthkerris's natural attractions.

More recently still the development and promotion of the West Country evolved in other ways.[37] Increasingly fashionable and stylish, by the early twenty-first century it housed a huge cottage industry of holiday homes, an increasing number of trendy boutique hotels, and coastal enclaves capitalizing on privileged markets. An extreme niche role was performed by the coastal village of Rock, famed as the retreat of upper-class teenagers escaping, at the end of their exams, from the clutches of public schools and parents. The establishment of the architecturally distinctive Tate Gallery in St Ives capitalized on the region's visual arts tradition. Its function as an area to experience nature in the raw advanced to include not only sailing and surfing but also other new extreme coastal sports and coastal walking. Other recent attractions made alternative uses of nature: the emergence of a modern sea-based regional cuisine literally consumed it; new aquaria put it on show; and the Eden Project, in a Cornish former china clay pit, an architecturally unique twenty-first-century version of the Victorian winter garden, transplanted nature from other parts of the world.

BEHIND THE FRONT

The sense of the seaside being represented as a paradise and then being altered into something unsavoury or undesired is common. The point may be made about the impact of Roger Vadim's 1956 film *And God Created Woman* in the transformation of Saint-Tropez from a 'serene' fishing village on the French Mediterranean coastline – although presented by Vadim as a site of sexual pleasure – into a fashionable and hedonistic jet-setting resort,[38] and, more recently, into a self-tanning product.

Du Maurier's disapprobation of the West Country seaside's working-class holidaymakers is one example of a common tendency for middle-and upper-class commentators to look at working-class holidaymakers and their seasides and not like or understand what they see, which is then vilified or dismissed. Frederick Treves appreciated the dignified, spacious and simple promenade in Nice in part because

> It is free from the robust vulgarity, the intrusions, and the restlessness of the parade in an English popular seaside resort. There are no penny-in-the-slot machines, no bathing houses daubed over with

advertisements, no minstrels, no entertainments on the beach, no importunate boatmen, no persistent photographers.[39]

Just occasionally in the first half of the twentieth century other social groups set out to research and understand working-class holidaymakers, as with the Mass-Observation researchers in their study of late-1930s Blackpool.[40] The wonderfully rich if partial results provided contrasting ideas and images often at odds with dominant representations of the resort and its users.[41] In their study of holiday sex they visited the 'traditional sex areas', under the piers, in hollows on the beach and in the dunes on the southern edge of the resort, sometimes pretending to be drunk and falling 'in heaps on couples to feel what they were exactly doing'. The prurient Mass-Observers sometimes became active participants, seeking to have intercourse with the holidaymakers they were studying, but whatever the research methods they 'scored only four records of copulation' in one summer season. The seaside authorities appeared positively annoyed when Mass-Observation announced to the press that despite the 'sexual myth' of Blackpool it was England's most moral town.

By the early twenty-first century, Blackpool, despite its determined marketing and promotional efforts and repeated renewal of its attractions, had been surpassed as a place of summertime hedonism by a number of Mediterranean resorts and particularly Faliraki on the Greek island of Rhodes, Ayia Napa on Cyprus and the Spanish island of Ibiza. Television series and newspaper reports detailed holidaymaking of 'hedonistic excess' in 'drink-and-sex' resorts, with Faliraki described as 'Europe's notorious beach-and-booze citadel',[42] and Ibiza as the nightclubbing capital of Europe with a 'reputation for drug and alcohol-fuelled

The dull and dispirited Brighton beach of the 1960s photographed in 1967.

The rejuvenated Brighton beach in the form of Fatboy Slim's 'Big Beach Boutique', July 2002.

excess'.[43] Across the Atlantic a similar process flooded southern resorts, most famously Miami, and Mexican seaside places such as Cancún with partying young people on 'Spring Break'. In Europe, the holiday companies, club owners, bar proprietors and voyeuristic media attention undoubtedly fuelled the process, but at its heart were the actions and behaviour of young people making their own holidays and holiday places.[44] Increasing concern that the excess and media interest would harm other aspects of the tourist industry led to local and national governments attempting to assert alternative images and roles for these seaside places, with Ibiza, for example, trying to stress the authentic and natural attractions of the island.[45]

As to British seaside resorts experiencing an erosion of traditional roles and markets, the representations of decline were varied. Some of the most powerful portrayals of Brighton, for instance, as a decaying and rundown resort appear in photographs and on film. Classic photographs of the resort from the 1960s onwards concentrate on two contrasting sets of images – old people in their declining years, perhaps asleep on the beach in a deckchair or wistfully paddling in the sea, and young people engaged in some beach activity, most famously in battles between Mods and Rockers.[46] Films of the period represented the cheap, cheerful and for most middle-class commentators tasteless Brighton seaside, captured in the 1971 *Carry On at Your Convenience* and a year later in *Carry on Girls*, through the violent youth culture in the 1979 *Quadrophenia* and Brighton as a gangland resort in the 1986 *Mona Lisa*, to the truly dreadful and murderous 1993 film *Dirty Weekend* with the denouement on the town's Palace Pier.[47]

But resorts and their representation change, and by the mid-1990s Brighton and Hove and its seaside had once more become fashionable and tasteful.[48] Perhaps most symbolic of all, in place of the depressing or violent beach photographs of three decades before, in July 2002 the national media captured in pictures a crowd of 250,000 at local resident Fatboy Slim's 'Big Beach Boutique'.[49]

Another alternative perspective, focusing on society at the seaside, forcefully argues that the experiences of some people living in or visiting resort towns are the reverse of dominant leisure and pleasure representations. Although often hidden from view, this seaside is a place of poverty and disadvantage and, often, violence and crime.

At least as far as the English seaside is concerned, such representations stretch back to the nineteenth century. In Brighton in 1859, a booming resort with more than 75,000 people, there were a recorded 325 prostitutes, 25 of them under 16 years of age, although the actual number was thought to be double the official figure. There were up to 400 brothels. While the quantitative dimensions of prostitution in the resort were uncertain – the figures implying, for example, that there were just one or two prostitutes working in each brothel – there were clear spatial and social consequences. One lane a short distance from the sea included a block of houses 'entirely garrisoned by females of the most depraved and abandoned class'. This seaside Brighton was closely related to the respectable resort on show during the day. Many of the prostitutes were former domestic servants, and their clients, presumably, included many visitors to the town. At night there was a different use of the seaside and its architecture. After 11 o'clock in the evening 'the women of the town' inhabited the colonnade close to one of Brighton's principal theatres, while the night-time scenes on the beach were said 'to beggar all description'.[50] Victorian attitudes to class, morality and sexuality provide a central theme to John Fowles's novel played out in the Dorset seaside at Lyme Regis.[51]

There has also been a minority literary concern to describe resident seaside communities. In the first decade of the twentieth century, Robert Tressell identified a despairing class war being fought in Mugsborough, in reality the Channel resort of Hastings. He complained bitterly how the upper-class 'patriots' had deserted the resort, instead holidaying on the Continent 'to spend the money they obtain from the working people of England'. Nonetheless, Mugsborough seemed a prosperous resort, still fairly full of 'good-class visitors, either holiday-makers or invalids', and the Grand Parade crowded with well-dressed people and carriages. But, argued Tressell, 'this fair outward appearance was deceitful. The town was really a vast whited sepulchre' with most local people in a state of perpetual poverty often bordering on destitution.[52] At much the same time, but 180 miles westwards along the coast, Stephen Reynolds wrote admiringly of the 'poor men's lives that scarcely anybody fathoms' of Sidmouth's fishing community, a resort he fictionalizes as Seacombe.[53] Three decades later Graham Greene, much to the discomfort of the resort's official place promoters, wrote about the 'shabby secret', 'the deformed breast' and the 'extreme poverty' of the other Brighton.[54]

Away from fiction, the developing historical genre of oral-history approaches allows local people, describing living and working in resorts and experiencing another dimension of seaside architecture, to have their own voices heard.[55] The poverty and deprivation experienced in many contemporary British seaside towns is well documented in other material,[56] with specific types of disadvantage strongly associated with particular English seaside places and forms of seaside architecture. Take the resorts of southeast England, for example. Despite contemporary Brighton and Hove's recovered stylish image, at night the beach and seafront shelters become the refuge of the homeless, drug pushers and addicts and the sexually vulnerable.[57] In towns like Bexhill dominant images are of the elderly and their carers sometimes equally housebound in seaside bungalows or apartments, or sitting on seafront benches.[58] Nearby Eastbourne, in contrast, includes a genteel separate-tables poverty of the private hotel. The seedy poverty and bad housing of disadvantaged people living in a derelict Hastings is revealed in Michael Winterbottom's 1998 film *I Want You*. Pawel Pawlikowski, in his 2000 film *The Last Resort*, portrays a barren, deeply unattractive Margate bereft of holidaymakers and a prison for illegal immigrants and asylum seekers.

One recent study of teenage sexual behaviour in contemporary English seaside towns quotes a young mother as saying: 'The fair, the pier, the arcades, even now I get excited when summer comes 'cos there are more men, and someone might fancy me.'[59] The nature and architecture of the seaside resort, the argument goes, are bound up with 'issues of fantasy, carnival and impermanence, encouraging often-vulnerable young people into exploitative casual sex'. The policy recommendation, that new 'adult-only' leisure and entertainment provision should be discouraged, identifies seaside architecture as the problem.

In this type of alternative representation the seaside and its architecture is not a lure but a place for the poor to escape from and a problem for government to address. The seaside and its buildings have become surrogate explanations of deeply rooted social and economic exclusion.

THE POSTCARD HOME

Although often derided as an insubstantial piece of ephemera, the picture postcard carrying a visual image on one side was the single most important way of representing

Taking photographs and refreshments on Blankenberghe Pier, Belgium. Postcard, *c.* 1920.

The promenade, a classic subject for the seaside postcard: Clacton-on-Sea, *c.* 1957.

of Scarborough's North Bay; a century later the most popular cards from one major postcard printing firm were of Blackpool's new roller coaster and the resort's 'Golden Tower' (also celebrating its centenary).[61] Postcards were an important part of the seaside business: the confidently estimated 35,000 cards per day sent from Swanage, a small English south-coast resort, in 1960 nowadays seems an unbelievably high figure.[62]

Unlike most forms of resort marketing, it was the individual consumers and purchasers of postcard views who determined which images would become popular. Commercial postcard manufacturers had regard to the market: the most successful images were endlessly reproduced while those that did not sell were quickly abandoned.

The postcard, though, was not simply a commercially produced artefact but was designed to bear the personal imprint of the purchaser. Through the space for a hand-written message, it allowed holidaymakers to create their own representation of what was important in their own holiday experience, or at least suggest in a few words what they wanted the reader to believe.[63] Rarely did people write about what they had seen, and instead other aspects of the sensory consumption of the seaside dominate, including, for British postcard writers, a confirmation of the perennial national fixation with the weather, amid

the twentieth-century Western seaside, its use and users and its architecture.[60] With the introduction of the pictorial postcard in the late nineteenth century, it and the coastal resort and seaside architecture quickly became accommodating allies. The first British picture postcard, of 1894, was

WE CAME AWAY FOR A CHANGE OF AIR, BUT ALL WE'RE GETTING IS A CHANGE OF RAIN!

mundane or personal messages to friends and relatives.[64]

Postcards were particularly significant in establishing and developing the image of a place, helping determine the essential resort sites and sights. In deciding which cards to purchase and the messages to write, the senders of postcards helped shape representations and understandings of the seaside. The most popular recurring images confirm the sights, themes and ideas most important to holidaymakers. But a series of design and subject-matter conventions also developed, with the image-makers not simply recording, but selecting, arranging and distilling. Some images were carefully made, photographers waiting for the right conditions and posing their figures, and printers retouching and tinting. Although there were many precursors, the manipulation of the seaside postcard image reached one extreme in the John Hinde company's colour postcards of the 1960s featuring meticulously created and posed resort views and scenes of Butlin's Holiday Camps.[65]

By the middle of the twentieth century most seaside postcards represented resorts as warm, sunny and dry, the beach, sea and resort architecture as crowded and enjoyed, and holidaymakers as numerous and classless: it was as though the seaside was devoid of poverty and decay and never empty, cold or wet. Postcard images reflected and

The misery of wet weather, c. 1925.

A storm battering the promenade in front of the Queen's Hotel, Eastbourne, c. 1910.

confirmed the iconic resort buildings and sites, and apart from perennial beach scenes, singled out piers and pavilions, pools and promenades. There was a self-fulfilling process at work: the iconic sites drew the most visitors and dominated postcard images and purchases, so reaffirming the status of the site and judgment of the holidaymaker.

WAITING FOR THE REST TO COME OUT.

THE WATER IS NOT QUITE UP TO THE MARK!

Gender roles at the seaside stereotyped in two early
20th-century postcards.

Nature at the seaside was explored through a variety of
images. The might of nature was revealed in views of rough
seas battering promenades or piers, a particularly popular
theme in the early twentieth century. The taming and transformation of nature was evidenced in postcards of seafront
floral beds and parks and gardens. The romance of nature
shows on the more dominant contemporary images of
sunsets over the beach or sea.

The authentic, original and often
romanticized seaside could be seen in
pictures of harbours, the paraphernalia of
the working beach, fishing boats and local
working people. There were also generic
images, often relating to no particular
place or overprinted with a resort name,
representing some assumed essence of
the seaside – perhaps as a place of leisure,
relaxation, non-work or health. Although
to contemporary eyes perhaps the most
boring of views,[66] in the early post-war
period postcards showed caravan parks,
chalets and boarding houses, and were
sometimes personalized by the sender
marking with a cross their own place by
the sea.

Postcards mostly presented positive
visual images of the seaside and specific
resorts, although alternative and contradictory images were also sometimes
created. An important genre was the
comic cartoon seaside postcard,
lampooning at a range of seaside characters and situations and a descendent from the seaside
caricatures of the late-eighteenth century. One variety,
'saucy' or 'naughty' postcards, satirized the seaside as a
place of sexual titillation, promise, adventure or misadven-
ture played out in the sea or on the beach, pier or
promenade. The most prolific and famous of the saucy postcard artists was Donald McGill.[67] Writing in the early
1940s, George Orwell believed that McGill's cards were a
release valve, 'a sort of saturnalia, a harmless rebellion
against virtue',[68] in much the same way that throughout the

"The comic postcards down here are positively disgusting! I *must* send you one!!"

" —YOU'VE GOT A COUPLE OF NICE HANDFULS ! "

"OKAY, IT'S YOU JIM, — I WASN'T SURE IF I'D COME TO THE RIGHT CHALET."

Comic postcard by Donald McGill (above) and two postcards exploiting sex and gender at the seaside.

twentieth century some commentators had explained the cultural role of the boisterous popular resort and the funfair and amusement park. There were alternative positions, however, and after the war conservative seaside authorities disagreed, seeing McGill's cartoons as a confrontational challenge to their own resorts and partly to blame for a continuing national moral decline.[69] His cards labelled as obscene, McGill was the defendant in high-profile obscenity trials in the mid-1950s. Censorship faded over the following decades, McGill was posthumously celebrated and the saucy postcard became ever-more obviously risqué and blatant.

The mass-produced commercial seaside postcard, for all its dominance, had more individualized and personalized rivals. Particularly in the first four decades of the twentieth century, real photograph postcard portraits, mostly produced by local professional photographers, revealed holidaymakers as individuals and members of

A Donald McGill comic postcard.

The distractions of a Swedish beach. Similar topics continue to be exploited by postcard designers.

photographers to create an image of their own choosing. The 'snapshot' – and the term itself is revealingly dismissive of the image-makers – allowed holidaymakers to determine the visual aspect of the seaside and their own holiday they wished to record. The resultant pictures were hugely diverse, ranging through the intimate portrait of a family on the beach to views of a resort. Such photographs had the significance of providing 'a representation of the present for the future consumption of the past',[72] and, as Elizabeth Edwards says, 'a self-generated history . . . a people's "voice" about themselves, for themselves'.[73] These personal photographs of the seaside might in later years be displayed, reminisced over, handed from one generation to another, stored and then lost in some attic trunk, and perhaps eventually consigned to the rubbish tip or car-boot sale, the original image-makers and subjects forgotten.

social groups directly engaged with the camera and photographer. The genre included both interior studio sets with a seaside image backcloth – to be found in inland as well as resort studios – and pictures taken on the front or beach, perhaps of a couple strolling along a promenade or a posed group of bathers in the sea.[70] The 'democratisation and informalisation of photography'[71] also permitted amateur

The work of other photographers of the seaside more surely and lastingly entered the public domain, and particularly from the 1920s there was a rich tradition of Western photographers attempting to capture some aspect of its essential quality, albeit defined by chronology or geography. The results were iconic images that continue to attract media and public attention, perhaps arrested by the nostalgia and revelation of past times and places. They

A beach photographer's group scene at Margate, Kent. The sender of the card, in 1913, wrote: 'Can you find us here? The boy and I've had a week at Margate. Had a nice time. Shall be pleased to see you any time.'

right: A found photograph. Image of an interwar promenader taken by a resort photographer, Margate, Kent.

A family photograph taken on an English south coast beach, c. 1930s.

include Jacques-Henri Lartigue's celebrated photographs of a sensual and sun-drenched French Riviera between the wars;[74] the *Picture Post* images of the sun and fun of 1930s seaside England created by the likes of Bill Brandt, Felix Man and Kurt Hutton;[75] Weegee's mid-century tumultuous Coney Island beach scenes; Tony Ray-Jones's pictures of a depressed and seedy English seaside from the 1960s;[76] Martin Parr's mid-1980s portrayal of New Brighton, a decayed resort close to the then equally decayed Liverpool, its visitors seemingly oblivious to the hopelessness and unease obvious to the viewer of the images;[77] and, more recently still, photographers such as Roger Bamber's more complicated pictures of decay and regeneration at the English seaside.[78]

As to the commercial postcard, although for over a century it dominated popular representations of the seaside – to provide a feast of valuable images to be avidly consumed by commentators on seaside architecture – by the early twenty-first century it was close to being a redundant cultural artifact and, in the process it was both celebrated and belittled.[79] Sales fell dramatically,[80] as the postcard was swept aside by new electronic technologies enabling seaside holidaymakers to say, show and represent what they wanted, when they wanted and to whomever they wanted.

CHAPTER 4

THE SEASIDE AS ANOTHER PLACE

Western seaside resorts have always sought to provide out-of-the-ordinary experiences and, particularly from the early nineteenth century, architecture was used to intimate other exotic and pleasurable places and times. Visiting the seaside came to mean not only journeying to the edge of the land – in itself a unique experience – but also encountering a fantasy architecture designed to transport users to alternative worlds. Although no single architectural style for seaside leisure and pleasure buildings dominated – there was a continual jostling of alternative ideas and visions – seaside Orientalism, a protean style, and related exotic design motifs including the palm became an important architectural theme. Many iconic resort buildings and classic seaside design details were the result.

THE EXOTIC AND THE ORIENTAL

The formative building in the invention of seaside Orientalism was Brighton's Royal Pavilion, designed by John Nash for the Prince Regent (later George IV). In origin a farmhouse on the edge of the town and with views of the sea, in 1787 the earlier structure was remade into a Palladian 'Marine Pavilion' designed by Capability Brown's son-in-law, Henry Holland. On the enlarged royal seaside estate, huge royal stables and a 'riding house' were built in the early 1800s to the designs of William Porden. Although monumental and functional structures, the exteriors were 'after the eastern style of architecture'.[1]

In 1815 Nash was employed to transform the Pavilion itself. With the agreement of the Prince Regent, the strategy was to clothe the older and plain structure in a fantasy of Oriental dress.[2] Charles Wright, the author of an 1818 guidebook to Brighton, described the works being undertaken and how the previous year 'the most splendid additions to the Pavilion were undertaken, and these are two wings to the north and south, covered with pagoda towers, terminating in a conical point, with stone pedestals . . . The architecture of these towers excite the attention of the observer.'[3] The fawning Wright went on to say how in another year or two, with the 'ornamental designs' completed, he would be able to give 'an authentic description, which will display the splendor that cultivated taste and refined art can produce, suitable to the grandeur of an edifice promising to be an ornament to the architecture, and a specimen of the superiority of the arts and manufacture of Great Britain'.[4]

According to Nash, it was the Prince who decided on the 'Hindoo style' of the Pavilion's exterior 'in the expectation that the turban domes and lofty pinnacles might from their glittering and picturesque effect, attract and fix the attention of the Spectator'.[5] There was no attempt at exact replication of Indian buildings or design detail, with Nash being more concerned with mood and appearance. Indeed, the exterior combined different architectural motifs, among them a dash of Gothic. The exterior architectural elements included minarets (for effect, not practical use), onion domes, tent-roofs, verandahs and perforated stone screens –

The West Front of the Royal Pavilion, from John Nash, *Views of the Royal Pavilion, Brighton,* 1826.

the last based on Indian *jali*, designed to provide shade and ventilation. The illusion extended to the stucco of the walls being painted to imitate blocks of stone.

The interior adopted another Oriental theme: fantastical Chinese-inspired decoration including huge dragons was combined with opulent Eastern and Western furnishings. New technologies and building materials were also important, Nash drawing on the most modern of early nineteenth-century British construction methods and materials. Inside, the 'bamboo' staircases were a cast-iron imitation, while one of the large domes was supported by 'one of the earliest instances in domestic building of a cast-iron frame construction'.[6]

By 1821 the Pavilion, as a critical site for Brighton and, indeed, when the monarch was in residence, British society,

had been transformed into an extraordinary and spectacular fantasy. Just two years later the resort's Chain Pier opened and this structure, too, looked to the East for its design inspiration, although in this case it assumed an Egyptian style. It was not for another four decades, however, as the seaside market broadened and demanded new leisure buildings, that seaside Orientalism began to take hold and subsequently spread around the coast and was exported overseas.

Seaside leisure buildings lacked any dominant architectural or stylistic convention, in part because the form and nature of leisure beside the sea were fast evolving and developing. Unlike, say, banks and town halls, such buildings had no architectural or stylistic 'symbolism of function'.[7] The quest for a distinctive architecture to set

Salon.

The innovative construction techniques used in the Royal Pavilion. Detail from John Nash, *Views of the Royal Pavilion, Brighton*, 1826.

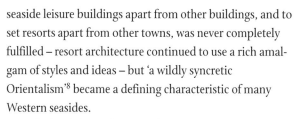

Brighton's West Pier of 1866 made inventive use of Oriental designs and cast iron. Left: serpent lamp, 1999; right: screen embellishing a pier kiosk.

seaside leisure buildings apart from other buildings, and to set resorts apart from other towns, was never completely fulfilled – resort architecture continued to use a rich amalgam of styles and ideas – but 'a wildly syncretic Orientalism'[8] became a defining characteristic of many Western seasides.

The breakthrough in popularizing seaside Orientalism came with Brighton's West Pier of 1866. Drawing on the nearby Royal Pavilion for its inspiration, the pier's designer, Eugenius Birch, made great use of decorative cast iron in a partly copied and partly invented style that at the time was called 'ornamental'. Cast-iron lamp-posts encircled with serpents, Indian-style openwork screens (an almost direct imitation of the Pavilion's own screens, although in iron rather than stone), minarets, pinnacles and domes were all in a 'vaguely oriental conception'.[9] Following his West Pier experiment Birch took the Oriental theme further, for example, in the large Hastings Pier pavilion of 1872. Seized by other pier designers, pleasure-pier Orientalism in Britain reached its apotheosis with R. St George Moore's Marine Palace of 1901 built on Brighton's third pier. From piers, Orientalism was unfolded on to an increasing range of seaside buildings, including bandstands, seafront shelters, pavilions, winter gardens, theatres and concert halls.[10]

Although the Royal Pavilion provided the inspiration for the flowering of Orientalism at the seaside, the Orientalism in the second half of the nineteenth century and later was an altogether different project. Whereas the Pavilion was architecture for a privileged elite, its subsequent form was 'demotic Orientalism'.[11] This was a popular, spectacular, mood-forming and modern architecture for a widening mass of holidaymakers.

A medley of architectural styles adorning Eastbourne Pier, c. 1910.

The spectacular Oriental pier-head pavilion, Morecambe, ultimately destroyed by fire in 1933.

Hugely eclectic in the range of architectural elements and ideas and usually remote from the real thing, seaside Orientalism became endlessly adaptable. In muted form, as the ubiquitous bungalow, it dressed the domestic dwelling. It migrated to Europe to disguise hotels and villas and jour-neyed to the United States to dress buildings ranging from attractions in Coney Island's early twentieth-century amusement parks to, on the west coast, the 1912 bathhouse at Venice Beach and the Santa Cruz Beach Casino of 1904 – destroyed by a fire within two years and replaced with an equally elaborate confection in 1907.[12] While Orientalism led to the creation of some iconic seaside buildings, elsewhere it became just one of a number of design elements to be used, for example, in a dome, cupola or arch. Oriental architecture could be equally at home for interior design: a classic example was the Indian Lounge in Blackpool's Winter Gardens; close by, it provided inspiration for one section of theming for the River Caves attraction on the Pleasure Beach.

At the nineteenth-century British seaside, cast iron was the most important material used in Oriental architecture. Raymond Lister, writing in 1960, likened Brighton seafront's cast-iron decoration to 'gigantic cake-icing' and described how it could transport people to another distant or imaginary place. For Lister the 'lacy lattice work' of the King's Road bandstand of 1883 had 'much the same effect that is given by the arches of the Court of Lions in the Alhambra at Granada, or the king's sleeping apartment in the Alcázar at Seville', while the 1890s Madeira Terrace from the sea gave the impression of

The Oriental pier-head theatre, Palace Pier, Brighton, 1901.

The diffusion of seaside Orientalism along the south coast of England, here adorning shops at Bexhill-on-Sea in 2001.

'an enormous grotto stretching along the Drive, hewn from the cliff and decorated with fanciful lattice work. It appears cool as it invites us to rest from the sun-drenched parade . . . submarine grottoes, salty mermaids and tritons with their horns of shell, and plunging seahorses do not seem far away.'[13]

And yet cast-iron decoration was never universally endorsed. John Ruskin, a critical arbiter of mid-nineteenth-century taste, bemoaned 'these vulgar and cheap substitutes for real decoration'.[14] By the inter-war years of the following century architectural critics often saw seaside cast iron and Orientalism as unfashionable, fussy Victorian mediocrity and a hindrance to the development of modern and progressive seaside places. Writing in the mid-1930s, Wesley Dougill criticized the architecture of the established resorts for their 'shoddy buildings steeped in Victorian mediocrity' and 'designs of bandstands, ornamental railings and seats taken direct from old catalogues' and seaside buildings that were 'mean parodies' of the Brighton Royal Pavilion.[15]

There were equally diverse views about seaside Orientalism elsewhere. In the 1920s Frederick Treves was initially captivated but then dismayed by the pier at Nice:

A little pier – the Jetée-Promenade steeps off from the main parade. On it is a casino which provides varied and excellent attractions. The building belongs to the Bank Holiday Period of architecture and is accepted without demur as exactly the type of structure that a joy-dispensing pier should produce. It is, however, rather disturbing to learn that this fragile casino, with its music-hall and its refreshment bars, is a copy of St Sophia in Constantinople. That mosque is one of the most impressive and most inspiring ecclesiastical edifices in the world, as well as one of the most stupendous. Those who know Constantinople and have been struck by the lordly magnificence of its great religious fane will turn from this dreadful travesty with horror. It is the burlesque that hurts, as would the 'Hallelujah Chorus' played on a penny whistle.[16]

James Hunekar, in contrast, was entranced by Atlantic City's Oriental Marlborough-Blenheim Hotel, constructed out of reinforced concrete:

If Coleridge, in 'Kubla Khan', or Poe, in 'The Domain of Arnheim', had described such a fantastic structure, we should have understood, for they are men of imagination . . . The architecture might be Byzantine. It suggests St Marco's at Venice, St Sophia at Constantinople, or a Hindu Palace, with its crouching

left: The other-worldly River Caves experience, Blackpool Pleasure Beach.

middle: The hybrid Casino, part-Oriental and part-Classical, Blackpool Pleasure Beach, 1925.

bottom: An alternative version of Oriental architecture: the extraordinary Elephant Hotel, Margate, Atlantic City, New Jersey, c. 1919. The sender comments: 'This is our Blackpool here.'

dome, its operatic façade, and its two dominating monoliths with blunt tops. Built of concrete, the exterior is a luxurious exfoliation in hues, turquoise and fawn.[17]

While Treves would have loathed the comparison to St Sophia at Constantinople, George Orwell would have found the reference to Kubla Khan equally unwelcome. In a 1946 essay imaging a modern-day entrepreneur remaking Kubla Khan's pleasure-dome in Xanadu, he describes how 'Kubla Khan's project would have become something quite different. The caverns, air-conditioned, discreetly lighted and with their original rocky interior buried under layers of tastefully-coloured plastics, would be turned into a series of tea-grottoes in the Moorish, Caucasian or Hawaiian styles.'[18]

Oriental seaside architecture could, then, be applauded or reviled. However, what were its consequences on the holidaymaking users of the architecture? Answering the placid question risks being engulfed by the maelstrom of contemporary debate about the nature and role of Orientalism more generally in the West.[19] For Edward Said, the meaning of Orientalism was twofold: it was 'a Western style' that implied 'dominating, restructuring, and having authority over the Orient',[20] thereby supporting Western imperialism and colonialism, but it also signified *another*

place distinguished from the West, a place of leisure and heightened sensuality. Viewed this way, the Orientalism of seaside architecture offered visitors the illusion of being in a place that was far and away from the West, a place of leisure and sexual promise.

Others contend that it was just not like that. David Cannadine, for example, argues that in Britain gradations of class were more important and that empire was often disregarded or taken for granted.[21] John MacKenzie addresses the Orientalism of seaside architecture directly, arguing that it was nothing to do with belittling or subjugating the East but a significant new style, 'grand, mysterious, fantastic and opulent all at once',[22] removed from any reference to a specific culture, in any case often mixed with or butting onto other architectural styles, and bound up with the development of the important seaside holiday business.

There is no evidence that architects had anything other in mind than to build spectacular, fashionable and competitive leisure buildings for the seaside. For holidaymakers thronging the astonishing piers and pavilions, seaside Orientalism must have helped generate a sense of excitement, confirming that the seaside, with its devotion to pleasure and health, was different from ordinary and everyday inland places. There was also the conjunction of an architecture suggestive of other places and worlds looking onto, in the case of piers built over, the very seas and oceans that led to foreign lands.

However holidaymakers as individuals and members of social groups mediated buildings in Oriental style, the British seaside was also a place where signs of empire and the nation's military might were endlessly on display.[23] The classic use of seafront Oriental bandstands, for

A Californian version of seaside Orientalism: the Casino at Santa Cruz, California, built in 1907.

The 1896 Indian Lounge, anteroom to the Empress Ballroom, Blackpool Winter Gardens, echoing the design themes of the Dunbar Room at Osborne House, Isle of Wight.

example, despite being eminent architectural symbols of leisure and pleasure, was by military bands. Past combats could be remembered in the war memorials located in seaside parks and gardens, and on many coastlines there were architectural reminders of military coastal defences from past or anticipated conflicts. The seaside was island Britain's front to other places and peoples, the promenade and cliff-top conjuring images of what lay over the horizon, and the coastal waters a 'protective barrier' as well as the

'An enormous grotto', Madeira Terrace, Brighton, 2002.

Cast-iron visions, from the 1890s, of Neptune and Aphrodite: Madeira Terrace, Brighton, in 2002.

primary resource for the seaside resort.[24] There are also links to be made between the British seaside and ideas of empire and racial superiority. In one well-developed late-nineteenth- and early-twentieth-century perspective it was 'the invigorating temperate climate which stimulated enterprise and spawned civilization';[25] and it was at the seaside where the climate was at its best, most readily consumed while enjoying the pleasures of the seafront. Unsurprisingly, perhaps, many seaside resorts became the preferred places of retirement for the returning servants of empire.

Whether despised or acclaimed in the past, in Britain the surviving nineteenth-century Oriental architecture at the seaside has been increasingly represented as valuable architectural heritage, its eclecticism in sympathy with post-modern hybridity. Seaside Orientalism is not, however,

simply a historic architecture of leisure but continues to be reinvented for modern purposes. Although Atlantic City's Marlborough-Blenheim Hotel was demolished in 1979, by 1990 the resort boasted the Trump Taj Mahal Hotel Casino and Resort, one of the largest casinos in the world. Part of the regeneration of a previously declining seaside town, this Taj Mahal is richly themed with Orientalism: '70 colorful minarets adorn the roof-tops', while 'seven two ton elephants of carved stone greet visitors'. Imitating the Atlantic City process, in the early 2000s plans were announced for an Egyptian-themed Pharaoh's Palace casino in Blackpool.

The appeal of the exotic as a symbol of the seaside has other manifestations. Venice has been evoked at both the British and North American seaside because of its exotic

La Jetée-Promenade et la Promenade des Anglais   Nice

St. & Co. à D.   L. Gross, Nice

Nice pier, c. 1904.

right: The Oriental Blenheim Hotel, with Boardwalk crowds, Atlantic City, New Jersey, 1911.

and romantic connotations, architectural distinctiveness and role as a bridge and meeting point between the East and the West. As van Leeuwen remarks of the United States, although the point applies elsewhere, Venice was 'an obligatory point of reference for all sorts of pleasure colonies from St Augustine and Miami Beach to Los Angeles and Newport Beach'.[26]

The American architectural visions of Venice could be audaciously unrestrained. On the shores of southern California, in the first years of the twentieth century, Abbot Kinney developed the remarkable planned resort of Venice of America, drawing its architectural inspiration from its Italian namesake.[27] Kinney not only attempted a reproduction of Venice's architecture and canals, but also imported both gondolas and gondoliers from the original Venice.[28]

The Californian version of Venice, however, was rooted in the boisterous seaside resort: the reproduction of the city jostled with amusement parks and bathhouses, piers and sideshows. In Florida, the Miami suburb of Coral Gables, with its Mediterranean-inspired architecture, features the 1924 Venetian Pool designed by the Corporation architect

The Trump Taj Mahal Casino and Resort, Atlantic City.

The Venice of America, California, c. 1910.

Phineas E. Paist with artistic input from Denman Fink and created in a former quarry. Praised by present-day commentators as the world's most beautiful, the innovative and richly themed pool includes a grotto, waterfalls, fountains and observation towers; architecturally, though, the feel is more tropical Spanish than Venetian. At the British seaside, in contrast, the muted evocation of Venice included, for example, Great Yarmouth's mile-long Venetian Waterways – constructed as an attraction to veil what was seen by the local authority as an unattractive coastal margin of sand dunes – the Venetian Boating Lake forming part of Ramsgate's inter-war Marina Bathing Pool – Venetian by name and little else – and Southport's transitory 'Venetian Nights' illuminated evening attraction, 'of exceptional beauty', on the resort's Marine Lake during the 1930s.[29]

As to Brighton's Royal Pavilion, once transformed into an Oriental make-believe, George IV visited it on just two further occasions. Two decades later neither the building nor its location, in the centre of a rapidly changing resort embracing new visitors and new technologies, enraptured the inheritor of the marine palace, Queen Victoria. The railway from London had reached the resort in 1841 and on

Easter Monday 1844 one of the new excursion trains, pulled by four engines and with more than 40 carriages, carried 1,100 people into the town. On 11 February 1846 William Henry Fox Talbot took the first photographs of seaside Brighton – of a seemingly desolate and empty Royal Pavilion.[30] Indeed, the new queen had made her last visit the previous year. Retreating from the invasive crowds brought in ever greater numbers by the railway – in a letter to her aunt she wrote 'the people are very indiscreet and troublesome here really, which make this place quite a prison'[31] – and perhaps with a premonition that the invention of photography would threaten her valued privacy still more, she moved to a new seaside home, the secluded Osborne House on the Isle of Wight.

The Pavilion, emptied of its contents and stripped of its fixtures and fittings, came into the ownership of the town in 1850 and, in a step in the transition from a royal leisure residence to a demotic tourist site, was opened to the public the following year. The building was to serve a variety of roles for the town and by 1865, according to one press comment, had 'alternated through the various gradations of lecture-

The Venetian Pool, Coral Gables, Florida, c. late 1920s.

'Venetian Waterways, Great Yarmouth', *c.* 1947.

Southport's late-1930s 'Venetian Nights' attraction on the resort's Marine Lake, from a painting by Fortunino Matania reproduced in *Sunny Southport: Official Guide, 1938–39*.

Osborne House, Isle of Wight, 2001.

monstrosity',[34] while by 1913 it was 'a bizarre pile'.[35]

Over the following decades into the late twentieth century, the exterior and interior of the building were repeatedly repaired, remodelled and restored – between the 1960s and '80s, for example, some of the Bath-stone minarets were replaced with fibreglass imitations – redecorated and refurnished. In part because it was in sympathy with contemporary design ideas and styles including a rediscovered fashion for Chinoiserie, from the 1920s the building was positively re-evaluated along with the Regency period. The influential judgement made by Osbert Sitwell and Margaret Barton in 1935 was that there was no other building in England or Europe 'to compare with it in individuality and exotic beauty'.[36] By the early twenty-first century, the Royal Pavilion and surrounding gardens had been restored to a close approximation of the original Nash designs. The earlier stables and riding house had long been transformed into the city's cultural and artistic centre, while

hall, ball-room, wild-beast show, and all the seedy and ephemeral occupations of an overgrown, ugly, and deserted building, too tawdry for posterity and too costly for use'.[32] The most extraordinary yet sympathetic use of the Pavilion and associated buildings and gardens was as a nursing home for wounded Indian soldiers during the First World War.[33]

Nineteenth-century commentators openly disliked the Pavilion's Oriental architecture, in part because of its association with what was viewed as a debauched and dissolute period of the monarchy. The sentiment was duplicated in commercial guidebooks: one 1900 guide described it as 'architecturally contemptible', another as 'a tasteless

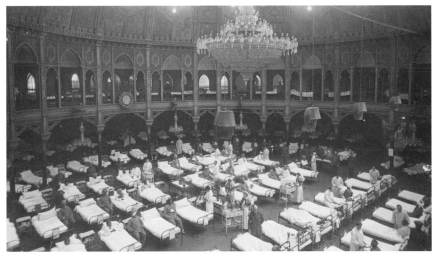

Brighton Pavilion as a military hospital for First World War Indian soldiers, c. 1916.

the Pavilion itself was considered as 'one of the great European royal pleasure palaces evoking images of Empire and the exotic, unmatched in its variety of styles and sheer inventiveness'.[37] It was also one of the most important tourist heritage sites in seaside England.

The Royal Pavilion – a product of the rich and powerful building at the seaside, the architectural pretence at being of another place or time, the abundance of art from other parts of the world, the sheer grandeur and opulence of the project, and the ignominy of the transformation into a tourist site and sight – had later seaside parallels. Queen Victoria's coastal retreat of Osborne House was built in the fashionable Italianate style in the 1840s. In 1852 the Queen described the 'calm deep blue sea, the balmy air, *all* quite Italian'.[38] A Durbar Room with luxurious Indian interior decoration was added in the early 1890s as a state banqueting hall; it was subsequently used to display gifts to the Queen from her Indian subjects.[39] Inspired by the royal example, the Indian style was copied at the northern seaside, in the Blackpool Winter Gardens Indian Lounge, and next to the equally splendid Empress Ballroom. Following the death of Victoria, in 1902 Osborne House and the associated estate were presented to the nation, and a century later it functioned as one of the island's major tourist attractions.

On another shore – that of California – from 1919 the media magnate William Randolph Hearst set about creating his own vision of an alternative holiday world at San Simeon, this time modelled on an eclectic mix of Mediterranean architecture and furnished with a financially unrestrained and prodigious art collection gathered from around the world.[40] Hearst died in 1951, and seven years later Hearst Castle opened to the public; transformed into a state historical monument, in less than four decades 25 million people visited the previously exclusive and private seaside realm.

THE PALM

The designers of the Western seaside also used exotic vegetation in the quest to create another place. Tropical vegetation, and particularly the palm, has been woven into the design tapestry of the seaside, although in northern resorts the thread has often been artificial and emblematic rather than real. The palm has been an idea and symbol of the exotic and the pleasurable other.

Brighton's Royal Pavilion used the palm in various ways. Cast-iron columns to support roofs and ceilings were decorated as palm trees, the designs sometimes abstract and sometimes uncertain: in one case the trunk appears as bamboo, the fronds as palm. Even the columns supporting the kitchen roof, necessary to make a large open working space, were embroidered with copper palm leaves. The motif is at its strongest on the ceiling of the Banqueting Room, used to entertain important dignitaries, decorated with huge tropical plantain fronds.

While the Pavilion's palms were imitations, from the same time there were also repeated initiatives to use real palms and other exotic plants at the Western seaside. In the earliest British resorts architects and garden designers planned vast cast-iron glasshouses to create a suitable artificial environment and alternative world. Early plans were not always successfully implemented. In Brighton, in August 1833, the Anthæum – 'an immense circular conservatory constructed entirely of cast iron and glass, extending over an area of an acre and a half and covered with a dome 160 feet wide and 64 feet high, which was designed to be the largest in the world'[41] – was nearing completion. The artificial pleasure garden included a lake and a hill, tropical and Oriental trees, captive birds and seating for 800 people. Inadequately designed and constructed, the building collapsed as the scaffolding was removed, the ruins remaining on the site for two decades.

The exotic kitchen. From John Nash, *Views of the Royal Pavilion, Brighton*, 1826.

The Royal Pavilion's Banqueting Room, the ambience dominated by the enormous plantain fronds.

The Rock Walk, Torquay, *c.* 1930.

As technology and design improved, the winter garden and associated structures were to become a standard part of the architecture of nineteenth-century resorts, part separate artificial worlds displaying the subjugation of exotic flora – the plant collectors' spoils of empire – and part places of entertainment. One of the best examples surviving into the twenty-first century, albeit in a transformed state, is Eastbourne's Floral Hall of 1874. The Blackpool Tower's roof gardens also evolved from an exotically vegetated environment to wonder at and in which to listen to concerts, through the introduction of Punch and Judy shows, to its development into Jungle Jim's children's adventure playground.

But the emergence of the resorts in the milder south-west of England, combined with the importation and cultivation of hardier exotic plants, also allowed the palm tree and its cousins to prosper out of doors. From the early twentieth century Torquay, in particular, promoted the 'stately palms' and related sub-tropical foliage in its

On the reverse of this postcard, sent in April 1910, E. writes to A: 'How are you dearies. I have just got the writing fit, so thought I would write and ask you if your garden is ready for these plants yet. Don't you wish you were going to the other side of this card tonight?'

The original Blackpool Tower Roof Gardens.

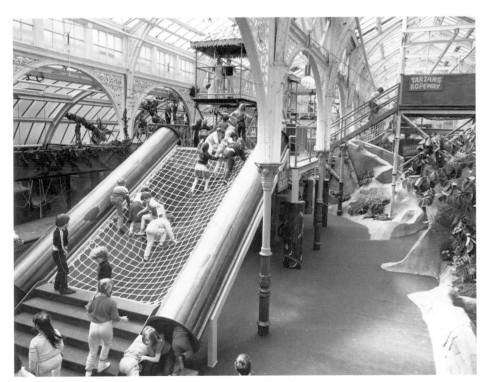

Blackpool Tower Roof Gardens transformed into Jungle Jim's.

The CORNISH RIVIERA

Cornwall promoted as a lush foreign seaside: the frontispiece of S.P.B. Mais's *The Cornish Riviera*, 1934.

'popular and picturesque' gardens and promenades.[42] A 1925 guidebook described how the 250 acres of public gardens in the resort 'abound in rare exotic plants, verdant lawns, and paths that wind in sunny or shadowy mazes among the myrtles and the palms'.[43] The palm became a significant element of a notable twentieth-century promotional campaign to establish Torquay as 'The Queen of the English Riviera', beguiling 'would-be visitors with an impression of a resort enjoying mild winters and warm summers, characterised by palm-tree-lined promenades and offering both elegance and luxury'.[44] The image, though, was backed by substantial local-authority intervention in the built environment and its use, including the creation of new parks and gardens mostly laden with palm trees and associated vegetation. An abstracted palm motif – in fact of a New Zealand cabbage tree – was subsequently repeatedly used on the area's late-twentieth-century guidebook covers and in publicity campaigns, often casting its shadow over some more usual seaside building or experience as if to say Torquay and the neighbouring resorts of Paignton and Brixham were altogether different from the remainder of seaside England.

But even the original Riviera needed to be invented as a place of leisure and then clothed in exotic imported vegetation – including, in 1864, the palm tree *Phoenix canariensis* – that came to be thought of as a natural part of the place and was an essential ingredient in the luxurious and diverse private and public gardens that embroidered the landscape.[45] And like Torquay, the palm tree came to feature in the place promotion of this part of the French Mediterranean coast, mixed together with images of the sea and sun, architecture and the ideal holidaymaker.

As the Western seaside reached further afield, Western holidaymakers increasingly encountered real palms in their

MENTON - Jardin

The French Riviera clothed with vegetation from around the world. An undated postcard of Menton.

Great Yarmouth fibre-glass palm, 1993.

'Every serious beach has palm trees' – Waikiki, Hawai'i, in 1902.

The Caribbean transplanted to seaside England in an attempt to revitalize Cliftonville Lido, Margate, 1973.

left: Coney Island palm, 2004.

natural environment. The development of Hawai'i as a tourist destination in the twentieth century was especially important since 'after Waikiki with its groves of coconut palms any serious beach had to have palm trees'.[46] Even less hospitable seaside places from Great Yarmouth to Coney Island turned to artificial palm trees in a playful attempt to transform the beach or promenade.

The definitive architectural use of the palm at the seaside, however, is in Dubai. The Jumeirah, Jebel Ali and proposed Deira 'Palms' are the world's largest artificial islands and construction projects, each in the shape of the date palm. The Palms, as 'iconic mega-projects', have more

than doubled the coastline of Dubai and are designed as huge seaside leisure complexes, with 'hotels, residential villas, shoreline apartments, marinas, water theme parks, restaurants, shopping malls, sports facilities, health spas and cinemas'.[47] This ultimate vision in designing the seaside, part of a strategy to turn the emirate into a global tourist destination, is proclaimed as the inspiration of the Crown Prince of Dubai, Sheikh Mohammed bin Rashid Al Maktoum.[48]

The scale of these projects is immense, with the largest scheme, The Palm, Deira, designed to be more than 14 kilometres long from the base of the trunk to the tip of the

The Palm, Jebel Ali, Dubai.

outer protective breakwater crescent, the arc of the crescent stretching 21 kilometres, and the 41 fronds varying in length from 0.8 to 3.3 kilometres. Deira will house 8,000 villas in addition to hotels and varied leisure facilities.

And yet in seeming admission that the palm itself is not enough, the designers of The Palms have resorted to a cacophony of other architectural and design themes from around the world. Nature, too, has been engineered and architecture both above and below the sea used to recreate other places. The crescent of the Jumeirah Palm includes three themed hotels: 'Brazilian Tree Houses', 'Okinawan Gardens' and the 'Venetian Village Resort', the last promising a 'vacation like a tropical trip to Venice'. Perhaps unknowingly, there is also a reference to Blackpool, the quintessential English working-class resort, with one section of the Jumeirah trunk containing 750 luxury apartments and 220 boutique shops called 'The Golden Mile', a phrase long used to describe Blackpool's rowdy central seafront packed with entertainment and amusement venues. Just off The Palms, Jumeirah, artificial reefs will provide the world's largest synthetic dive park. Some of the reefs will simulate the topography and habitats of dive sites from around the world, while one, 'The Lost City', will function as an underwater theme park, with diving attractions ranging through sunken planes and ships, an Egyptian pyramid and Roman ruins.

It is ironically satisfying that the palm, for two centuries an architectural symbol of the exotic used to help transform the Western seaside into other places, has been adopted by the Arab world as part of an ambitious strategy to revolutionize the very idea of the seaside as a place of pleasure and to market it to Westerners.

CHAPTER 5
DESIGNING RESORT OPEN SPACES

The seaside resort is structured by its open spaces. Apart from the sea itself, the critical spaces are the beach, the seafront with its promenade or boardwalk, and parks and gardens. In varied measures resort open spaces provide ways of experiencing nature and society, entertainment, leisure, pleasure and health. Although sometimes merging into each other – an English esplanade often includes a garden, an American beach also a boardwalk running along its landward edge – each site has distinctive architectural and design elements. As the ideas of the seaside and resort developed and evolved during the nineteenth and twentieth centuries, these open spaces became core attractions of the seaside experience, heavily marketed in promotional material, with individual resorts proclaiming the distinguishing features of their own beaches, seafronts and parks.

Necessary sea defences, protecting resorts from the worst excesses of nature, combined 'business with pleasure', as one early twentieth century guide to Ramsgate described it, also serving as promenades and leisure areas or embellished with coastal parks and gardens as bold statements of how the boundary between land and sea had been tamed and made into places of pleasure. Equally, though, the development of the seaside has involved transforming existing open landscapes. What were perceived as marginal or valueless places – cliff tops and faces, sand dunes and marsh – were claimed for resorts and often transformed into invented and exotic landscapes. These new resort landscapes were beside and fronted the sea, a separate environment, but providing sea air, breezes and views that could all be consumed from the shore in comfort and safety.

Seaside resorts and the society they represent confront nature directly at a sharp, precise edge or front. At a finer scale, however, the linear edge itself, and especially the

SOUTHPORT.
PROMENADE
GARDENS.

The ever-expanding beach at Southport transformed into promenade gardens.

Polite society and the splendours of Brighton's Regency architecture at the water's edge, with beach, esplanade and gardens. George Bryant Campion, *Lewes Crescent*, c. 1838, watercolour and bodycolour.

seafront and beach, can be seen as an anomalous category between nature and society moving in zones from the cultivated resort through seafront garden and promenade on to the beach, then into shallow water and finally into natural deep water.[1] Such transitions and gradations also often occur along the length of a seafront open space running parallel with the sea, typically from the resort centre, where the promenade and beach are most designed, through to the fading and lessening of artificial interventions and increasingly natural seaside.

But the architecture and use of seaside open spaces change with time. On a daily basis, how a seafront shelter is used at night is radically different from its daytime role. There are also seasonal rhythms and disjunctures in use and users of beach and seafront. And over longer periods the design and utilization of these spaces have evolved and sometimes changed more radically, perhaps as one style and purpose has been swept away and replaced by another. Similarly, the changing flows of holidaymakers to a resort have implications for the use of open spaces with, perhaps, a previous select esplanade turned into a rumbustious space. There may be other subtle but significant alterations, such as the contemporary use of the car in some resorts as a private and secure seafront viewpoint (and a place to read and snooze) in contrast to the dominant use of the communal seaside bench in the past.

BEACH

Underlying the difficulty of capturing the essence of the beach is that it is an ambiguous open space, capable of being defined, designed and used in different ways.

The prim and sedate respectable Victorian beach with donkey rides, as pictured for children *c.* 1860s.

right: Unrestrained fun and sun. Cover illustration by F. S. Ash for the children's book *On the Sands*, mid-20th century.

Photographs and other images reveal some of this complexity in the evolving use and design of the beach by holidaymakers at different times and in different places. Scarborough beach in the eighteenth century, for example, appears as a promenading and bathing place for 'the company' visiting the resort. By the middle of the next century William Powell Frith's minutely detailed panorama, *Life at the Seaside (Ramsgate Sands),* stresses the themes of family relaxation and play, social harmony at the water's edge, and the parade of seaside characters – Frith was particularly attracted to the 'all sorts and conditions of men and women'[2] found on the Sands – although also combined with references to national power and the defensive importance of the sea and coast.[3] Eighty years later, and on the other side of the Atlantic, in 1934 Paul Cadmus portrayed a heaving, joyful, boisterous and hedonistic 'Coney Island' beach, with bath house and amusement park to be glimpsed in the background. In contrast, Charles Meere's 'Australian Beach Pattern' of 1940 reveals the beach users –

The new fashion for donkey rides. James Gillray, *Morning Promenade upon the Cliff, Brighton*, published 24 January 1806.

despite their pleasurable activities – as heroic, austere and isolated individuals. The point about the multiplicity of visions and purposes that the beach can fulfill could be repeatedly illustrated from around the Western world.

Until the discovery of the seaside as a place of health and pleasure there was no need, of course, for seashore architectural structures for other than functional maritime purposes. The beach was also a hazardous and unwelcoming environment for architecture, a risky marginal zone in danger of being swept by sea or storm. With the development of the seaside resort, the beach became the site for a range of new architectural structures. More permanent beach buildings are discussed in the next chapter. But there were also arrays of transient beach structures. As sites of business, commerce and performance, beaches in nineteenth-century British popular resorts, for example, could be littered with a higgledy-piggledy pattern of temporary booths, kiosks, stages and children's rides. Although the

early twenty-first-century British resort beach is commercially an altogether more orderly and tidy affair, there remain threads of continuity with the past: donkey rides – established in Margate by 1790 and initially a select entertainment for fashionable ladies – are still to be experienced, as are the miniature and collapsible architectural splendours of Punch & Judy booths.

The primary purpose of the beach in the embryonic resorts was as the starting and return point for the therapeutic journey in the bathing machine to consume the sea. But the beach itself became increasingly valued for other holidaymaking purposes. By the mid-nineteenth century the British beach was a place to walk, ride, stand and lie, but, for the respectable Victorian, most of all it was a place to sit and, from that position, to watch, contemplate, converse and read. Sitting on the beach itself or on a chair or bench often took a particular form, the sitters adopting a correct, upright posture, presumably simply repeating what

The early and elite beach as promenade and bathing place. T. Ramsey, *Holidaymakers on Scarborough Beach*, *c.* 1770, oil on canvas.

The mid-Victorian family beach. William Powell Frith, *Ramsgate Sands: 'Life at the Seaside'*, 1852–4, oil on canvas.

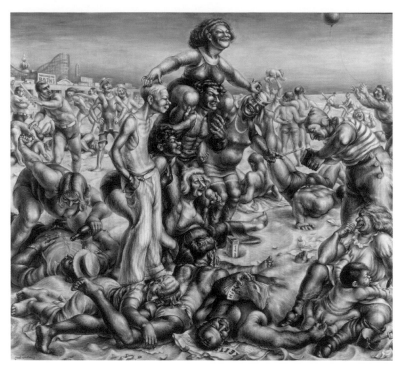

The crowded excessive city beach. Paul Cadmus, *Coney Island*, 1934, oil on canvas.

The symbolism of the beach for a nation at war on the far side of the world. Charles Meere, *Australian Beach Pattern*, 1940, oil on canvas.

Donkeys at Blackpool, 2004.

Design and furnishings for the fashionable private beach.
Cannes, 2003.

But even beaches imagined as places of complete freedom and unrestraint still involved particular designs and
unwritten expectations and rules: the Californian beach of
extreme sexual hedonism had its own distinctive social
geography and methods of self-regulation.[12] However, as the
following chapter illustrates, the beach could also be a site of
intense control and manipulation by seaside authorities
from medical practitioners to local councils. In turn, there
were sometimes bitter struggles between beach users and
seaside authorities, or among different groups of users, to
assert and realize alternative visions of the beach.

The symbolism of the beach, capturing the essence of
summertime leisure and pleasure, could also be used for
commercial and political purposes away from the seaside.
Architecture and technology allowed it to be replicated in a
variety of inland locations, from theme parks and water
parks to casino resorts and capital cities. In Las Vegas – a
resort surrounded by sand but far from the sea – the
Mandalay Bay casino and resort opened in 1999 with a
South Seas island theme, enticed visitors to 'Dive into
Mandalay Bay's lush, 11-acre tropical sand beach' ringing a
water park with pools, wave machines and a 'lazy river'.[13]
In 2002 the beach concept was used in Paris in an attempt
to lure visitors to the capital and to persuade residents to
stay in the city during the traditional summer holiday
period of the great French exodus to the seaside. 'Paris-
Plage' transformed the banks of the Seine with 3,000
tonnes of fine white sand, potted palm trees, sun loungers
and parasols.[14] The success of the venture – 2.3 million
people visited the beach in 2003 – led to it being repeated
in subsequent years and copied in other European cities.
Although Paris-Plage was claimed as 'one of the most
successful examples ever of instantaneous urban

The regulated beach at dusk: Beer, Devon, 1999.

top left: The early-morning beach as a religious space, Brighton, 2003.

top right: The family beach, Lancing, Sussex, 2002.

above: The crowded, youthful beach: Brighton, 2004.

Use of the beach and the bathing costume in transition in an inter-war beach scene on a postcard.

Inter-war beach scene, 'Côte d'Azur. Scène de Plage.'

Venice Lido, *c.* 1956.

The regulated beach, Skegness, 2002.

The Mandalay Bay Hotel, Las Vegas, 2002.

transformation',[15] London had done much the same thing immediately after the Second World War, sand being imported to Tower Beach, and allowing Londoners the curious pleasures of lazing on a sandy beach and swimming in the tidal Thames while in the shadow of Tower Bridge and a bomb-ravaged city all around.

PARK AND GARDEN

In 1818 Brighton's most significant open space away from the beach, the Steine, was described as 'the fashionable promenade . . . unrivalled for the beauty of its lawn, and the crowds of nobility and gentry which assemble there every evening'.[16] Just inland from the seafront and ringed by the resort's principal buildings, including the adjacent Royal Pavilion, the open space had been transformed from a working area used by the fishing community into a respectable resort promenade ground:

Fifty years ago it was called Stein Field, and nothing more than common waste land, indiscriminately used by the inhabitants for the repository of heavy goods, sale of coals, boat building, net making, &c. The Steyne was levelled and enclosed, and, as the company invariably promenaded in this field, the nuisances gradually disappeared.[17]

Despite continuing opposition from the fishing community, the initial enclosing of the Steine with wooden railings and accompanying turfing occurred in 1776. This open space for pleasure was an essential element in the creation of Brighton as a resort; early on there were no seafront spaces designed for promenading and, in any event, the initial fashionable visitors to the town appeared to prioritize society above sea views. Subsequently the Steine as a pleasure ground was re-made in more elaborate versions through the addition of iron fencing, floral beds and shrubs, paths, lighting, the encasement of a stream, varied commemorative

The pinnacle of designing Brighton's Steine as a seaside park and promenade. The opening of the Victoria Fountain, from the *Illustrated London News*, 30 May 1846.

'View of the Subscription Gardens, the Clock Tower and Maize Hill', St Leonards; in the middle distance, the new resort; an engraving of *c.* 1835.

The sedate and educative Dreamland gardens, Margate, *c.* 1920s.

statues and memorials and, in 1846, a centrepiece in the form of an ornamental fountain, 32 feet high with large cast-iron dolphins. This was a regulated space, for the elite visitors to the resort, governed by rules that prohibited unwelcome users and inappropriate activities.

The story of the appropriation of the Steine by seaside authorities and its transformation into a respectable and regulated space for visitors was repeated for resort open spaces elsewhere in Britain. In nearby Hastings, for example, the working fishing beach was endlessly tidied, ordered and

regulated by the town council to make it a seemingly more attractive place for visitors to the resort. This had partly been achieved by 1858, when the author of one guide commented: 'the beach has been vastly improved by the removal of the quaint-looking old fishing huts, that formerly so much obstructed the sea view'.[18]

The Steine, though, was unusual in being an early designed pleasure ground that was publicly provided and – at least to the respectable – freely accessible. More typical, until the mid-nineteenth century, were subscription gardens associated with private seaside estates, such as Kemp Town in Brighton and the St Leonards new town close to Hastings, and fee-charging commercial pleasure grounds open to all, or at least to those that had the price of the admission charge.[19] But from mid-century the growing significance of the seaside authorities in designing and regulating resorts was associated with the increasing public provision of seaside parks and gardens. Land was purchased or given to town councils (sometimes in self-interest) by local landowners, made into public parks and gardens, and subsequently promoted as resort attractions.

A pattern of public provision followed in many established British resorts included a string of parks and gardens integral to the seafront proper; large inland parks often some distance from the front; and, especially in the first half of the twentieth century, the development of new leisure open spaces at a resort's built-up extremities. Each of these spaces had a specific role to play in the design fabric of a resort. The interior parks – for example, Stanley Park in Blackpool, Preston Park in Brighton and Alexandra

Park in Hastings – offered rational recreations and entertainments from bowling, tennis and boating lakes to rose gardens, rockeries and cafés. Scarborough's Peasholm Park was especially distinctive, its Japanese gardens with a pagoda surrounding a lake on which naval warfare battles were fought with miniature warships. In contrast, the typically later outlying extensions, in part land-use planning devices restricting and controlling the growth of a resort, usually concentrated on the popular new-found interests in open-air physical sporting activities or simply provided green swathes for coastal walks.[20]

The seafront parks and gardens, intricately related to the promenade, were a particularly critical dimension in designing the British seaside resort. They clothed and furnished the stark edge of the resort through a combination of elements. Grass lawns and paths, perhaps made of crazy paving, were the stable ingredients. They were enlivened with various themes. Ornamental gardens and flowerbeds might include floral architectural elements such as a clock or steamer, Italianate gardens or rockeries, or specialized gardens for roses or alpine plants. Artificial water features ranged from fountains, waterfalls and cascades, ornamental lakes with stepping-stones and coloured lighting, to children's paddling pools and boating lakes. There were bandstands, shelters, refreshment rooms and toilets. The past was referenced through memorials and commemorative statues, the present through floral clocks and clock towers, other places through a riot of theming and exotic planting, and the mastery of nature through the sustained magnificence of the planting.

Floral Ship, seafront, Tauranga, New Zealand, 1973.

The Pine Walk, Bournemouth, c. 1916, shortly after a name change from Invalids' Walk.

If domestic gardens 'were extensions of the house in architecture as well as decoration',[21] seafront parks and gardens became grand open-air extensions of the seaside hotel and boarding house. The seaside park and garden domesticated the seaside, in a familiar and comfortable way but at the same time in a manner more adventurous, wondrous and elaborate than could ever be attempted in the ordinary home. The seaside garden also become 'a mediator of sociability',[22] with the promenade spaces and

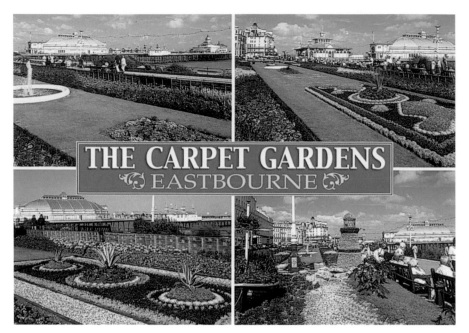

nature. Initially a mid-nineteenth-century private garden for a seafront hotel, they were taken into ownership of the Corporation in the mid-1890s. Essentially unchanged since then, this most manicured of seafront gardens includes various architectural floral features such as intricate 'Persian Carpet' panels.

Postcard of the Carpet Gardens, Eastbourne, *c*. 2000.

walks and arrangements of benches and seats, the positioning of the bandstand, floral clock or fountain, and the main garden features all helping to throw holidaymakers into contact with each other. But the seaside garden also, ideally, provided views and experiences of nature, in the form of the beach and sea, albeit at a distance and separated and bounded by the seafront railings and sea defences. There were safety and domesticity here, but also a grandeur that might otherwise be experienced only in a stately home or palace: seafront parks and gardens copied a private and elite experience and translated it into a public attraction that was shared and democratic.[23] Seaside parks, gardens and associated open spaces could provoke intense personal responses from individuals and their families, most obviously revealed in the use of memorial seats, marking the death of a loved one, their engraved plaques capturing in a few words why the person and the place was so important.

Eastbourne's carpet gardens more so than most demonstrate this combination of elements from the domestication of nature through gardening and the creation of spaces for respectable sociability to the very edge of raw untamable

PROMENADE AND BOARDWALK

Behind the pleasurable seafront is another purpose, of defence against nature. In most resorts there was a critical need to make safe and solidify the otherwise permeable and shifting boundary between land and sea. Without the front — and it is sometimes tantalizingly unclear whether the word refers to the front of the land or the front of the sea — resorts would be imperilled. This concern with safety and protection from the sea has involved the construction of 'coastal defences', the phrase revealing the underlying anxiety of an attack by nature, using groynes, breakwaters and sea walls. This alternative seaside architecture has its own history, typically involving progressively larger, more permanent and extensive structures and maintenance and renewal with, for example, original sea walls built of stone being re-made or replaced in concrete.[24]

But the inhospitable natural coastal margin often proved difficult to comprehend and tame. At New Brighton in north-west England, the building of the Marine Promenade in the inter-war years of the twentieth century was planned both to provide a new promenade and protect the town's beaches. The unfortunate opposite result led to the erosion of local beaches and contributed to holidaymakers

PRINCESS PARADE

NORTH SHORE. BLACKPOOL

THE TOWN'S RECORD OF MUNICIPAL ACHIEVE-MENTS STANDS UN--EQUALLED BY ANY CORPORATE BODY.
[BELFAST TELEGRAPH·]

THE THREE FINE ESPLANADES ON THE NORTH SHORE IS THE MOST POPULAR PART OF THE 75 ACRES OF SMOOTH ASPHALT WHICH STRETCHES FOR THREE MILES ALONG THE SHORE, ON WHICH 100,000 PEOPLE MAY PROMENADE WITH EASE : THIS HUGE UNDERTAKING IS A SPLENDID EXAMPLE OF MUNICIPAL ENTERPRISE : EXECUTED AT A COST OF £390,000, THROUGH THE BOROUGH SURVEYOR (MR. J. S. BRODIE.)

Early 20th-century postcard displaying Blackpool municipal pride at the re-making of the North Shore seafront.

deserting the resort: 'New Brighton cut its own throat – a long suicide, but a sure one.'[25]

Apart from being a defensive measure against the sea there were equally practical commercial reasons to improve seafronts. In resorts such as Hastings, Blackpool and Coney Island, where original sea walls butted against resort buildings leaving minimal open space, new and more secure sea walls were constructed seaward to provide more expansive seafronts. As a local paper commented in the early twentieth century on the completion of a massively expensive scheme to broaden Blackpool's seafront, 'We can well afford to sink a third of a million in perfecting our sea-front. It is our principal market-place, and must be our greatest attraction.'[26] Elsewhere, the artificial or natural accretion of a beach took the sea ever further from a resort – Southport is the classic English example of organic beach accumulation – with subsequent architectural and design interventions to enliven new open spaces, perhaps with promenades, gardens and lakes.

Seafronts provoked other functional responses. Even the classic boardwalk of seaside America probably began with the purpose to keep sand from being trodden into Atlantic City's hotel carpets.[27] In resort landscapes with cliffs as a barrier to be negotiated between beach and resort, the architectural and engineering reaction included lifts and cliff railways, steps and pathways, and protective railings against a fall.[28]

But whatever the utilitarian functional purpose of the seafront, its other major role as a primary seaside pleasure zone ensured that the front was designed, clothed and made suitable for the holidaymaker. The promenade and boardwalk became a major space through which holiday-makers interacted with both society and nature. Just on the landward edge of the boundary between land and sea, the promenade allowed society collectively to experience the magnificence and awe of nature.[29] But it also allowed individuals the memorable and perhaps equally awesome experience of participating in seaside society in the form of the promenade crowds. Essential architectural elements included the spaces and paving for walking and seeing and being seen, and facilities for resting, sitting, viewing, sheltering and, in the twentieth century, sunning. Additional elements included bandstands for listening to music, manicured seafront gardens and, especially in the twentieth century, children's boating lakes, paddling pools and playgrounds.

There were various design strategies. In nineteenth-century British resorts, for example, decorative cast-iron was the material used to embellish the seafront promenade; in the twentieth century concrete came to the fore. Cliffs also needed to be embroidered with brickwork, terraces or vegetation. Chalk cliffs, with their daunting baldness and stark whiteness, were deemed particularly unattractive. One technique, employed in Brighton, was the creation of the

The Beach & Boardwalk from Steel Pier. Atlantic City, N.J.

Atlantic City's Boardwalk in the early 1900s, and in 2004.

opposite: Cliff lift at Blackpool, 2004.

richly decorated cast-iron Madeira Terrace, horizontally dividing the cliffs and thereby providing a third promenading space. At Folkestone, with the Zigzag Path of 1921 traversing the cliff face, and Ramsgate, with its 1893 Madeira Walk descending from cliff top to beach level, the naked chalk was transformed into the picturesque through the careful planting and artificial rock features rendered with Pulhamite. A 1910 guide described the Madeira Walk effect as:

A cleverly contrived 'pass' overhung by solid blocks of Pulhamite rockwork, interspersed with shrubs and flowers. It is very artificial, but none the less very pleasing. The geologist and antiquary of the far future will probably be at his wits' end to account for stone of this nature being imbedded in chalk. The waterfall is the most perfect of shams . . . Here, even in the droughtiest of droughts, the water is never 'off', unless the engineer directs so, or the gas-engine breaks down. When the fall is illuminated at night by revolving lamps of various hues the effect is charming.[30]

Seafronts, promenades and boardwalks soaked up the character and ambiance of specific resorts and their holidaymakers. In the United States, for example, an Atlantic

SUNKEN GARDENS, N.S., BLACKPOOL.

PAIGNTON
GLORIOUS SOUTH DEVON

"THE MOONLIGHT PROMENADE."

Oh! the moonlight Promenade, with a nice girl by your side,
While the jolly old moon is shining round,
Throwing your shadows upon the ground,
You can kiss, squeeze, cuddle and spoon, for outsiders you've no
    regard,
And there's many a Miss who has had her first kiss
On the moonlight Promenade.
                Songs of the Season Series

top left: Embroidering a previously ragged edge, The Sunken Gardens at Blackpool, *c.* 1955.

left: 'Business with pleasure': sea defence as promenade at Paignton, Devon, 1949.

above: An early 20th-century postcard of 'The Moonlight Promenade'.

opposite: Madeira Lift, Brighton, 2004.

Margate, Kent, seafront shelter, photographed in 1999.

Plymouth Hoe, Devon, also in 1999.

City observer in 1900 described how the boardwalk, a structure that was repeatedly re-made, extended and enlarged, divided the resort's boisterous society from nature. On the landward side:

> Booths run the gamut from home missions to vaudeville; from oysters to photographers. They also include book stalls, sun parlors, Japanese stalls . . . and fortune tellers, who invariably prophesy wealth and a large family for a reasonable fee of fifty cents. And there, almost bordering on this gingerbread, clapboard creation of man, is the sea – its surf sparkling in the sun as if smiling to itself at the thought that with one sweep of its long, green arm it would wipe the beach clear.[31]

At much the same time a very different promenade experience was to be had on the other side of the Atlantic – on the Leas in Folkestone, an eminently respectable cliff-top, open promenading space and the centre of a still aristocratic resort:

> On the Leas on a Sunday one may see the Distinguished and the Wealthy rub shoulders in pleasant contiguity, instinct with the satisfactory knowledge that they have achieved their weekly devotions and that a good dinner awaits a good appetite. The edges of the prayer-books gleam along the smooth grass, the sun shines, the dresses rustle discretely, the voices simulate the murmur of the sea. The sea itself keeps at a respectful distance, acts as a good servant, silently supplying the necessary ozone . . . This is the real philosophy of a Folkestone season. This is the town's justification, its apologia pro vita sua.[32]

Brighton's rather plain older seafront, *c.* 1906.

The new elaborate Italianate seafront gardens in Brighton from the Oriental birdcage bandstand of 1884, *c.* 1930s.

Magnus Volk's electric sea train, nicknamed the 'Daddy-long-legs', Brighton, 1896–1901.

Nice, 2003, with a free public beach in the foreground and a private beach beyond the fence.

Artificial Pulhamite rock and the waterfall feature, Madeira Walk, Ramsgate, from a postcard, *c.* 1906.

mind (a public convenience was provided beneath the bandstand) – and Ramsgate's Madeira Walk with its Pulhamite artificial rock, designed gardens and waterfall were identified as seafront heritage to be restored for the future. Other projects have re-made promenades, combining a strong public art emphasis with architectural and engineering changes. One of the most highly praised schemes was Bridlington's remaking of its south promenade completed in 1998 and the product of an architect-artist collaboration between Irena Bauman and Bruce McLean.[38] Blackpool's neglected southern promenade was also re-engineered and redecorated with a series of large works of public art. In Brighton, the central seafront between the two piers was subject to a radical redevelopment involving both public and private sectors. The public elements included a fishing museum, a new curved boardwalk with idiosyncratic public sculptures, and basketball and beach volley-ball courts; the private-sector investment ranged through a health and fitness centre, shops and artists' studios, pubs and clubs, and cafés and restaurants.

But, in the early twenty-first century, the intriguing question is whether the nature of the seaside promenading experience has radically changed. In one view with the development of postmodern society the promenading experience

A Blackpool South Promenade improvement: Michael Trainor, 'They Shoot Horses Don't They?', 2002; the world's largest mirror ball.

Public art on Blackpool's South Promenade in 2004.

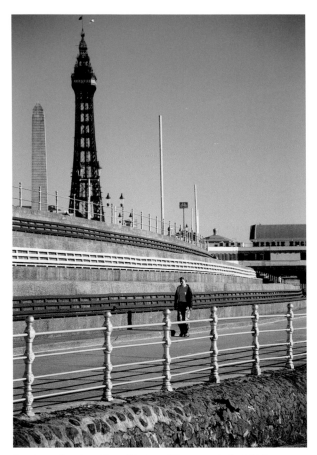

Empty seafront seating, Blackpool Promenade in 2004.

has been transformed from a shared and collective to an individual one.[39] Certainly, though, the experience of promenades in different resorts has changed over time. Even on the busiest and sunny summer day, nowadays Blackpool's extensive promenades are mostly under-used, a shadow of a crowded, jostling past, while in a Mediterranean resort such as Cannes, the summer-evening seafront promenade remains a significant feature of the seaside.

CHAPTER 6
ARCHITECTURE FOR SEA AND BEACH

The sea, although a strange and alien environment distinct and separate from the land, was the primary reason for visitors seeking health and pleasure to journey to the coast and for the emergence and development of seaside resorts. To be bathed in, however, the sea also had to be entered, and Western countries developed a range of alternative vernacular architectures designed to provide access to the ocean. These seashore architectures evolved over time, revealing much about changing uses of the sea and the beach, and radical shifts in attitudes to nature, notions of decency and pleasure, gender and the family, and the public and private.

BATHING MACHINES

In Britain, for two centuries from the 1730s, the architectural icon of the use of the sea for health and pleasure was the bathing machine. This radical invention was in use on the sands of the coastal spa town of Scarborough, Yorkshire, by the 1840s. It could still be glimpsed as an anachronism, engulfed by a sea of holidaymakers, on the beach at Blackpool in the 1930s. Outwardly, it looked substantially the same in the 1930s as it had 200 years earlier: a small rectangular wooden structure tall enough for a person to stand comfortably, with a pitched roof, a door at both of the narrower sides with steps leading either up from the land or down to the sea, and small windows set high in the longer walls, all fixed on a undercarriage mounted on axles and four wooden and usually large wheels. By the end of this

long period, however, the bathing machine had become a redundant and antiquated piece of architecture, falling into disuse as the domination of private bathing for health as a way of consuming nature gave way to new forms of consumption around the communal use of the sea and beach, public swimming and sunbathing for pleasure.

Early accounts struggled to describe bathing machines. In the mid-eighteenth century it was both 'a curious contrivance of Wooden Houses moveable on wheels'[1] and 'a conveniency made for safety and privately bathing in the sea, of late much used and found beneficial'.[2] Tobias Smollett's more detailed description of the Scarborough machines in his semi-autobiographical fiction, *Humphrey Clinker*, published in 1771, still conveys the novelty of using bathing machines – 'ranged along the beach, with all their proper utensils and attendants':

> Image to yourself a small, snug, wooden chamber, fixed upon a wheel-carriage, having a door at each end, and on each side a little window above, a bench below – The bather, ascending into this apartment by wooden steps, shuts himself in, and begins to undress, while the attendant yokes a horse to the end next the sea, and draws the carriage forwards, till the surface of the water is on a level with the floor of the dressing-room, and then he moves and fixes the horse to the other end – The person within being stripped, opens the door to the sea-ward, where he finds the guide ready, and plunges headlong into the water – After having bathed, he re-ascends into

the apartment, by the steps which had been shifted for that purpose, and puts on his clothes at his leisure, while the carriage is drawn back again upon the dry land; so that he has nothing further to do, but to open the door, and come down as he went up.[3]

Guidebooks, a major mechanism for selling and representing the first seaside resorts, quickly adopted the number and quality of bathing machine as a measure of the size and excellence of a resort. In Hastings, in the mid-1790s, for example:

The Bathing Machines (of which there are twelve or fourteen very good ones) stand to the westward of the town, close to the parade, on which is a small box, called the Bathing-room, for the use of company, while waiting for the Machines. No watering place can excel Hastings in the convenience of bathing; few can equal it.[4]

A piece of moveable and moving architecture, the physical distance travelled by the occupants of bathing machines was usually no more than a few tens of metres. But the bathing machine had a significant symbolic and cultural role as the apparatus for venturing from the landside into the seaside of the beach. It was the vehicle from which bathers immersed themselves, or were immersed by others, in the sea, and in doing so consumed nature. People paid for the privilege of being transported in a bathing machine, with the direct monetary transaction commodifying and privatizing nature. The bathing machine became an essential

'A curious contrivance of Wooden Houses moveable on wheels', from *The South Prospect of Scarborough in the County of Yorkshire*, 1745.

Hidden amongst the crowded beach, a few surviving bathing machines, Blackpool, 1938.

instrument for regulating and controlling the use of the sea – when, where and how people bathed. In designing their ideal seasides and how they should be used, the early resort physicians concentrated on bathing in the sea, usually medically prescribing its consumption in great detail.

In this early period in the larger and more successful resorts, the 'bathing-room' was an essential adjunct to the machines themselves, a building where prospective bathers – members of polite society and the elite 'Company' – would gather, waiting for a bathing machine to become available. The relationship between the two pieces of architecture was most developed in Margate, where the half-dozen bathing rooms sandwiched between the High Street and the Sands included galleries looking out over the bathing beaches and steps providing direct access into the machines. Margate was at the forefront of bathing-machine architecture in other ways. In the middle of the eighteenth century Benjamin Beale, a Quaker living in the resort, invented the modesty hood, a canvas canopy shielding bathers from prying eyes and creating a private, individual bath. Society appropriated nature for a specific purpose and with little explicit recognition of the vastness of the ocean lying beyond the confines at the machine:

The architecture of late 18th- and early 19th-century bathing at Margate: machines with their modesty hoods, the bathing houses with galleries and stairs to the machines.

> The Machine moves on 4 Wheels, on which is erected a commodious Dressing-Room, furnished in a genteel Manner. The Machine is so contriv'd, that the Persons who bathe descend from out of the above Room into a Bath, which forms itself in the natural Sea 7 Feet in Length and 5 Feet Breadth; all inclosed and railed, which renders it both secure and private.[5]

But over the two centuries of its use, the bathing machine and all that went with it was never accepted with complete unanimity. Some people contested and resisted this control, asserting other views and ideas about how the sea should be used. Bathing machines and the seashores across which they rolled were also sites where the evolving relationships and schisms around gender and class were played out. Age, marital status and sexual relations were often explicit added ingredients. These divides were also cut through by rifts around whether the seaside as a place of health and leisure was essentially public and communal, on

Structures for bathing without machines: Plymouth Hoe in 2002.

the one hand, or private and individual, on the other. Many of these sustained tensions are apparent in enduring antagonisms and conflicts between two groups: the decency regulators – those asserting that the bathing machine was essential for decency, propriety and respectability; and the pleasure seekers – those arguing that bathing machines restricted freedom and pleasure.

Smollett, writing in the mid-eighteenth century, captured the tension between the control and constraint imposed by machines and the freedom sought by the pleasure seekers. His fictional character, Jery Melford, discusses the use by women bathers of 'a dress of flannel . . . for the support of decorum' and the use of 'tilts' on some machines 'to screen bathers from the view of all persons whatsoever'. But Melford then continues that for his part he loves swimming 'without the formality of an apparatus', describing the sea as a 'noble bath, for health as well as pleasure. You cannot conceive what a flow of spirits it gives, and how it braces every sinew of the human frame'.

For most of the nineteenth century the decency regulators dominated, at least if measured by the almost ubiquitous presence of the bathing machine in British resorts as an instrument for controlling the use of sea bathing and regulating the consumption of nature. In a few places the use of bathing machines was impracticable because of the nature of local beaches, and instead there were seashore architectural interventions to allow bathing in sea water. On the rocky shoreline of Ilfracombe, an isolated resort on the north coast of Devon, for example, the Tunnel Beaches featured bathing pools – one for women, the other for men – constructed in 1823 'by building up walls to connect various rocks',[6] thereby retaining sea water at each high tide and creating permanent bathing areas. Elsewhere in the south-west of England there were similar primitive tidal pools, including those on the Plymouth Hoe foreshore created by the mid-nineteenth century, with a 1888 guide describing how 'There is a large and well provided bathing place for ladies underneath the Hoe, but the rocky nature of the coast renders the use of bathing machines impracticable.'[7]

The emergence of the seaside in England went hand-in-hand with the early cultural hegemony over the seaside in other parts of the West. Northern European countries, for example, had avidly adopted and sometimes adapted eighteenth-century English seaside cultural practices. As part of the process the bathing machine, as a significant cultural artefact from the seaside, was also exported to northern Europe and parts of the British Empire, particularly the Dominions. Margate machines reached the East and the West Indies in the eighteenth century,[8] and in the following century bathing machines were on the far side of the world, along with many of the British regulatory practices associated with bathing.[9]

The debates in Britain about seaside decency were also entangled with questions about whether people should bathe naked or use costumes and whether men and women should use the sea together. The evidence is fragmentary and argued over, but initially in the eighteenth century men and perhaps also women often took to the sea naked and also often bathed together.[10] Bathing machines, sometimes equipped with modesty hoods, acted as substitute costumes. The privately published guidebooks to individual resorts provided sometimes-graphic accounts of tensions around bathing machines. Take Worthing on the Sussex coast south of London. One commentator, in 1805, was aghast at bathing in the otherwise quiet and sedate resort:

> Worthing is yet in its infancy, consequently we cannot expect to find there perfection, but in the course of a few seasons, I trust, some better regulations will be adopted in respect to bathing; the present practice of ladies and gentlemen going in, sometimes nearly in the same place, and always at a distance sufficiently short, to distinguish each others features, being perfectly indecent and inconsistent with the rules of propriety and morality. I should also recommend to the gentlemen, to recollect the delicacy that is due to the female sex, and instead of lounging upon the beach, and indulging in unpleasant observations, to direct their attention to amusements more manly and becoming.[11]

Little more than a decade later, decency on Worthing's beaches appeared to be appropriately regulated: 'The machines are used separate from each other, with a proper attention to decency; and their guides are universally extolled, for the care and civility.'[12] Other writers, however, were not quite so sure about the nature of the Worthing bathing experience, contrasting the bather's private travails with the public pretence of the joyful bathing experience:

> Having picked his way over the shingles, he ascends that intolerable nuisance a bathing machine; and after a jolting of two or three minutes, violent enough to discompose the frame of an Hercules, wishes that he were in bed again. With a reluctant jump he commits himself to the wave, and upon recovering the effects of the first plunge, while gasping, and endeavouring to keep his feet upon the sands, an overgrown wave gives him a gratuitous mouthful of salt water, and a slap in the face, which knocks him against the wheel of the machine. This is too much for his nerves; he pants and blows, and hurries up the steps of his house of correction, with more celerity than he walked down them. The shaking now is patiently endured, though it gives an occasional impetus to the towel, to the danger of his eye. Released from his purgatory, he retraces the beach, and meets his neighbour going the same journey. The sea has already conferred its strengthening benefits upon him, for he expatiates upon the excellence of the bath, and professes to envy his equally reluctant friend, who is about to undergo a like saltation.[13]

While people might have disliked bathing and bathing machines, social pressure forced them to put up with 'that intolerable nuisance'. A similar sense of private scepticism together with uncertainty about the medical benefits of bathing came from John Marsh, writing in his diary about a

MERMAIDS AT PLAY; OR, A NICE LITTLE WATER PARTY.

seemed to dabble about like a fish, for a quarter of an hour together, by which she however weakened herself and brought on a complaint in her lungs that in ye course of ye following year proved fatal to her.[14]

Bathers were well aware of and openly discussed the ambivalent and contradictory attitudes to the therapeutic use of the sea, as indicated by the conversation of the waiting assembly in one of Margate's bathing houses, just four years later:

> Most of the company had talked over their own case, which invalids are particularly fond of doing, and all had given a judgement on the sea, but in general so contradictory, that [it] amounted nearly to this – it thinned and it thickened the blood – it strengthened – it weakened – it made people fat – it made them lean – it braced – it relaxed – it was good for everything – and was good for nothing.[15]

John Leech, 'Mermaids at Play; or, a Nice Little Water Party', from Leech's *Pictures of Life & Character, c.* 1860.

The transformation of a woman into a mermaid and society into nature as represented in *Judy; or, the London Serio-Comic Journal,* 6 September 1882.

visit to Bognor, on the Sussex coast, on Wednesday, 22 August 1798:

> Went into a machine from whence, with the Guide's assistance (ye sea being rather rough) I had 2 very good dips, but being not used to it, as many people pretend to do, and particularly Mrs Carpenter, who used, it

Equally, though, there were representations of bathing and bathing machines being a public pleasure. Charles Dickens, writing of the neighbouring resort of Ramsgate, described 'Three machines – three horses – three flounderings – three turnings round – three splashes – three gentlemen, disporting themselves in the water like so many dolphins.'[16] While men might become dolphins, a more dominant Victorian representation was of women bathers as mermaids, both demure and, especially if their hair floated freely in the sea or was worn down while drying on the beach, erotically alluring and sexually available.[17] In such visions the bathing machine turned society into nature and women into untamed and sexually charged mythical creatures. The bathing machine perhaps liberated – although for whose benefit is debatable – rather than controlled.

Along with mermaids, cultural representations of bathing machines incorporated a host of other stereotypes including the bawling child, the staid or ever hopeful old maid and the know-it-all gent. Fun could be poked at all, and in the process the role of the seaside authorities resisted and undermined. The sexual relationships around bathing and bathing machines were especially open to comment and ridicule, from Thomas Rowlandson in the early nineteenth century, through humorous illustrations in satirical magazines such as *Punch,* to seaside comic postcards of the twentieth century.

The bathing-machine guides, in some places called attendants, bathers or dippers, emerged as another unique seaside character. The guides were an important part of the early bathing-machine ritual, essentially helping control how the sea was consumed. As an adjunct to bathing machines, they ensured the safety of bathers and administered the therapeutic treatment prescribed by doctors. Most resorts claimed one or two renowned dippers, who were mostly presented as lovable, eccentric and long-lived local celebrities;[18] it was as though working literally in the sea created extraordinary personalities. But there were alternative views. The artist John Constable thought Brighton's female dippers 'hideous amphibious animals',[19] and a male visitor to Teignmouth in 1846 thought they were 'the most horrid-looking creatures I ever beheld – good heavens, to be dipped by one of them, and soused like a condemned puppy or kitten! The idea is dreadful.'[20] A decade later Philip Henry Gosse delighted in describing 'the thalassine immolation' taking place at Tenby in Wales:

He sees me! He sees me!!

The cruelty of life at the seaside. A comic postcard of *c.* 1906.

In the midst of the crowd stand a dozen of white bathing-machines, and the busy bathing-women – uncouth, uncorsetted figures – in blue serge gowns with a fringe of rags below, are moving to and fro; while far off, within the verge of the breaking sea, the profane eye that dares wander that direction, catches a glimpse of one of these brawny priestesses of Neptune offering a sacrifice to her divinity, in the shape of a slender figure with long sable robe and dishevelled hair. We cannot hear the shrieks, but we see with horror the arms dashed up in despair, as the helpless victim is ruthlessly seized and plunged beneath the whelming wave. – We look no more; it is too dreadful![21]

SUMMER AMUSEMENT AT MARGATE, OR A PEEP AT THE MERMAIDS.

MRS TWIST DOES NOT APPROVE OF MR TWIST GOING FOR SOLITARY STROLLS.

Two versions of the male holidaymaker as a voyeur, incurring the wrath of his spouse:

Thomas Rowlandson, *Summer Amusement at Margate, or A Peep at The Mermaids*, 1813, pen and watercolour.

A postcard of *c.* 1904.

Mother says: "So tight you musn't wear
'em, or else you're sure to tear 'em!"

An aspect of the revolution in bathing costumes in the early
20th century, seen here in a postcard of *c.* 1915.

I'm having all sorts of sport, so glad I came.

But these sacrifices, deliciously agreeable to many male eyes, were on the wane as the medical profession's grip on sea bathing loosened and doctors turned their attentions to other ways of exploiting nature. By the 1860s the profession of dipper had largely vanished. The characters lived on in local histories, along with the general notion of dippers and other people working on the beach as delightful, idiosyncratic and unusually long-lived products of the sea.[22]

The therapeutic bathing-machine rites, the very notion of sea water as an omnipotent cure-all and the representation of resorts as places of health and pleasure were also undermined by the foulness of some resorts' bathing waters. Margate's tribulations described by the caricaturist James Gillray in 1807 – writing of 'Muddy water, dead dogs, Fish Guts, Greens and filth swimming about'[23] – continued into the nineteenth century, despite investment in the sewerage disposal infrastructure. Similar sanitation problems were repeated in many other older, poorly planned and under-invested British resorts, making the use of the sea both unsavoury and potentially risky. An 1850 inquiry into Worthing's public health painted an unpleasant picture of the seashore used by the resort's 40 bathing machines with Mr Wicks, 'the proprietor of several of these moveable bathing-houses', complaining of the offensive 'odour which proceed from the sands in the immediate neighbourhood of the wooden troughs that conveyed away the drainage of the town'. Worse still, there were 'several very large cesspools sunk in the beach that were very offensive, and it was necessary to avoid their locality, for the odours were constantly complained of'.[24] The resort became infamous for its 'sloppy sands'.

Despite such difficulties, dominant Victorian mores provided the decency regulators with increasing power and

left: A postcard of *c.* 1910, one of a series using a studio set.

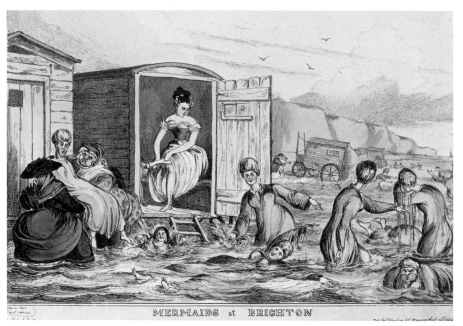

Bathing machines and bathing guides administering the treatment. William Heath, *Mermaids at Brighton, c.* 1829.

authority. Social pressure increasingly combined with legal sanction aimed at forcing people to use bathing machines and to use them in particular ways. Most resorts introduced byelaws designed to ensure the use of costumes and that men and women bathed separately from machines zoned by gender. But the paradoxical eventual outcome of this strengthening of the power of conservative seaside authorities, in the face of growing resistance from the pleasure seekers and a series of contextual factors, was to undermine the use of bathing machines. Whether for reasons of choice, fashion or social pressure, most women did indeed wear bathing costumes; in contrast, many men resisted their use. Although around the coast there were continued complaints from the decency regulators about the 'disgraceful and indecent scenes in regard to bathing'[25] by men, and despite the sanctions against bathing naked, the persistent tradition of men eschewing the use of bathing costumes was slow to die. The male pleasure seekers continued to protest about the enforced use of costumes, instead wanting 'to have pure bathing unfettered by clammy, wet rags'.[26]

But 'the market mattered more than morality at most seaside resorts',[27] and the fear of losing pleasure-seeking holidaymakers meant that byelaws were often not enforced, with male nude bathing and mixed bathing persisting throughout the nineteenth century. By the 1880s, however, in many resorts both activities were marginalized and away from the main bathing beaches, or allowed only at the start or the end of the day.

Worthing was typical of how municipal authorities tried to control bathing through the licensing of bathing machines and detailed byelaws regulating public bathing. By the late nineteenth century, the resort required bathers to use the machines licensed at specified stands; girls above the age of eight were prohibited from bathing within 50 yards of males, and vice versa; and, 'indecent exposure' was prevented by keeping the doors of machines closed while out of the water, ensuring machines were at a suitable depth in the sea while bathing took place, and through the use of 'Regulation costumes'.[28] Such segregated bathing rules reflected a particular view of 'decent' society and its relationships with nature; enforcement of the rules had various consequences, including separating members of the same family while they were in the sea.

As the seaside was opened up for new classes of holidaymaker, so the dominant use of the bathing machine was challenged. This architecture could not cope easily with the requirements of mass seaside holidaymaking. In some places there were simply too few machines to handle the influx of visitors. In other places there were so

Walter Fagg's patented bathing machine on rails, including individual changing rooms and a 'bathing crate' for non-swimmers, Folkestone, Kent, *c.* 1900.

many machines that, like losing a child on a crowded beach, bathers might quite easily lose sight of their own machine, sometimes with farcical results. In response, there were occasional attempts to improve the design of machines. An 1880s innovation was 'Fagg's Patent Bathing Carriage' at Folkestone, which ran on rails up and down the beach according to the state of the tide, and included 20 compartments in a long narrow carriage and a long boom carrying a large rope cage for use by non-swimmers.[29]

The new working-class visitors sometimes could not afford the expense of hiring a machine; on other occasions they were unaware of or simply disregarded the conventions around bathing. Working class day-trippers, in particular, challenged the bathing regime status quo. Francis Kilvert recorded girl rail-trippers at Seaton on the south coast of Devon in 1871, 'with shoes, stockings and drawers off, wading in the tide, holding up their clothes nearly to their waists and naked from the waist down,'[30] while in 1887 a respectable visitor to Torquay was shocked when 'a number of working men . . . whisked off their clothes and ran like savages to the sea'.[31] But there could be gender- and class-based double standards in such observations. Kilvert himself enjoyed bathing naked and wrote that 'the young ladies who were strolling nearby seemed to have no objection'.[32] In helping to preserve the exclusivity of particular beaches for more powerful social groups, the bathing machine and its associated regulations could be used to keep unwelcome working-class holidaymakers from reputable resorts.

The decency regulators were also criticized in popular text and images. From the mid-nineteenth century, there was a consistent flow of comic literary and visual representations attacking the bathing-machine regime and the prudery, dishonesty and discomfort that often went with it. The criticisms became increasingly severe as the century drew to a close. A satirical poem, 'A Study of a Rare Old Conservative', in *Punch* in 1883 concludes: 'that horrid contrivance, the Bathing machine!'[33]

Once men – or most of them – were clothed and the public decency lobby assuaged, the arguments for segregated bathing and the use of bathing machines were weakened – why should machines be used, or the sexes segregated, if bodies were covered by costumes? The family as a unit also became an increasingly important focus for seashore pleasure, making the segregationist rules around bathing machines progressively more dysfunctional. Attitudes to consuming nature at the seaside altered in other ways, with a growing emphasis on active pleasure. The growing popularity of swimming – and demand from holidaymakers to learn to swim – and playing in the sea also made the notion of being tethered to a bathing machine

increasingly ridiculous. Some bathing-machine proprietors adapted to the challenge by employing swimming instructors and offering swimming lessons; but this was but a respite from the challenge to machines.

But the initial external impulse undermining the supremacy of the bathing machine in Britain came from the northern resorts of mainland Europe, where, during the nineteenth century, use of bathing machines increasingly disregarded segregation of the sexes. As early as mid-century a few lone English voices found the French style of 'mixed bathing' quite acceptable:

> To an Englishman of the present generation, this strange mode of bathing, and mixture of the sexes, waves, sands, sea-weed, jelly-fish, and conversation, is a decided novelty; but that is all, for I never heard of any impropriety occurring in consequence of the custom; and I always found these *réunions* in the water equally agreeable with those in the salons of Caen. Some of the ladies who were very careful of their complexions . . . invariably took their parasols into the sea with them.[34]

It took another half-century for such contrasts to be forcefully used on behalf of the pleasure seekers. And yet in 1896 at the public

top: A *c.* 1910 postcard of an 'Ostende Baigneuse', posing for bathing at the Belgian resort.

left: An early postcard of Etretat – the French style of bathing at a small resort.

ÉTRETAT. — La Plage à l'heure des Bains

Inter-war postcards showing the variety of bathing tents at two Kentish resorts: Folkestone and Palm Bay, Cliftonville.

bathing station on one beach in Hove, actually Brighton's respectable neighbouring resort, 'men and women bathe together' and there were 'naked men talking to nursemaids', although this nakedness was probably a reference to the wearing of revealing costumes rather than to be taken literally. One journalist feigned uncertainty as to whether such activities were 'rather advanced or else quite primitive', noting how mixed bathing 'excites no surprise when one is, say, in Dieppe (what a difference sixty miles or so make in one's notion of propriety), but is really very, very awful when we are in England'.[35]

In Britain the introduction of bathing tents for changing, in tune with the notion that men, women and children could bathe and swim together, was the first architectural novelty to challenge the bathing machine status quo. In 1892 the *Boy's Own Paper* carried an article on how readers could make a portable bathing tent, the author arguing that 'there are some folks who object to using bathing machines, and have a corresponding antipathy to the half-dried towels supplied therein, and I think that not only they, but every one fond of swimming . . . would appreciate the possession of a portable tent . . . which would render them independent of bathing machines'.[36]

Across the nation, sections of the press increasingly attacked regulated and segregated bathing, much preferring the relaxed mixed bathing in France.[37] Municipal authorities were also apprehensive that visitors would be lured to the Continent rather than remain in British resorts. Increasing pressure from determined and vocal visitors eventually led a few innovative resorts to sanction the groundswell of popular sentiment and officially allow mixed bathing. Llandudno on the Welsh coast was the first in 1895, quickly followed by a string of small and then larger resorts.[38]

The demise of segregated bathing was also to become the death knell for the bathing machine: the introduction of mixed bathing meant the removal of its remaining decency protection function. Visitors flocked to the pioneering resorts, opening the floodgates for other resorts to follow suit or otherwise lose visitor numbers and market position. At first segregated bathing was maintained on some beaches in most resorts, but these beaches were mostly quiet, with the mixed bathing beaches packed with holidaymakers. But there was also substantial local variation that could run ahead or tail behind such wider changes, and in some resorts the dominant social groups, usually in control of town councils, acted as conservative forces; the pleasure seekers resisted, and change was adopted reluctantly and late. In the south-west of England the laggardly resorts were Ilfracombe and Lynmouth, finally accepting mixed bathing in 1906 and 1907 respectively.[39] At Worthing on the Sussex coast the bathing regulations had eased by the early 1900s, but there were continual demands for the remaining restrictions to be removed. In 1906 one businessman had a vision of 'Dieppe at Worthing', combining lock-up tents and 'plenty of bright music while bathing was in progress so that we might in that respect more nearly approximate to the Continental model', while six years later a writer to the *Worthing Gazette* lambasted the remaining bathing machines as 'antediluvian relics of early Victorian barbarism', urging that councils 'remove all restrictions as to when and where bathers should enter the sea and should encourage mixed or family bathing as much as possible'.[40]

Although from the early decades of the twentieth century costumes alone were needed to bathe in British coastal waters, and despite radical changes in attitudes to nature, traditional medical opinion and some seaside guidebooks continued to offer conservative advice on sea bathing. A 1905 guide to Hastings, for instance, asserted that for children, 'The practice of paddling should not be allowed, it is most injurious.'[41] There were also debates – duplicated throughout the West – over what constituted appropriate costumes, how much of the body should be covered and what material should be used.[42] In Bexhill in 1904, and despite its reputation as a fashionable and forward-looking new resort, following complaints from the proprietor of one of the town's private girls' schools, argument raged about whether male bathers should use 'University costumes', covering them from neck to knee, or the more revealing 'slips' or bathing drawers. One correspondent writing to the national *Daily Mail* was horrified by the Bexhill situation: 'first, for ladies, it was a costume with a tunic, then a costume without a tunic, then the material got thinner, till now we read of white silk (about as thick as another skin) . . . For the general public to meet under such conditions as these will not long continue possible in England.'[43]

The unravelling of the relationship between costume and machine was accompanied by still more radical changes in holidaymaking at the Western seaside. Sun rather than sea bathing had no use for the old bathing machines. The stress on sunbathing, swimming, and play and exercise, in public and in the open air, made bathing machines, in design architecture for private sea bathing, redundant. Naturism was at the forefront of the discovery of the sun, helping the long-established British seaside tradition of bathing naked to survive the twentieth century

with remarkable resilience. Although in one view by 1914 'the last diehards finally gave up the old custom of nude bathing',[44] in reality local custom and practice ensured that some remote or private beaches remained places for naked bathing. The new naturism, however, gave renewed impetus to the activity by both men and women.

By the mid-1930s, the commentator Ivor Brown saw the bathing machine as 'one of the great vehicles of the nineteenth century. Now it can be seen shelved on the shingle, mouldering to decay . . . unwanted by a Lido-haunting generation'. Brown captured nicely the tension between the 'shabby, sandy, grubby boxes' and how, in the past, in them 'we were delirious passengers'.[45] Other inter-war observers were less sympathetic, with George Ryley Scott regretting how bathing for the masses had coincided with Victorian Puritanism, making nudity and immorality synonymous: 'The greater the area of flesh exposed the more immoral was the woman – and the man.' It was the segregated bathing machine's 'regulations and restrictions, imposed in the blessed names of modesty and morality, that acted as cold blankets and did so much to retard the growth in popularity of bathing'.[46]

Whatever the analysis of the past, by the 1930s most bathing machines were left literally high and dry at the top of the beach. Some were burnt in huge bonfires; others were sold to local people for garden and allotment sheds and chicken houses – in the late twentieth century a few were reclaimed, restored as seaside heritage and placed on show in museums – and many, with wheels removed, were converted into beach huts. If they had not already disappeared, the start of the Second World War, and the need to clear obstructions from beaches to help protect against sea-borne invasion, acted as an efficient bathing-machine removal agent.

A postcard, c. 1920, of the 'View from Pier, Shanklin', Isle of Wight, showing bathing machines high and dry.

Shanklin beach huts, probably converted from bathing machines, photographed c. 1999.

Australian architecture for the sea: two views of the Sea Baths, Queenscliff, Victoria, *c*. 1910.

BEYOND BRITISH SHORES

With the growing internationalization of the seaside resort, there were comparisons to be made with the practice of bathing beyond British shores. Seaside holidaymakers in other countries found alternative – and preferable – ways of using the sea that had no need for the bathing machine, especially as it was used in Britain. In consequence, the British cultural hegemony of the Western seaside faded, and increasingly the British seaside was influenced by what happened elsewhere.

This was especially the case in Australia, with the few bathing machines that had arrived in Australian resorts, such as St Kilda, quickly giving way to an alternative Australian architecture of the beach and sea, in the form of public baths or 'bathing establishments', which gave access to the sea itself and sometimes to buildings providing hot-water baths and medical treatments. Although dispensing with bathing machines, other aspects of the English bathing tradition, including regulation and segregation by sex, were maintained into the early twentieth century. Usually built in the sea and accessed by a pier, the public baths, along with their attendants, tickets and changing rooms, became an important feature of the Australian seaside resort. They included an additional feature – a fence enclosing the bathing area – to ensure bathers were 'perfectly safe from the attack of those sea monsters – sharks',[47] the creatures being one reason why the bathing machine was such an ephemeral feature in the colony. Australian resorts were anxious to extol the virtues of their bathing establishments, with one mid-1870s guide, for example, describing how Sorrento's baths were 'equal to any artificial enclosure in the colony':

> The picket fence extends into the Bay 850 feet. The rise and fall of the tide secures the perfect purity of the

Baths carved out of the shore, Bondi Beach, Sydney, Australia, 1922.

> water. The sloping bottom and the sandy beach add comfort and safety to the luxury of a bath, while every possible element that leads to strength and enjoyment are present to make up the sum total of the whole.[48]

Looking back four decades to the 1920s, Graham McInnes graphically described the 'shark-proof enclosure of piles and netting through which the sea vigorously slopped' of various men's and women's baths along the Melbourne seafront:

> The baths presented . . . much the same entrance as that to an English pier: an arch, flanked by ticket booths and a turnstile. Beyond this lay a wooden hall where you could buy 'lollies' or ice-cream and also rent locker keys, towels and an exiguous male bikini known as a pair of Vees. Thus equipped you entered the baths proper, a wooden oblong with a runway and a series of cubicles at the shore end and down each side. Cubicles

Bondi Beach Surf Bathers' Life Saving Club, 1907.

The ritual of the surfing beach, Western Australia, 1951.

thickly encrusted with a heavy growth of mussels, like fungus on an old tree, but gleaming jet black in the troughs between incoming waves.[49]

And yet by 1900 more and more Australian bathers deserted the public baths in favour of bathing from the beach itself, leading to developments that were to have international significance. In some parts of the coast baths were in any case impracticable because of the huge waves crashing onto the shore. Instead the surf itself became an enduring attraction. At Bondi Beach, Sydney, the combination of the challenging waves pounding the shore and the initial impetus given by meetings to resist restrictive bathing laws led to the formation, in 1907, of the world's first surf life-saving club, the Bondi Surf Bathers' Life Saving Club. Along with its central purpose of saving the lives of surf bathers, the Bondi club became an enduring ornament of the beach, with the patrols of the uniformed volunteer life-savers, its equipment, including surf boats and the Surf and Line Belt invented at Bondi, and a rich tradition of displays, competitions and carnivals. Elsewhere in Australia and other seaside places where surf was the norm and an exciting lure to ever more beach users, hundreds of other life-saving clubs followed the initial Bondi example.

At much the same time, another Australian architectural bathing innovation was the 'bathing box', 'a symbol of

were shared by two or three boys, and after climbing into your Vees and hanging your key around your neck on a piece of salt-toughened string, you entered steps at the shore end. The entire structure was weathered ash grey with a permanent scurf of salt . . .

Where the bottom shelved into deeper water, ropes strung across assisted non-swimmers. As the protecting piles progressed seaward they became more

some status' and 'a private change room, a storehouse and a refuge from the heat',[50] remarkably similar in form and function to the beach huts that subsequently became increasingly popular in Britain.

The European version of the bathing box, the beach cabin or *cabana*, had already become a significant feature of the most elitist Mediterranean resorts by the early twentieth century. In *Death in Venice* Thomas Mann describes how the beach cabin, with its awning and wooden platform providing a veranda and protection from sun and sand, performed as a piece of architecture from which to view 'the scene on the beach, the spectacle of civilization taking its carefree sensuous ease at the brink of the element'.[51] The private hotel beaches on the fashionable Venice Lido with its imposing leisure architecture described by Mann were the preserve of wealthy European families, separated by nationality but drawn together by their membership of the aristocracy and enjoyment of the new-found pleasures of relaxing on the sunny sands and playing and swimming in the shallow, warm sea. Mann develops the coalescence of society and nature on the beach into a mechanism for Aschenbach, the story's protagonist, to fall in love with the beautiful Tadzio, a fourteen-year-old boy he admires from afar. Aschenbach allows the revitalization he receives 'from the sun and leisure and sea air to burn itself up in intoxicating emotion'[52] for the object of his affection. He is unable to break free of his obsession, which proves fatal, and Aschenbach dies while sitting on the beach watching Tadzio on one last occasion. On the emerging summertime French Riviera, too, the bathing cabin became increasingly familiar.

Decoratively embellished changing huts at Nice in the early 20th century.

Cabana, Venice Lido, 2003.

Sea-bathing for the New York masses: Coney Island, 1900.

An early 20th-century postcard of bath houses at the 'Shore Line, East from Dreamland Chutes, Coney Island'.

Late-nineteenth-century English visitors to another continent, North America, knew that the bathing machine was little used there, since 'by far the most popular method of bathing is that in the open sea, or surf-bathing'.[53] In the largest and most working-class resorts, the bath house developed as an architectural feature of the seaside, providing changing rooms and costume hire for the masses wishing to enjoy the sea. New York's Coney Island had both private bath houses and, from 1911, a huge solid Municipal Baths with 12,000 lockers: poorer New York families might queue for hours waiting for the chance to use the baths and the sea.[54]

The Australian bathing establishment and bathing box, the mainland European beach cabin and the American bath house were eventually translated, as beach hut and bathing pavilion, into common architectural features of the British seaside.

BATHING PAVILIONS AND SUN TERRACES

Despite the demise of the bathing machine, during the decades before 1950, some British local authorities – deeply traditional and conservative Eastbourne was one of the most notorious – continued the attempted regulation of beach bathers, trying to enforce the use of huts and tents for changing and banning both changing on the beach and 'mackintosh bathing', the practice of wearing a waterproof coat over one's costume when going to and from the beach. This regulation continued in some places until after the Second World War.[55] But it was ultimately unsuccessful. Public pressure and practice and commercial realities ensured that such attempts to regulate the use of the beach and sea were eventually abandoned. Central government gave little support to local authorities, like Eastbourne, that wished to pursue a conservative restrictive and regulatory approach, viewing such ideas as old-fashioned, an unnecessary constraint and likely to disadvantage poorer visitors to the seaside.[56] Other local councils proclaimed their relaxed bathing rules. The 1934 Folkestone Guidebook, for example, boasted that 'mixed bathing is permitted, as it is on the Continent, and visitors appreciate it greatly. A large number of convenient cabins are available, and open free bathing can also be enjoyed.'[57]

Rather than tents and cabins strung along the beach, an alternative strategy had to be adopted in Plymouth with its rocky shoreline. Over five decades from the late nineteenth century, repeated investment was made in a series of changing and rest rooms and bathing terraces flowing over the broken and steep coastline into the sea. Most of this bathing architecture, the forerunner of the bathing stations and pavilions that became common in inter-war English resorts, survived into the twenty-first century, becoming part of plans to regenerate Plymouth's seafront.[58]

With use of the sea and beaches less restricted and an increasing interest in seaside sun, in the 1920s and '30s many British resorts developed a new architecture of bathing stations and pavilions. Copied from resorts in continental Europe and from Australia and across the Atlantic, superficially the bathing station had the utilitarian purpose of providing a place to change and keep belongings before the users ventured onto the beach or into the sea. And yet this was also an architecture that mediated between the land and the sea, society and nature, and suggested a new family-centred and relaxed use of the seaside: many of the bathing stations included refreshment rooms and terraces to sit, watch or sunbathe. Searching for an appropriate style for these new structures the architects, usually municipal engineers, drew on eclectic sources. Sometimes the new bathing stations were located on the beach itself and, designed for seasonal use only, were simple, functional structures dismantled in the autumn and re-erected again in the spring. The more permanent buildings with minimal decoration used Mediterranean or modernist design themes or a more traditional Municipal-Classical style reminiscent of local government offices.

Margate claimed its Marine Bathing Pavilion of 1926 as the first of its kind in Britain. The 214-feet-long structure, built on a steel frame to take it well above sea level, included a surrounding promenade with a pitch-pine deck and six flights of stairs to the sands.[59] An early 1930s guide described how the new pavilion had 'taken the place of the old-fashioned "machines" formerly ranged along the sands. The pavilion is equipped with shower baths and a hot water supply and a refreshment department has popularized afternoon tea on the sand.' Elsewhere in the resort there was 'a long range of bathing establishments with their platforms and lines of dressing-boxes'.[60] There was still a

The Marine Bathing Pavilion of 1926, Margate, *c.* 1960s.

newest and fastest expanding seaside towns. In the 1920s and '30s Poole, an emerging resort on the south coast of England, developed an array of new beach structures, for sea- and sun-bathing and for summer and winter use. The Corporation was particularly proud of the Branksome Chine Solarium, designed by the borough engineer following a visit to similar facilities in Germany,[63] boasting that it was the first of its kind to be built in Britain: 'In summer the Solarium, which has its own vita-glass tea-lounge, is used as a bathing pavilion; in winter one may enjoy within its walls artificial sunshine and summer heat.'[64] The sheltered flat roofs of the building gave 'undisturbed facilities for basking in the sun' and so allowed 'concentrated sun bathing'. The café 'was designed in order to introduce something of the continental "touch" to the country'. At nearby Sandbanks, 'until recent years a solitary spot visited by adventurous picnic parties in summer and almost deserted in winter', the Corporation built an additional extensive bathing pavilion. Branksome Chine and the other bathing pavilions became the centrepieces of a radically new seafront architecture for a sun-based use of the beach and sea, 'designed for the crowds who come here for bathing, picnicking and other seaside delights',[65] and including a new sea wall doubling as a broad promenade, 'day bungalows for hire ', boating pools for children, parks and gardens and a 'Motor Park' for the increasing number of visitors driving their own vehicles to the seaside.

problem at Margate and some other resorts, however, where the sea receded a considerable distance at low tide, separating pavilions and their users from the sea itself; the response in Margate in 1937 was to construct unadorned pools on the foreshore, the simple structures replenished by the sea with every incoming tide.[61] Respectable but modernizing Southport on the Lancashire coast, in 1938, made much of the municipal 'modern Bathing Centre' on Ainsdale Beach. The building, with a classical-style entrance, provided 'splendidly appointed dressing pavilions for ladies and for gentlemen', a café with a Beach Tray Service, tuck shop, deckchair hire, deck tennis and other games on the terrace and, nearby, a large car park.[62]

The resorts most able to respond to the new demands for an architecture for sun-focused seaside pleasure were the

'The Sands, Cliftonville', Kent: postcard sent in 1924.

The same site and its changing architecture half a century later.

Artist's impression, c. 1932, of the 'The New Solarium and Café at Branksome Chine, Poole', Dorset.

The bathing stations represented a moment of transition in the use of the Britain's resort beaches: municipal provision and guidance for a hoped-for mass use of the beach that within a few decades was to prove out-of-touch with holiday-makers' demands and, in consequence, uneconomic. Margate's beach bathing establishments were to disappear as the resort declined in the post-war decades. Southport's Ainsdale Beach bathing centre was not mentioned in the resort's 1957 guide. Poole's bathing pavilion buildings survived, albeit without the changing rooms for bathing. The once innovative solarium at Branksome Chine was converted into a cafeteria, although in the early twenty-first century it was renamed as Branksome Beach and transformed into a restaurant, café and bar, making much of its 1930s decor and feeding off the emergence of Sandbanks as a south-coast enclave for the rich and famous, tagged the 'Golden Riviera' and the 'Palm Beach of Britain'.[66]

BEACH HUTS

As the bathing machine fled the coast many British beaches became the home for another type of 'Wooden House', the

beach hut. Like its predecessor it became part of the architecture of the respectable family by the sea, reflecting both social relations and attitudes to nature. Outwardly the two structures looked remarkably similar, and indeed old bathing machines were sometimes put to new uses as beach huts. But purpose and function were radically different, with the beach hut bound up in the process 'of the sea becoming a focus for shared family enjoyment rather than part of a regulated regime of medicinal bathing for isolated individuals'.[67]

Providing a safe, home space beside the sea, probably alongside other huts occupied by similar people, contemporary British beach huts also provide seaside councils with the opportunity of income generation. Some councils provide a stock of beach huts and chalets for the use of residents and visitors, renting them out for just a few days or annually. Even when beach huts are privately owned, there is income to be had from annual ground rents and rates. And along with local-authority control come vestiges of beach regulation: the size and spacing of beach huts, the exterior colour – in many resorts it is white – and restrictions on their use (no overnight sleeping, for example). But in other ways beach huts allow for an uninhibited flowering of individual seaside design skills. Interior design can range from some nautical or natural theme, through chintzy home-from-home decoration including flowery curtains and resurrected lounge sofa, to the beach hut as miniature art gallery or the uniquely themed Dame Barbara Cartland memorial beach hut in Hove and the Barry Manilow beach, hut in Bournemouth. And once the occupants and their possessions flow out on to the beach a tiny part of public space is appropriated, however temporarily, as a private personal and family place.

A prelude to beach huts? Grays Beach, Aldwick, near Bognor Regis, Sussex, 1895.

A postcard of Wells Beach, Wells-next-the-Sea, Norfolk, showing tents, huts and redundant bathing machines nestling at the foot of the sand dunes.

In the 1990s beach huts were increasingly represented in the newspaper weekend colour supplements as newly fashionable and much sought-after architectural icons: 'Californians have beach culture, the British have beach huts'.[68] One persistent theme in these representations is surprise that beach huts are popular, along with recognition that they provide a get-away-from-it-all haven for rest and relaxation – 'It's our piece of paradise'.[69] Another theme is that in the jostle to acquire a beach hut, local people are likely to be swept aside by wealthy incomers, members of metropolitan society: 'If you have had your eye on a beach hut, the bad news is that you could already be too late. The classy burghers of Fulham and the trendy denizens of East London have most probably got there before you.'[70] There is now an annual media competition to find the most expensive hut among the estimated 750,000 – a surprisingly huge number – ringing the British coastline.[71] In January 2002 most national newspapers carried stories about a £120,000 beach hut on inaccessible Chesil Beach in Dorset. This, though, was a chalet rather than hut: a 12 by 40-foot building with double-glazing, plumbing and bedrooms, and just 100 feet from the sea.[72] Two years later Dorset 'live-in' beach huts were being sold for £145,000 and £160,000.[73] Southwold, on the Suffolk coast, is often chosen by the media to represent both the contemporary beach hut and fashionable resort. Gleeful press reports link soaring and exorbitant prices – figures of £30,000 being quoted in 2000 and £45,000 in 2003 – to the influx of 'London media types'.[74] The British beach hut had by then become a powerful icon representing the summer, closeness to a friendly nature and family-centred leisure in the sun, and used to advertise a diversity of products from ice cream and beer to clothing.

The beach hut in one variety or another proved to be a widespread and sustained emblem of contemporary

Beach huts at Wells-next-the-Sea, Norfolk, 2004 (top), and Lancing, Sussex, 2003.

Southwold beach huts, at the inexpensive end of the resort, in 1999.

Western beach life. By the early twentieth-first century beach huts could be found, for example, around the coasts of northern Europe and in North America, South Africa and Australia, and were often associated, as in Britain, with an exclusive, relaxed and family-centred use of the beach and the sea. They were also increasingly prized by architects, valued for their heritage, the vernacular design simplicity and as 'an exemplary architecture for idleness'.[75]

Elsewhere, and particularly in Mediterranean Europe, the southern United States and in tropical Western resorts, the *cabana*, an exotic name for an individual beach shelter, became an even more powerful architectural symbol of the contemporary beach. Representations of the ideal cabana surrounded it with nature, not society – it could be presented as a primitive structure of wooden posts support-ing a palm-leaf-clad roof situated on white sands just metres from the gently lapping waters of a remote tropical lagoon. The cabana, in this form, captured the presumed pleasures of a Robinson Crusoe vacation away from the West and its

society, even if the viewer of the image knew that comfort and safety in the form of an exclusive resort hotel was just a short distance away, albeit hidden from view behind a curtain of exotic vegetation.

The cabana concept could also be captured, taken inland and appropriated for other purposes with the Las Vegas Mandalay Bay casino, for example, featuring cabanas for hire draped with acrylic canvas and 'equipped with a TV, refrigerator and other amenities'. Seemingly unabashed by the irony of cabanas in the middle of the Nevada dessert, the casino's guest information proclaimed that 'For your comfort, there is a ceiling fan and misters in every cabana.'[76]

Almost as a footnote, some reports suggest another dimension to British beach huts, noting the problems of vandalism, the petty bureaucracy, annoying neighbours, voyeuristic passers-by, and the dangers of huts being swept away by storm and tides.[77] Alternative representations of beach huts sometimes appear in contemporary art. Most powerful, dramatic and puzzled-over by the British press

Tracey Emin, *The Last Thing I Said to You is Don't Leave Me Here (The Hut)*, 1999, mixed media.

The Forty-Foot bathing place, Malahide, Dublin, in 1997.

The Forty-Foot bathing place, with 'Women Welcome' seen faintly on the stone.

was the artist Tracey Emin's London gallery installation, *The Last Thing I Said to You is Don't Leave Me Here*, using her own Whitstable beach hut, and subsequently sold in 2000 to the contemporary art collector Charles Saatchi for £75,000. Installed in a stark London gallery, Emin's work symbolized the beach hut as icon of the seaside. But in contrast with Southwold's beach huts, the epitome of respectable families relaxing by the sea, hers represented a seaside of decay, nostalgia and loss.

But there were other alternatives to the home-from-home contemporary British seaside represented by beach huts. In Britain and elsewhere one persistent, albeit minority, claim on the beach has been asserted by naturist pleasure seekers. Naturism, like naked sea bathing before it, was still often represented as indecent and perverted. Nonetheless, it became more popular in the second half of the twentieth century, and during the 1970s and '80s naturist use of the beach – the 'unfettered bathing' of a century before – moved more centre stage.[78] In England a few innovative local councils officially designated naturist beaches, in part attempting to regularize existing unofficial practice, but also responding to Continental examples and local pressure, and trying to maintain the popularity of their resorts. In the face of local controversy and considerable national media coverage, Brighton was one of the first in 1980. The beach remains today, shielded from the outside world, or vice versa, by an artificial shingle bank.

Skirmishes continued between the decency regulators and pleasure seekers over naked bathing and whether it should be allowed and who could do it. One antagonistic scrap in the mid-1980s concerned a proposal to designate a naturist beach at Littlehampton, a quiet residential seaside town in Sussex. Proponents argued: 'nudism is becoming the norm on nearly all the beaches of the Continent . . . troublemakers would keep away if there was a stretch of beach officially designated as a naturist beach which perfectly respectable people used'.[79] Opponents voiced the emotive criticism that such a beach 'would encourage perverts and homosexuals, and lead to a risk from AIDS. "There is already a sign at the harbour entrance saying Beware Rabies. Now there will have to be a notice saying Beware AIDS".'[80] The local police chief superintendent feared the beach would be a threat to law and order.[81] The proposal was rejected, although unofficial naturist use of the beach continued.

Elsewhere, local social relations had contrasting results for how people bathed. One notable struggle – remarkable evidence of the survival of bathing practices rooted in the past clashing with the present – occurred in Ireland in the 1970s and '80s over the use of the Forty-Foot bathing place at Sandycove, Dublin, a bathing site with its own unique architecture. A traditional all-male preserve used for naked bathing, it drew the ire of Ireland's developing women's rights movement. Groups of women took direct action, including swimming naked, in protest at the discrimination of men but not women having their own long-established bathing area where they could swim without costumes.[82] A short story by Michael Collins captures how the traditional use of Forty-Foot by 'a fraternity of men, naked creatures inhabiting a place of men that had been handed down through generations' fell foul of the fast-changing social relations between Irish men and women.[83] Following this struggle both men and women swam at Forty-Foot, with the use of costumes becoming the norm.

CHAPTER 7

FROM BATH HOUSE TO WATER PARK

For the builders and users of the early resorts, the sea, despite its enormous attractions, had disadvantages. It could be inaccessible, dangerous or unpleasant, and, apart from the bathing machines, it was difficult to make a profit from it. New ways of domesticating, adapting, using and commodifying sea water were invented, involving the construction of baths and pools. Over the years to the present day these artificial structures, in varied architectural forms, became a chief attraction of the seaside resort. Their history reveals the evolving use of resorts by holidaymakers and changing attitudes to nature, health and pleasure by the sea.

THE INDOOR BATH

Margate, in 1736, was the first resort to boast an 'enclosed' sea water bath, fed from the sea by a 15-foot-long 'canal', and invented and owned by Thomas Barber, a local carpenter. The bath and 'a neat Dressing Room, and Dresses' at beach level was accessed by descending from the dining room of a seafront lodging house. Barber advertised the benefits of the innovative 'enclosed' bath as being convenient, private and comfortable. Bathing could take place whatever the state of the tide or the nature of the weather; bathers were not on public view; and the building above also provided a summerhouse and 'a pleasant prospect of the sea'.[1] Although the contemporary descriptions are unclear, Barber's bath was almost certainly a single bath accommodating one person, establishing a pattern of

personal, private bathing – like that offered from bathing machines – that was to continue until the 1820s, when larger and communal baths at the English seaside were first constructed.[2]

Perhaps because the lure of the sea and shore was so great and the technology to build baths by the sea so poor, the other principal eighteenth-century English resorts were slow to follow Margate's lead.[3] Brighton's first baths, for example, were constructed in 1769 to the plans of Dr John Awsiter. The small building in classical design, modelled on an example from the inland spa town of Bath, included six cold baths and separate hot, showering and sweating baths, all supplied with sea water rather than spa water. Awsiter asserted the therapeutic purposes of the establishment: for example, it was valuable for invalids too poorly to use the

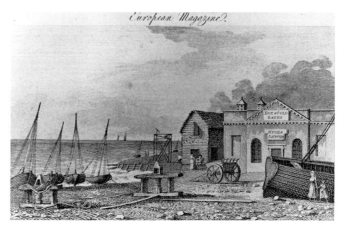

Awsiter's 1769 'Baths at Brighton', as pictured in 1803 in the *European Magazine*.

The fortress-like Clifton Baths, Margate, Kent, 1829.

sea, while the warm sea water bath opened the pores of the skin, so allowing the extraction of all 'poisonous humours'.[4]

Over the following decades into the nineteenth century, each resort developed its own complicated history of artificial indoor baths.[5] Expensive of time and money, the specialist indoor baths were an attraction to affluent elite visitors alone. Close to or on the seafront and designed to exploit the medicinal virtues of sea water, there was often intense competition between the proprietors of these privately owned establishments. Each extolled the attractions of their own buildings and baths, the particular bathing methods, which ranged from 'cold water shower baths' to 'air pump vapour baths', and the curative successes of their own enterprise.

Margate's Clifton Baths, constructed in the 1820s, were an immense undertaking involving what for the period were massive excavations of chalk cliffs and associated sea defence works. The complex was unusual in trying to have the best of both worlds, providing artificial baths and carefully planned and integrated access to bathing machines. There was an innovative – because of its size and because it was communal rather than private – 80 x 40 feet 'plunging bath' for women and children, various vapour, shower and medicinal baths, and dressing, waiting and reading rooms. A huge domed structure cut into the chalk provided standing room for 20

bathing machines that, when the tide was suitably low, could be driven through a tunnel down to the beach. The exterior architecture referenced the fashionable and exotic Egyptian style, with a tall pyramid-shaped chimney.[6]

The most famous Brighton bathing establishment in the first half of the nineteenth century, Sake Dean Mahomed's Indian medicated vapour baths, had a formative influence on the development of bathing treatments. Dean Mahomed, an Indian, arrived in Brighton in 1814 and added shampooing to the repertoire of existing bathing techniques. His ethnic origin helped generate the enormous professional success he enjoyed in Brighton, because being an Indian distinguished 'him in the eyes of his patrons: the British gentry and nobility'.[7] Shampooing, a body massage with oils, was an exotic treatment, described in an 1818 guide to Brighton as 'an expedient neither known or understood in this country, but generally used in India and the Levant as a luxury, and often resorted to as a remedy in very high estimation'.[8]

Conflicting representations emerged, with the bathing process being seen either as a luxury for pleasure or as a treatment for ill health, that were to become a consistent theme in the history and architecture of seaside baths and pools. In Dean Mahomed's case, for example, one view asserts that the aristocracy besieged the doors of his establishment because although 'ostensibly these vapour baths were for the cure of rheumatism and allied ailments, actually they were frequented by voluptuaries of both sexes'.[9] Dean Mahomed avidly promoted his practice using written testimonials and, like Dr Russell before him, publishing a medical casebook extolling his treatments. His achievements in the town allowed him to construct a grand new

Mahomed's Baths, Brighton, 1823, by Joseph Cordwell.

structure, Mahomed's Baths, in 1821. Architecture and design were used to distinguish the new baths from those of the competition and to emphasize their exoticism. The imposing building stood in the centre of the resort on a seafront promontory. In keeping with his Indian identity so valued by his customers, and echoing the Oriental style of the nearby Royal Pavilion – occupied by one of his own patrons, George IV – the internal decoration of Dean Mahomed's baths was opulent and redolent of the East. The walls of the reading rooms looking out over the beach and sea, for example, pictured an imaginary Indian landscape with pagoda, temple, a Rajah's mausoleum, lake and mountains, figures in Indian costumes, birds and rich vegetation.[10] It was as though the combination of sea views and the internal decor allowed Dean Mahomed's patrons to conjure images of other distant and exotic places.

Dean Mahomed's baths gradually failed as a business and were acquired by a new owner in 1841. By then the railway had reached Brighton and, as the resort attracted a broader range of visitors, it fell from royal favour. The baths

themselves were demolished in 1870 and the site used for a hotel. The shampooing and Indian medicated vapour baths techniques developed and made famous by Dean Mahomed persisted and merged into British society, but their origins were lost, appropriated by white British experts, and then transformed and renamed as the 'Turkish bath'.[11] The first Brighton Turkish Bath, the 'Hamman', opened in 1868, almost two decades after Dean Mahomed's death.[12]

Turkish baths were to become an enduring feature of the treatments offered in the municipal resort baths of the mid-twentieth century. Although they had disappeared from the British seaside by the end of the century, their present-day successors are to be found in the leisure club with indoor pool, gym, sauna and steam room, and associated beauty salon often offering full body massages, that feature in the most expensive of today's resort 'grand hotels'; like the seaside baths of two centuries before, these are expensive luxuries for the wealthy.

In the third decade of the nineteenth century swimming began to emerge as a new activity for elite seaside

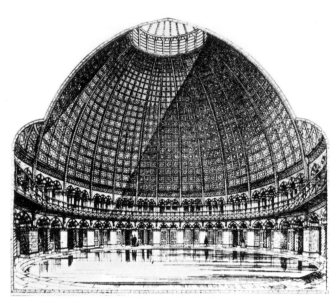

Brill's Baths, Brighton, the 1866 design for men, as illustrated in the *Civil Engineer and Architect's Journal*.

visitors. Although at first they were few in number, new communal rather than personal baths were constructed, the proprietors making much of the innovative swimming lessons they were able to provide. In Brighton, a circular and domed swimming bath was opened in 1823, and in 1861 the site of Brighton's first bathing establishment, Awsiter's, was used to erect a building that was both 'the only sea-water swimming baths for ladies in the Kingdom, and in Europe' and also specifically designed to 'give instruction in the elegant and valuable art of swimming'.[13] Eight years later, on land adjacent to the ladies' bath, a red-brick building was constructed housing another circular but larger swimming bath, in this case for men. Designed by the architect of many iconic British buildings, Sir George Gilbert Scott, the new baths were 65 feet in diameter, contained 80,000 gallons of sea water – drawn from nearby Hove because Brighton's sea water was thought to be polluted – and surrounded by a balcony designed to hold 400 spectators. Scott's innovative structure was a first indication that the transformation of the private bather into the public swimmer might entertain onlookers as well as the direct participants. Both the circular baths were demolished in 1929 to make way for a

cinema. These examples from Brighton and Margate may be replicated, with variation, around the coasts of Britain and mainland Europe.

By the early twentieth century, municipal enterprise had largely replaced the private sector as the generating force behind the public architecture of bathing at the British seaside. Architecturally, the indoor public baths conformed to a municipal tradition and followed an established pattern used, for example, in schools and town halls: classical architectural references, especially for entrances, were common. Resorts, in continuing intense competition, engaged in an endless rivalry over the quality of their indoor baths. In 1938, for instance, Southport Corporation proclaimed its Victoria Baths on the promenade as 'the most up-to-date in the North of England'.[14] Apart from the swimming and private baths with both sea and fresh water, there were Turkish, Russian, foam and pine bubble baths. A year later, on the south coast, Hastings' White Rock Baths, which had been reconstructed by the Corporation in 1933,[15] were advertised as having the 'largest and finest tepid sea-water bath in Britain', as well as 'Hot Sea or Fresh Water Private Baths, Seaweed Baths, and various Medicated Baths, Turkish Baths, Lounge and Rest Rooms'.[16]

By the 1930s, however, the holidaymakers' imagination had been seized by the sun. The architects of the newest indoor baths at the seaside responded with some innovative design features. The 1937 Pier Approach baths in Bournemouth, for instance, included the usual amenities but also featured a large solarium and an exterior sun bathing terrace: the solarium was to 'be available at all times of the year and in inclement weather will produce the equivalent of natural sunlight for the benefit of bathers and spectators', while the sunbathing terrace, overlooking

Bournemouth Bay, allowed sunbathing during fine weather 'in most ideal surroundings' with the interior swimming pool becoming 'in effect equal to open-air premises'.[17]

THE OPEN-AIR POOL

However modern and whatever the attractions of the indoor baths, as holidaymakers, and society more generally, fell in love with the sun and with physical exercise and relaxation out of doors, the open-air pool and lido emerged to become the preeminent architectural symbol of the British seaside in the first half of the twentieth century. New popular ways of using nature – swimming, diving, sunbathing and spectating on those doing so – demanded new architectural structures. Technology played an important role. Innovative construction techniques and building technologies, including steel frames and reinforced concrete, enabled the architecture of the seaside resort to be made in new ways and new styles.

Society, though, was ambivalent whether open-air pools were for health, for pleasure, or a combination of the two. The government and respectable society thought they were or should be places of health and exercise. Some commentators and users thought they were, first and foremost, places of pleasure.

The Government avidly supported the open-air pool building movement. Swimming and sunbathing were in the national interest: they aided public health and promoted physical and mental fitness. As Sir Edward Campbell MP put it on the opening of Weston-super-Mare's swimming pool in 1937, the government was 'determined to do their utmost to encourage physical exercise for all classes and ages', with exercise taking 'no better form than swimming in clean sea-water open to the sun and air'.[18] Sir Edward

hoped the spectators would be so stimulated by the prowess of those using the pool that they would emulate their example, so helping to build a 'Fitter Britain'.

The contemporary concern with public health had various design manifestations in the technologically and architecturally more sophisticated pools and lidos. The water needed to be safe. Filtering might be used to ensure 'the complete clarification and cleansing of the water',[19] the settling tanks and filtering and chlorination plants hidden away and the external structure used to house ranks of seats for spectators, a sunbathing terrace or a place for communal physical exercise. Elsewhere the water was 'purified' using electronically produced ozone, 'without any dangerous effect upon the bathers, and at the same time destroying the most dangerous bacteria'.[20] Fountains were both a decorative feature and used to aerate water. Bathers, too, needed to be cleansed before entering a pool. In the mid-1930s the 'best modern practice' for the proposed Black Rock pool in Brighton included a complicated admission and changing process with locker keys, towel issue counter, showers and a 'compulsory soap foot bath'.[21] With a hint of the old regulated beach, even the most modern of pools, such as Ramsgate's 1935 structure, included separate changing rooms for men, women and children.[22]

In a period of great municipal enterprise and competition at the seaside, the seaside authorities were eager to invest in the physical infrastructure and public architecture of their resorts.[23] The larger and more impressive the open-air pool – and most were designed not by architects in private practice but by borough surveyors and engineers – the better it was as a symbol of forward-looking municipal enterprise. Resorts, through the official handbooks and guides, tirelessly promoted the attractions of their pools and lidos. The dimensions of their pools, the number of

A *c.* 1950s postcard of Black Rock Bathing Pool, Brighton.

On the site of the Victorian station, the 'Bathing Pool and Sands, Ramsgate' – from a postcard sent in 1947.

gallons of water held, the depth of the water, and the height of the diving boards were all-important. Hastings Corporation argued of its new pool in the 1935 visitors handbook that 'there is certainly no finer or better equipped pool in England';[24] four years later it had become 'the finest open-air swimming pool in Europe'.[25]

Representations of swimming pools and lidos, particularly from town councils and railway companies in their publicity posters, laid great stress on the new pools and their

architecture as sites of extraordinary spectacle and display, physical activity, excitement and bodily exposure with healthy young people revelling in the experience. The pools and lidos were represented as places of modernity, social and sexual equality and liberation. Shorn of their everyday clothing, the pool users appeared classless. Typically in these images, women were numerically and visually dominant and often seemingly unattached, suggesting that at the new pools men would meet fun-loving young women with the

THE FAMOUS BATHING POOL
AT HASTINGS & St LEONARDS
FREE BOOKLET FROM Q.P. INFORMATION BUREAU. HASTINGS
TRAVEL BY THE THROUGH LMS SUNNY SOUTH EXPRESS FROM THE NORTH & MIDLANDS-CHEAP FARES

'The Famous Bathing Pool at Hastings and St Leonards', LMS poster, c. 1930s, artwork by G.S. Pryse. The image suggests that female bathers far outnumbered male ones.

promise, perhaps, of much more. None of this is surprising given the manner gender was used to sell and design the seaside. But perhaps there was reality behind the image for, if one late 1930s expert commentator, George Ryley Scott, is to be believed, sea-water bathing had little to do with why people thronged the beaches and open-air pools 'in a state of semi-nudity' during the summer months. Instead, in 99 per cent of cases, people were there for 'pleasure, and pleasure alone'. Scott particularly disapproved of the role adopted by women:

Many of these supposed bathers do not enter the water at all. They have not the slightest intention of entering it. They are merely displaying, for the edification of the other sex, their physical charms with the aid of daring and attractive bathing costumes. This is a factor which no one engaged in the study of the popularity of seaside bathing can afford to overlook.[26]

Respectable Southport Corporation would have sympathized with Scott's comments, proclaiming that its Sea Bathing Lake was 'the only place in the country where the question of Sun Bathing has been successfully dealt with', through the provision of separate sunbathing areas for men and women, each in 'complete privacy'.[27] The sunbathing question was part of the undercurrent of debate over whether pools were for health or pleasure that continued into the post-war period.

Ironically, however, the available evidence suggests that in practice men were more likely than women to use the new pools. Ramsgate's 1935 seafront swimming pool, for example, used a wire basket system to store and safeguard the clothes of swimmers, and while almost 1,100 baskets were provided for men there were just 600 for women.[28] Perhaps the architects and the commissioning seaside authorities of these iconic structures had such faith in the work of the poster artists selling the experience that they knew that more men than women would succumb to the lures of the lidos.

Commenting in the late 1930s, one of Britain's most prominent architects and town planners, S. D. Adshead, believed the sea was losing its attraction and that swimming pools were a necessity for a modern resort:

> The provision of swimming pools at the seaside is now an absolute necessity; indeed, not only owing to the inconvenience of sea bathing, but also to the demand for diving facilities. In a modern swimming pool, diving, the attractions of fashion in bathing costumes, refreshment accommodation, sunbathing and shelters set in garden surroundings are the accompaniments of a great show.[29]

Although by the mid-1930s some small pools were built 'purely for recreational purposes without any attempt to cater for spectacular events',[30] Adshead's 'great show' pools were more common. They were to become a central element of the new forms of seaside leisure and in turn demanded a radically different theatrical architecture. Pools and lidos, and seating, sunbathing terraces and promenades became amphitheatres. The diving boards, water chutes and fountains were props and the water-cleansing plants, changing rooms and car parks essential backstage facilities. As to the bathers and spectators, they were transformed into performers and audience, although sometimes the prone sunbathers were as much a part of the performance as the swimmers and divers. Despite the sense that the sea as a place to bathe was at best inconvenient and at worst unattractive, the new structures were built as close to the sea as possible, and ideally on the foreshore. The pools touched and used nature, and tamed and remade it into a modern synthetic creation suitable for society's use. In the resorts with the most advanced pools the sea as a place to bathe was relegated to a subsidiary role: by 1932 in Blackpool more than twice as many people bathed from pools rather than the beach, and the estimated figure for Weston-super-Mare was more than five to one.[31]

Architecturally, the earliest twentieth-century British open-air pools drew on classical and neo-Georgian design themes, including columns, colonnades and pediments: an early example was Scarborough's South Bay Bathing Pool of 1915, claimed by the Corporation as the largest outdoor pool in Europe and the first provided by an English seaside town council. For a brief period this embryonic lido, a harbinger of developments around the coast two decades later, set Scarborough apart from other seaside places. The resort's 'most popular bathing-place',[32] at high tide the sea flowed over the outer wall and into the two-million-gallon pool. By the 1920s bathing at the pool was represented as an exceedingly popular pastime, because it is always safe, accompanied daily by a good band, and along the Shore side many tiers of seats are provided for spectators, who obtain a good deal of amusement from the antics of their friends in the water . . . The pool has its complement of water chutes, diving boards, and rafts, along with the laughter-provoking artificial horses, etc., which are very great favourites with the younger folk.[33]

The Blackpool Baths of 1923 were held within 'an elliptical embayment' built over the foreshore. The baths' design reflected the Beaux-Arts architectural fashion of the period with a central domed pavilion complete with Doric columns, and colonnades of changing rooms embracing the oval-shaped pool.[34] The professional press described how the bath was 'designed in the Renaissance style of architecture, and is built with ivory white terra-cotta, known as "Marmola"' and was 'well equipped with every comfort and convenience for both bathers and spectators'. A grandstand seated 3,000 people, the pool held 1.6 million gallons of filtered sea water, and the highest diving boards reached 32 feet above the water.[35]

Southport's Sea Bathing Lake of 1928, replacing an earlier structure of 1914, included a 'pergola carried on white pillars, and leading down to the lake there is a wide artificial stone stairway, on either side of which clear sea water falls in beautiful cascades over limestone rocks on its way to the lake'.[36] On the south coast, Margate's Clifton Baths of a century before were replaced in 1927 by an open-air swimming pool, later to be called Cliftonville

The delights of the South Bay pool used to sell the resort of Scarborough. Railway poster, 1933.

Lido, and large enough for almost 1,000 bathers and 3,000 spectators.[37]

By the 1930s the cult of the sun was literally reflected in modernist pool designs: flat roofs were designed for sunbathing; the extensive use of glass allowed light into buildings; and tiled surfaces, often in white, refracted the

Blackpool's classical pool, *c.* 1920s.

The Southport Sea Bathing Lake, from a painting by Fortunino Matania reproduced in *Sunny Southport: Official Guide, 1938–39*.

Margate's Cliftonville Lido, with the pier in the distance, *c.* 1950.

innovative features including underwater floodlights to illuminate aquatic sports, races and diving competitions, three promenades, space for 5,000 spectators, a sunbathing beach that faced and allowed access to the sea, and provision for deck games (copied from the sports and pastimes on ocean liners).[39]

One of the most visually arresting and stunningly located of the new modern structures was the Tinside pool of 1935 on Plymouth Hoe.[40] Startling architecture also featured in Weston-super-Mare's 'super new swimming pool' of 1937: much was made of the locally designed and constructed four-tiered and seven-platformed diving stage, described as 'Europe's finest diving stage' and 'a unique achievement'.[41]

heat and light of the sun. The Nautical Moderne style was especially significant and redolent of the avant-garde, adventurous and international. It was at this point that 'lido' sometimes replaced 'pool' to represent the modern, adventurous and even exotic, the word borrowed from the beach resort in Venice, and ultimately from *litus*, the Latin word for shore.[38]

Hastings had one of the first more modernist structures. Rather akin to the municipal pride that went with the opening of nineteenth-century piers, the opening of the resort's open-air bathing pool in 1933 was celebrated in style. Civic dignitaries watched as 250 people dived into the pool, an exhibition of high diving and, with a sense of the pool representing both a continuation of and a radical departure from what had gone before, a 'mannequin parade' featuring costumes past and present. Although smaller than some earlier pools, holding just a million gallons of sea water, the Hastings reinforced-concrete structure had many

The new pools also captivated the local and regional press. In the south-west of England, Penzance's Jubilee Pool

'No finer or better equipped pool in England': the Outdoor Bathing Pool, Hastings, *c.* 1934.

'The Bathing Pool and Tinside Lido, Plymouth', Devon, c. 1930s, postcard.

The Jubilee Pool, Penzance, c. 1992.

of 1935 was described in the *Cornishman and Cornish Telegraph*:

> Jutting out into the sea, exposed to the full violence of the south-easterly and southerly gales, it was necessary to take advantage not only of every natural asset, but of every other idea that modern engineering science could devise . . . but the interior of the pool is not only a fine

piece of engineering – it is also a work of art. The monotony of straight walls and right angles – the domain of the compass and ruler – has been entirely and utterly avoided. Instead, there are graceful curves and pleasing lines – an adaption of cubism to the terraces and platforms which enhances the effect and makes the whole so pleasing to the eye.[42]

There were some exceptions to the pools being of municipal origin to the design of a resort's own surveyor and engineer. Although mostly austere and unembellished by municipal standards, they were to become an essential feature of the privately owned holiday camps that were an increasingly prevalent feature of the inter-war British seaside. By the mid-1930s an open-air pool could also form the centrepiece of a far larger new seaside development. In designing the 1937 Saltdean Lido for a private estate company, the architect R.W.H. Jones was inspired by Bexhill's De La Warr Pavilion of two years earlier to produce an unashamedly modernist, streamlined and curvilinear style. The lido formed a centrepiece of a larger ambitious estate plan, including the equally modernist and Jones-designed Ocean Hotel, for a previously undeveloped stretch of the coast to the east of Brighton. The estate company's publicity described how the lido's 'luxurious equipment and surroundings' were 'unrivalled in southern England', the blue tiles imparted a 'beautifully coloured effect on the water' and how sunbathing facilities were provided on 'real

Artist's impression for a promotional brochure of the new Saltdean Lido, Brighton, late 1930s.

crisp seashore sand'.[43] Just two years later the wonders of Saltdean Lido, like those of many open-air pools around the British coastline, were to be snatched from the grasp of holidaymakers as the lido closed with the outbreak of the Second World War. Uniquely, it was not to reopen again until 1964, and by then it was in council ownership.[44]

In this onslaught of new modern structures the earlier pools looked increasingly out of place. In the mid-1930s the Scarborough pool was 'lidofied'. Higher walls both kept out the sea and provided further extensive terraced seating for bathers and spectators; a modernist 32-feet-high series of diving boards and platforms soared above the pool, its depth more than doubled to accommodate the plunging divers, while shallow pools, each with a four-tiered fountain, served younger and less confident bathers. The pool entered a period when it was celebrated in postcards and posters as one of the resort's great places of display and spectacle.

Despite the changes, however, by 1938 the pool was damned with faint praise in a development plan for Scarborough prepared by Adshead and Overfield. The authors maintained that the pool 'serves its purpose as such, but the dressing accommodation and approaches to the pool are objectionable, and in due course considerable improvement

might be made in this regard'.[45] Adshead and Overfield went on to propose the conversion of a 1935 children's boating lake at North Bay into an open-air bathing pool, 'retaining the present main entrance and the very attractive shelters which have been so universally admired'. By 1950 the North Side Bathing Pool was operating as envisaged: 'There is accommodation for 800 bathers and 700 spectators, with sunbathing terrace, promenade and cafés. The temperature of the water is maintained at 10° above surrounding air temperature.'[46]

The open-air pools and lidos continued as attractions of the post-war English seaside into the 1950s and '60s. The pools remained the stage for a variety of events, including the traditional bathing beauty contests. In 1964, for example, Blackpool, the most popular of English resorts, still presented its 1923 pool as 'the world's finest open-air swimming pool' and as 'incomparable' and a 'wonder pool'.[47]

But such grandiose claims were increasingly out of tune with what people expected and wanted from the English seaside in the last three decades of the century. The pools became less attractive to holidaymakers more interested in the relaxing warmth of overseas holidays or the comfort of the enclosed 'sub-tropical water paradise'. In the context of late-twentieth-century local government politics and the high costs of maintenance and restoration, municipal authorities were less able and willing to invest in the structures. Despite local and national campaigns to preserve the pools and lidos, one by one they were threatened with closure and demolition.

Saltdean Lido, Brighton, in 1993.

A *c.* 1950s postcard of South Bay and the Bathing Pool, Scarborough, with the modernized pool.

Artist's illustration of the proposed North Bay open-air bathing pool, Scarborough, 1938.

From the late 1970s Scarborough Council began to restrict spending on the South Bay Bathing Pool, arguing declining use and rising costs. The pool closed a decade later, and although plans were announced to convert it into England's largest 'undersea world' they came to nothing. Erased from the town's tourist maps, it was as though the pool no longer existed, although local politicians and national heritage groups knew otherwise. In 2002 the Twentieth Century Society proposed the listing of the pool for its architectural interest and cultural heritage. In contrast, councillors maintained that the derelict pool was 'disgraceful, an albatross and a carbuncle'. Responding to the listing proposal, the council leader argued: 'I'm sick of people with big ideas who have no idea where the money is coming from to pay for them. People like that are holding the town back. It's pie in the sky.'[48] The holidaymaking spectacle had been transformed into 'a major scar on the landscape'. In 2003 the pool was filled with 60,000 tonnes

The Sea Bathing Lake at Southport, early 1950s.

of rubble and the surface grassed over. All that remained in view were the surrounding walls separating the pool from beach and sea.

Although Blackpool's 'elliptical embayment' remained, the open-air baths themselves were demolished in 1983 and replaced by 'The Sandcastle' of 1986, an indoor leisure pool. Weston-super-Mare's swimming pool's seven-platform rein-

Miss Mermaid competition at Cliftonville Lido, Margate, Kent, 1959.

A few of the great inter-war pools and lidos – and some smaller, simpler pools – survived into the twenty-first century, albeit sometimes in disguise. Scarborough's North Side pool was transformed into 'Atlantis', 'A most fun packed, exciting heated outdoor waterpark'.[50] The original 1935 'universally admired' buildings remained, encircled by the snaking blue ribbon of two water slides. In Scotland, the Stonehaven open-air pool of 1934 was restored in the 1990s and, uniquely, continued to offer heated sea-water. On the south coast of England, the combination of under-funding and ever fewer visitors led to the closure of Saltdean Lido for three years in the 1990s. Then, as the century drew to a close and desperate for a solution to the problem of what to do with the listed structure, the city council leased the site to a private company for 125 years. As part of a £300,000 restoration, the pool's water was heated and the original pool split in two, making one shallower pool for paddling and a deeper one for swimming; the agreement involved using the lido's car park to build a £1.8 million pub. The

forced-concrete diving board of 1937 was demolished as a hazard in 1982, the huge pool largely filled in and the site transformed into the Tropicana Pleasure Beach, with green plastic slides snaking from a giant yellow pineapple into what was left of the pool; by 2005 the Tropicana, too, was waiting redevelopment. Post-war, Hastings' swimming pool was briefly reinvented as a holiday camp, the pool mostly filled in and the changing cubicles converted to chalets;[49] it was eventually wiped from the landscape. Southport's Sea Bathing Lake of 1928 and Ramsgate's pool of 1935 were similarly obliterated. Cliftonville Lido, the site of the 1820s Clifton Baths, slowly stagnated; the pool was finally in-filled, covered with a layer of sand and renamed 'Lido Sands', a desolate and eerie reminder for those who knew of what had gone before.

The closed Scarborough South Bay pool in 1993.

Just before demolition of the diving boards: Weston-super-Mare open-air swimming pool in 1982.

The railway site of Ramsgate Pool (and before that the station), 2002.

Government's sports minister officially reopened the lido in 1998. Commentators were lyrical about the restored structure, describing it as 'the most beautiful building in Britain',[51] and proclaiming the beauty 'in its graphic simplicity, framing the contrasting exquisite complexity of the snaking mosaic of wave forms projected on the bottom'.[52]

The preservationists also celebrated Plymouth's Tinside Pool: 'jutting into the open sea with its smooth curves of Art Deco concrete. The great liners may have vanished, but the lidos can provide an equal romance.'[53] And yet the pool closed in 1992. A decade later architecture was increasingly seen as a tool of economic regeneration and, as part of a major rejuvenation of the city's seafront, the Tinside Pool reopened in 2003 following a £4 million restoration. Despite threats, and partly because of the consistent local support, Penzance's Jubilee Pool remains a feature of the town's seaside attractions in the twenty-first century.

The residual architecture of the grand open-air pool and lido is nowadays likely to be seen as a nostalgic reminder of a valued and perhaps more innocent, harmonious or communal recent past.[54] The preservationists present lidos as period pieces, for their 'delightful and evocative' architecture, as examples of civic enterprise, and for the 'more life-enhancing experience' they provided.[55] Looking back at the 'brief but dazzling era of lido life', Ken Worpole questioned what had generated the intense passion in the new architectural form:

> Such enthusiasm must have had deep political and cultural foundations. This shared international concern for a politics of the body could not have been conjured out of nothing, and it is extraordinary that architectural and cultural history so quickly neglected or forgot the great public passions that were created for such forms of urban hedonism and bodily delight.[56]

And yet in truth the idea of the open-air pool followed the example of so many British holidaymakers and migrated south to warmer and sunnier climes. Albeit sea water replaced by fresh, by the start of the twenty-first century open-air pools can be found in a diversity of forms stringing the shores of the Mediterranean and other Western tourist seas. Smaller pools in hotels, villas and beach houses are nowadays most often portrayed as luxurious, exclusive and romantic, close to and almost a continuation of the sea but separate from it. Grander and larger structures in campsites, holiday complexes and commercial water parks, closer in their ancestry to the inter-war British lidos, are more

The small pool in Brixham, Devon, 1999.

Scarborough's Atlantis, 1993, reusing the North Bay open-air bathing pool.

Plymouth's Tinside Lido undergoing restoration, 2003.

likely to be viewed as sites of pleasure, tumultuous fun and riotous adventure.

NATATORIUM TO WATER PARK

Beyond Britain the architecture of seaside pools has taken a diversity of forms over the last century. In the United States, the most iconic and innovative of seaside pools was the mid-1890s Sutro Baths in San Francisco, a remarkable water recreation and entertainment complex capturing an important turning point in the architecture of swimming. As much aimed at residents of the city as visitors, the baths recognized the increasing popularity of swimming as a communal activity to be enjoyed by large numbers of both participants and spectators. Proclaimed as the 'largest natatorium in the world', in 1896 the baths were advertised as 'no better sea-bathing in the world' and as 'the largest enclosed Baths and Winter-Garden in the world'.[57] The brainchild of Adolph Sutro, engineer, entrepreneur and later mayor of San Francisco, the baths were built on the edge of the ocean. The foundations were laid on a sandy beach of a cove and the surrounding cliffs remodelled to house a huge structure of iron and glass. The glazed roofs alone covered two acres. Sutro himself was ambitious for the baths, asserting that 'I must have it large, pretentious, in keeping with the environment, with the Heights, with the great ocean itself.'

This was an architecture that demonstrated the mastery of nature and particularly the ocean. There were six sea-water pools and one fresh-water plunge bath. The largest sea-water pool, 300 feet long and 100 feet wide, was at 'ocean temperature', while the smaller pools were heated.

Water park, Mallorca, Spain, 1997.

They were equipped with water chutes, diving boards and rafts and an array of gymnastic apparatus, including trapeze and rings. As a site of communal spectacle to be both participated in and watched, the structure had a capacity for 1,628 bathers with ranks of tiered seating soaring into the roof and providing spaces for 7,400 spectators.

In the first two decades the baths captivated spectators, still amazed by what humans could do in water, with a diversity of displays, exhibitions and competitions. The boundaries between theatrical performance and sporting feat were confused and visitors might enjoy Professor Karl, 'the marvelous Anthropic Amphibian, who eats, drinks, smokes, writes and sleeps under water, in full view of the audience', and witness world swimming records being broken. The baths assailed the senses in particular ways. Apart from the sight of the huge functional structure awash with visitors, 'all around was the echoing, enveloping sound of splashing and laughter and shouts; the close feel of heat and high humidity; the engrossing smell compounded of salt water dampness, wet cloth, human bodies and frying hot dogs'.[58]

Although technologically innovative and a functional modern structure, in interior design the baths attempted a variety of other messages. There was an imposing classical grand staircase gently descending from the entrance to the baths and dressing rooms. There were broad promenades encircling the upper storeys and with views to the baths below. The subsidiary winter-garden theme was developed using the humid and warm atmosphere to sustain tropical plants, including palm, pomegranate, magnolias and maguey. The cliff-top entrance building was in a classical style, supposedly the replica of a 'Grecian Temple', although at times draped with huge Stars and Stripes.

There was another dimension to the baths that was

Sutro Baths, San Francisco, c. 1898.

sustained throughout the life of the structure. Sutro combined his entrepreneurial motives with a strong philanthropic philosophy and was eager to 'help install in the minds of youthful visitors a desire for learning'.[59] This variety of philanthropy and profit-making was evidenced in the baths' museum. Arrayed on the upper floors and promenades were an eclectic range of artefacts from around the world, including displays of natural history from shells to sea lions – nature classified, understood and contained – exhibits varying from medieval armour to Egyptian mummies, and a picture gallery.

As a business the Sutro Baths began to falter early in the twentieth century, perhaps as the spectacle became less appealing and the technology and architecture more mundane. As a response in the mid-1930s the baths were given a significant design make-over. The classical references were swept away from the entrance building and replaced by two rather contradictory design themes. Visitors were welcomed both by two Art Deco towers topped by elongated domes – a reference to the future – and also a new 'Tropic Beach' façade – a reference to another part of the world that was further developed inside the baths with

the installation of a sandy beach and quasi-tropical decorations designed to detract from the bleak and functional interior. The new beach was represented as exotic and relaxing: 'Always as balmy and summery as mid-June on a South Sea Isle, whatever the weather outside. Here's the spot to loaf in tropic comfort like a Fiji Islander. No nudists and practically no missionaries, but everything else is Number One Triple A Tropic Style!'[60] Other counters to the declining popularity of the antiquated swimming facilities involved using the building for new leisure purposes: part of the large pool was turned into an ice-skating rink and dancing was introduced, on 'glassy-smooth' floors and with views of the Golden Gate Bridge.

These changes were but a respite to the long-term decline of the attraction. During the early 1950s the Sutro family sold the baths. The 1930s entrance was subsequently hidden away behind a more rustic exterior with domes removed and towers enclosed behind timber cladding. Inside were still more dramatic changes: the last of the old swimming pools closed and Sutro's offered just ice-skating and collections of curiosities as a remnant of the once-proud museum.

Sutro's closed in 1966 with the planned demolition hastened by a fire in the same year. Press reports mourned the loss of 'the closest thing to something out of the Arabian Nights this city has ever seen . . . Xanadu, the Hanging Gardens of Babylon and Madame Toussaint's Wax Museum all rolled into one'.[61] More recently still the city has made much of the history and archaeology of the baths, now part of the Golden Gate National Recreation Area, with the ruined foundations still to be viewed amid what is once more an increasingly natural edge of the ocean.

The Sutro Baths were a forerunner of the subtropical water paradises so common a century later and as at home

Disney's Blizzard Beach, Orlando, Florida, in 2000.

Blackpool's Sandcastle in 2002.

inland as on the coast, at a stroke seeming to undermine the natural locational advantages of the seaside: what purpose has the seaside when some of its chief attractions can be artificially reproduced miles from the ocean? The Disney-world theme-park complex in central Florida, for example, includes two brilliantly if bizarrely 'imagineered' open-air water parks. Blizzard Beach is themed as a ski resort built following a freak snowstorm and now slowly melting in the Florida sunshine. Visitors enjoy the classic theme-park disconnected experience of playing in water while the sounds of 'Santa Claus is Coming to Town' and 'Christmas in the Caribbean' drift over the public address system. Another water park, Typhoon Lagoon, is themed around another natural disaster storyline: this time a great storm wreaking havoc with the tropical Placid Palms Resort.

Typhoon Lagoon adheres, although extremely, to the recurrent water-park design and marketing motifs of the exotic and tropical seaside. In north-west Europe, for example, the inland Centre Parcs holiday villages, the successor of the coastal holiday camps, feature 'subtropical paradise' water parks: 'steam rising, stars in a frosty sky. Step out of one world and into another – a subtropical paradise. It's magic'.[62] At the real seaside, indoor subtropical pools have been built in many older and colder resorts and, unlike the lidos before them, provide an all-year and all-weather experience. In Britain, one of the earliest was Blackpool's glass-clad 'The Sandcastle' of 1986, built on the site of the resort's huge open-air pool. Proclaimed as the 'first "inside seaside"', the interior included exotic vegetation partner-

Ocean Dome, Phoenix Seagaia Resort, Japan, early 21st century.

ing 'computer-controlled tropical temperatures' and pink flamingos suspended above four pools, a wave machine, slides and fountains.[63] The Sandcastle concept was replicated in other seaside resorts and in the surviving holiday camps. Although architecturally often undistinguished and mostly indistinguishable from similar inland structures, the new indoor pleasure pools provided new ways of using water in themed environments.

But the most ambitious contemporary water-park reproduction of the seaside, both beside the sea and yet abstracted from it, is Ocean Dome in Japan. Part of the Phoenix Seagaia Resort located a few hundred metres from the Pacific, Ocean Dome is the extreme water park: 100 by 300 metres, a huge sliding roof, capacity for 10,000 visitors, 13,500 tonnes of water, a machine producing waves large enough to surf, and exotic coastal theming with the trappings of a backdrop of a deep-blue sky painted with cotton-wool clouds, white sandy beach, tropical vegetation, rocky islands and a volcano housing water slides, one with a 40-degree incline and taking riders to speeds of 40 kilometres per hour. The Dome's website describes how:

When you walk in, you are greeted by a beach of pure white sand and a paradise of eternal summer. You can watch the surfers on the artificial waves of The Great Bank or try body-boarding yourself. There are quite a

few differences between the Ocean Dome and the ocean, among them the heated indoor pool, the kids' pool, the floating pool, and three fast and thrilling water slides.

Despite the technological and cultural differences, a comparison with the Sutro Baths, a century earlier and a continent removed, also reveals surprising similarities: both close to the sea, both providing an artificial version of seaside nature, both making use of tropical vegetation, both praised as the largest of its kind, and both for visitors as active participants and spectators.

While the demise of the Sutro Baths was nostalgically mourned, the Ocean Dome has been criticized for its artificiality. Echoing George Orwell's dismissal, six decades before, of the supposed remaking of Kubla Khan's pleasure-doom in an early post-war Britain in cultural decline,[64] David Boyle rejects the Ocean Dome's 'fake paradise' in the context of what he presents as a present-day struggle between the real and unreal.[65] He criticizes the unnaturalness of it all, including the absence of 'real salt water, real crabs, real seaweed or fish'.[66] But whether to be close to or abstracted from seaside's nature, and the most appropriate relationship between society and nature, induces contradictory responses at different times and places: a century before Edmund Gosse railed against the ravaging of the real seashore – his 'fairy paradise' – by beach-goers.[67] Contemporary water parks, the architecture of the artificial seaside par excellence, may be unloved by many middle-class commentators but they are enjoyed by millions of people on holiday.

Another present-day variety of the water park uses the architecture of the artificial seaside to provide an intensely managed and manipulated interaction with real nature. Discovery Cove, an Orlando attraction that opened in 2000, is described as a 'family-orientated tropical paradise filled with a variety of unique animal interactions'.[68] The pretence of the architecture is that it is authentic nature. Every attempt is made to disguise the artificiality of it all and to hide away the evidence that it is the product of architects and designers. The cove replicates in synthetic form a tropical coastal landscape, providing a river and sandy beaches and a coral reef teeming with fish swimming through shipwreck remains and grottos (with shark and barracuda in deeper water and behind protective glass).

The main attraction is the Dolphin Swim, a controlled environment where 'guests can swim and play with dolphins'. A travel journalist's first impression was of a Caribbean resort: 'You cross a wooden bridge over a gurgling river to get to the dolphins, which were splashing about playfully in sparkling water in a huge blue lagoon, fringed by white sand.'[69] The owners of Discovery Cove, the Busch Entertainment Corporation, present the captive animals as ambassadors for their species, helping to entertain, educate and inspire people.[70] There is a curious exchange of roles with architecture imitating seaside nature while animals – although only those that will perform and are attractive to guests – are transformed into theme-park characters. In this design of the seaside the unpalatable parts of the natural world are hidden or ignored. Architecture forms part of the pretence that corporate America exists in harmony with nature rather than sanitizing and exploiting it in the pursuit of pleasure and profit.

CHAPTER 8
WALKING ON WATER

By the early nineteenth century there was a growing appreciation of the joys and benefits to be gained not just by being beside the sea but going out over it. Over the previous half a century, visitors had learnt how to understand, admire and enjoy the seaside, and a new architecture for coastal leisure eventually developed in response. Piers were one of its chief products and part of a process of 'attuning space with desire' that characterized the later stages of the Romantic consumption of the seaside.[1] Although with none of the disadvantages and dangers associated with boats, whether seasickness or the possibility of capsizing or even drowning, piers enabled visitors to leave the landward side of the sea and venture out to the water itself.

Walking on to a pier was to be transported ever closer to raw, untamed nature, heightening both the sense of admiration of nature and the accomplishment of the individual making the visit. Moreover, sea air was surely more beneficial over the sea than when breathed on land. And there was the camaraderie to be enjoyed by being with like-minded people. There were new panoramas of the coast to view, storms and sunsets to marvel at, and horizons to contemplate. The pier, as a platform from which to view the horizon, allowed people to reflect on themselves, other places and other times. Although it was of course an illusion, the pier was remarkable in seeming to enable people to journey a little closer to the unobtainable.

FROM PROMENADE TO PLEASURE PIER

Walking over the sea for pleasure at first used structures designed for functional maritime purposes. At Whitby, Scarborough, Ramsgate and other older coastal towns being transformed into resorts, stone breakwaters and piers – often very old structures – protecting or forming a harbour were explicitly adapted for parading by fashionable visitors. In *Persuasion*, written in 1815–16, Jane Austen describes the 'old wonders and new improvements'[2] of the Cobb at Lyme Regis, an ancient stone pier sheltering Lyme harbour, although by the early nineteenth century also a genteel promenade and one of the chief 'charms' to be enjoyed by visitors to the town. Austen makes use of the Cobb for a critical turning point in the story, the first of a rich literary tradition using piers as sites of leisure and happiness but also unforeseen danger or denouement. One of the novel's characters, Louisa Musgrove, jumping down 'from the high part of the new Cobb', misses the safe hands of Captain Wentworth, to fall and be 'taken up lifeless'.[3]

As Austen was penning her fiction, the pier at Margate, another stone harbour arm, was being rebuilt after earlier storm damage. Reopening in 1815, the pier included a new parade for visitors. An early instance of promenading over the sea involving a monetary transaction, on payment of an entrance toll visitors to Margate pier had access to a privatized, exclusive and separate space that included a gallery for a band to play.

In contrast to the necessarily strong, stone, harbour walls and breakwaters designed to rebuff the sea and provide

The ancient Cobb, Lyme Regis, in 1999.

The earliest example of these new dual-purpose piers was that of 1814 at Ryde on the Isle of Wight.[4] In 1824 Jarvis's Landing Place was built close to the stone Margate pier. In this case the name indicates the low-lying wooden jetty's primary purpose, to allow passengers 'to reach the shore when the water is too low for vessels to enter the harbour'. Despite the intent, an 1831 guide described how it 'is deservedly considered one of the most inviting marine walks which fancy can imagine, or experience realize'.[5] The promenade, though, functioned only between low and mid-tide since the structure was submerged at high water, often stranding visitors on the slightly higher pier-head and leading to either alarm from those above the sea or hilarity from those observing the scene from dry land.

The most iconic of these transitional structures, part landing stage and part select promenade, was Brighton's Chain Pier, opened in 1823. Apart from being Britain's greatest seaside resort, the town was also one end of an important cross-Channel route to continental Europe. The Chain Pier's enabling Act of Parliament emphasized the function of the pier for landing and shipping people and goods, but also recognized the 'Purpose of walking for Exercise [and] Pleasure'.[6] Indeed, the promoters of the enterprise anticipated that the revenue from promenaders would exceed that from passengers travelling to or from France.

The Chain Pier's chief attraction for promenaders was to be able to walk over the sea. It was here, as Corbin argues,

sheltered water, the principal function of landing stages and jetties was to get people and goods between ship and shore safely and easily. They were usually constructed of wood and built relatively cheaply and speedily, and the design challenge was to provide a bridge into deeper water where vessels could moor. In the early decades of the nineteenth century, landing-stage piers were built to facilitate sea-borne access to resorts. The promoters of such ventures increasingly saw promenading as a useful subsidiary income-generating function.

that aristocratic visitors to Brighton 'encountered the desire to see, feel, and experience the sea'.[7] A report in *The Times* on the pier's opening believed that 'to the man of pleasure and the valetudinarian, it offers a marine promenade unequalled'. Critically, however, this was a communal rather than a solitary activity. The seekers after health, for example, were 'dragged to the farthest extremity of the chain pier, to inhale to the greatest advantage the invigorating sea breezes, and concentrated upon a single spot, they give a decided colour to the place, rendering it an open hospital'.[8]

Apart from the pier itself, early on the only artificial attractions, mostly to do with consuming nature in one way or another, were a 'floating bath' at the pier-head, a camera obscura, sundial, two small cannon, some green benches and mineral-water booths.[9] At the root end of the pier a reading room and saloon was opened to offer traditional resort facilities, including a library, telescopes to view the coast and pier, and musical entertainments, while 'Meteorological results and prognostications were also posted daily for inspection'.[10] Over time, however, the simple and natural attractions of the elite marine promenade were supplemented with a range of other facilities and entertainments. In the process the Chain Pier was transformed into part promenade and part pleasure pier, becoming a major attraction in its own right, and in embryonic form pointing the way to what was to become a pleasure pier mania in the second half of the century.

In both architectural and engineering terms, too, the Chain Pier was an innovative and iconic structure. The designer, Captain Samuel Brown, drew on rapidly developing metal technologies and his own previous engineering inventions involving chain cables and suspension bridges. The deck of the pier was 1,154 feet long and 13 feet wide, hanging from cast-iron chains suspended from four pairs of cast-iron towers, themselves designed in the fashionable Egyptian style and 'modelled on the pylon gateways of Karnak in Egypt'[11] and resting on four clumps of wooden piles driven into the seabed. The chains were anchored into the cliff face, while the broader pier-head landing stage was paved with Purbeck stone. As a radical departure from what had gone before, the architecture of the pier responded to the demands of aristocratic promenaders for a grand, imposing structure. *The Times* review of the opening of the pier emphasized the national achievement it represented, commenting on the perfection of the English iron that formed the 'material part' of the structure and noting that 'whether viewed as a national monument or as a novel invention, it is a gratifying evidence of the resources and intellect of our country'.[12]

Within a few years of its opening both J.M.W. Turner and John Constable were to feature the pier in their marine landscapes of seaside Brighton, and over the following seven decades views of the pier were endlessly painted, drawn, engraved and photographed: there were more than 150 different prints of the structure.[13] For a third of a century at least, the pier was the most important and popular attraction on the seafront, and in the mid-1850s Thackeray wrote admiringly of the structure running 'intrepidly into the sea' and how 'for the sum of two pence you can go out to sea and pace this vast deck without the need of a steward with a basin'.[14] Despite Brown's innovative solution to building in the sea, however, his ideas were not widely adopted. Brighton had 'a uniquely numerous and opulent visiting public'[15] seemingly willing to support the venture, although in reality it was never a great commercial success.

Other resorts were necessarily content with more ordinary timber landing-stage piers with subsidiary

The Pier and Pavilion from Royal Terrace, Southend, 1938.
Blackpool's crowded North Pier, early 20th century.

authorities described as 'not made for trade'.[17] These piers became fashionable and select extensions to seafront parades and drives. The inevitable band apart, promenade piers had little in the way of artificial entertainment and, as Walton suggests, they were an 'established recreational institution with pretensions to gentility and even "rationality"'.[18] In reality, the middle-of-the-century pier builders underestimated the continuing radical transformation of many resorts and the business of being beside the sea. From the early 1870s a second wave, this time a tidal wave, of new fully fledged pleasure piers engulfed the coastal resorts.

One 1890s commentator remarked that if the speed of pier development continued it would be 'necessary to alter the map of England, and represent it as a huge creature of the porcupine type, with gigantic piers instead of quills'.[19] Looking back from the vantage point of the early 1950s to the pier-building obsession of the late nineteenth century, the economic historian John Clapham thought Victorian piers 'were as symbolic of what archaeologists call a culture as are axe-heads and beakers . . . There they stood. No visitor to the island could miss them. From them the least seafaring of the islanders could watch his ships go by with the joy of vicarious ownership.'[20]

The new middle-class and, increasingly, working-class seaside visitors generated a demand for new architectural forms. During the second half of the century not only did the number of British piers multiply seven-fold, but their structure and purpose also changed. Although the

promenading functions: one was erected at Southend in 1830.[16] By 1850 there were just a dozen piers in British resorts, most serving both as landing stages and promenades. And yet by 1900 Britain's seafront architecture had been transformed: by that date there were 80 piers, with some resorts having two or even three of the structures. The first wave, in the 1850s and '60s, in this deluge of pier building was of promenade piers proper, structures the harbour

The pier as another world. North Pier, Blackpool, entertainment programme, 7 September 1950.

ubiquitous enjoyment of a stroll over the sea was still available, in most resorts gone was the traditional landing-stage function for anything other than pleasure trips on the sea and, by the end of the period, gone too, from the largest and most popular resorts, was the open-deck promenade pier.

The pleasure piers – either newly constructed or transformed from earlier promenade structures – were sites of artificial entertainments and amusements, many of these echoing and developing what was to be found in inland cities, including theatre, orchestral music, music-hall and variety shows, dancing and roller skating. Pleasure piers burgeoned with pavilions and theatres, concert halls and winter gardens, refreshment rooms and shops. But there were still ways in which the seaside location was used to provide a unique experience, most pleasure piers hosting a plethora of maritime entertainments ranging from steamer excursions – providing for most voyagers otherwise unobtainable views and panoramas and a real sense of the sea – through aquatic entertainers and performing divers, to water fêtes and bathing facilities. It was the combination of maritime pleasures and indoor entertainments over the sea that made piers such an important feature of the British seaside experience from the late nineteenth century to the mid-twentieth.

Piers proved to be a flexible and evolving architectural form. Decking and structural elements were continually renewed because of the hostile coastal environment. Fire or storm damage, a repeated threat, would be seized as an opportunity to rebuild in a contemporary style. In the commercially most successful resorts, piers were repeatedly extended and enlarged, and as the composition and demands of seaside visitors changed so existing pier buildings were put to new uses. What was originally designed as a winter garden for musical entertainments might become a rifle range or roller-skating rink, and then be transformed into an amusement arcade, each transition perhaps also involving an architectural and interior design make-over. Ornate Victorian decoration might be hidden away behind a 1930s modernist facade. If existing buildings could not be adapted or were deemed too old-fashioned, they would be swept away and replaced with new structures designed for modern amusements.

Pleasure piers were also remarkably different from the early nineteenth-century structures in how they were made. The challenge of pleasure-pier building was to combine civil engineering for the extreme and inhospitable coastal margin with architecture designed to attract and entertain visitors. New technologies, some borrowed from the railway and ship-building industries, revolutionized pier construction and helped meet this challenge. Cast and wrought iron was critical in the construction of pier substructures. Problems inherent in securing a pier to the seabed were increasingly overcome, particularly through the use of innovative jetting techniques where the seabed was soft, and screw piling, originally patented in the 1830s by Alexander Mitchell as part of a floating dry-dock invention, into more solid strata.[21] Such methods and the prefabrication of materials, including cast-iron columns, perhaps made hundreds of miles away from the construction site, freed designers from earlier constraints and allowed the rapid construction of tall and wide load-bearing structures carrying wide promenades and large buildings on their decks.

The new piers were represented as modern and community ventures in which a resort and its inhabitants had an important stake. Since piers were speculative private enterprises, the shareholders often included both local and regional businessmen and other people of very modest means owning just a few shares.[22] The pleasure piers depended on luring toll-paying visitors through their turn-stiles, and then maximizing the revenue extracted from people once they were on the pier. Exterior architecture and interior design were important parts of the process, and pier buildings were designed to attract and entice, using various leisure motifs and symbols. By 1900 Oriental architectural styles, although not universal, became a classic decoration of pleasure piers. The most successful pleasure piers became architectural spectacles in their own right, while also offering spectacular entertainments.

But the pier development process was not always plain sailing. Sometimes pier proposals were abandoned because resorts were too small, finance inadequate or local political opposition too great. The class character of a resort also had consequences for pier enterprises. In 1874 Portsmouth's antagonistic class and political relations resulted in riots over the control of land by the entrance to Southsea Pier. The pier company wished to enclose the land, thereby excluding the undesirable local working people and turning it into an exclusive space reserved for respectable pier visitors. The several nights of protest included the burning of newly erected fences, attacks on the pier – the angry crowd pelted the promenaders and pier buildings with stones – and the quelling of the unrest by police, volunteer assistants and troops.[23]

The working classes already lived in Portsmouth and Southsea in large numbers. Elsewhere, some select and late-developing resorts eschewed piers because of the fear that such developments 'would drive away affluent visitors who wanted to avoid both noisy, flashy amusements and the working-class excursionists they attracted'.[24] There was no such concern in high-class and exclusive Eastbourne, a resort under the patronage and control of the Duke of Devonshire: in the 'Empress of Watering Places', 'the pier,

with its bands and its theatre, only offered the highest class of entertainment'.[25]

BRIGHTON'S WEST PIER

Each pier developed its own particular life history, responding to and reflecting local and regional circumstances and events, as well as broader national changes in seaside holidaymaking and architecture. Looking at one resort – Brighton – and one pier – the West Pier of 1866 – illustrates in microcosm many of the processes at work. In the later stages of its history, however, Brighton's West Pier was to assume an iconic and national status.[26]

A speculative private enterprise, the West Pier Company's object was 'to erect a handsome, commodious, and substantial Iron Promenade Pier . . . in the centre of that portion of the Esplanade which, at all seasons of the year, is the most thronged by residents and visitors'.[27] Reflecting 1860s Brighton's status as the leading British resort, but also the transitional state of pier technology, style and function, which was still being attempted, tested and searched for rather than taken for granted and assumed, the new pier was at once ambitious, innovative and uncertain on matters of engineering, architecture and purpose.

The West Pier's opening on Saturday, 6 October 1866 was celebrated with military music, processions the length of the pier and a 21-gun salute of the Royal Standard.[28] That evening the dignitaries attending an inauguration dinner in the Banqueting Room of the Royal Pavilion heard speeches in praise of what was represented as a wonderful, modern and mould-breaking piece of engineering and architecture. One poetic speaker described the pier as 'a kind of butterfly upon the ocean to carry visitors upon its wings and waft them amongst the zephyrs and balmy breezes of Brighton'.

James Webb and George Earl, *Brighton from the End of the West Pier*, c. 1870, oil on canvas.

The mayor of Brighton looked to the future, trusting

that the Pier would ever remain a benefit to the town, that the elements above and below it would be propitious; and that the healthy and sick, the rich and the humble, might alike enjoy the health-inspiring breezes to be obtained upon it; and that the weak might be restored to robust health. He hoped that the Pier might remain to future ages to prove what speculation had done.

The press agreed with such sentiments, *The Brighton Examiner*, for instance, arguing 'we now look upon the structure as artistic and elegant, outrivalling everything of the kind in this country, and perhaps the world'.

The component parts for the pier were prefabricated in a Glasgow ironworks to the instructions of Eugenius Birch, the pier's designer. The doyen of Victorian pier engineers, Birch was responsible for fourteen seaside piers, from Margate Jetty in 1853 to Plymouth Pier in 1884, as well as innovative aquaria in Brighton and Scarborough. It was Birch who made popular the innovative 'worm' or screw piling technique, so radically different from how the Chain Pier had been made.

Although much the same length, at its narrowest point the West Pier was four times wider than the older Chain Pier. Commentators admired the design strengths of the overall structure with its columns and piles 'braced and tied in such a manner as to ensure the greatest amount of stiffness to the Pier, and least amount of resistance to the sea',[29] and marvelled at the expanse of the open deck, providing 'altogether over 100,000 superficial feet of promenade'. Simulating a promenade on land, the deck of the pier was of close planking covered by 'gravel laid upon bitumen'.

The unwanted were kept off the pier by money, architecture and social convention. Turnstiles, ornamental iron gates and two imposing identical square tollhouses in Italianate style guarded the entrance and marked it out as a separate place. Standards of behaviour were carefully regulated. There was strict dress code for promenaders (although other orthodoxies applied to male bathers from the pier-head, who could enjoy the sea unencumbered by costumes). The tollhouses were the most contentious feature of the new pier, nearby residents arguing that they were so large 'the whole vista of the sea was cut asunder',[30] and one press critic agreeing that 'no beauty of structure can compensate for the loss of sea view'.[31]

The pier had other innovative and distinctive architectural features designed to capitalize on the nature of promenading and the mid-Victorian seaside holiday. There was 'ample and continuous seat-accommodation', including curved cast-iron pier bench seating along the edge of the pier, 'for 2,000 to 3,000 persons',[32] facing inwards rather than outwards over the sea, allowing visitors to the pier to rest, talk and look. There were untrammelled panoramic views out to sea and along the coast, and visitors could also enjoy the sight of crowded beaches and people using bathing machines at the water's edge. Addressing the Victorian anxiety with health and the

The New Pier from Regency Square, Brighton, c. 1866,
engraving.

conviction that the most beneficial aspects of the seaside
came from breathing sea air, Birch provided innovative
ornamental weather screens on the pier-head around a
small open platform for band performances. The distinctive architecture of the screens represented design for
health, comfort and social mixing:

On a sunny winter's day invalids can enjoy the mild
temperature and life-prolonging air with perfect freedom from chilling blasts . . . In summer the screens will
shade the visitors from the sun without putting up an
awning, which gives closeness and an air of confine-
ment. It might be thought that with all this shelter the
head of the pier would be confined in appearance.

Brighton's early West Pier, as originally designed, at low tide, with Oriental kiosks and open deck promenade, *c.* 1870s.

Nothing, however, could well be more open. The manner in which Mr Birch has obtained the maximum of accommodation and weather protection with the minimum of air-stoppage and light-obstruction, is a charming specimen of engineering skill . . . As a sanatorium, this part of the Pier must be productive of the most beneficial effects to invalids and persons of delicate constitution.[33]

Another feature of the pier's architecture also proved to have a lasting reflection in pier design elsewhere. There were six 'ornamental houses' integral to the deck of the pier, used when individuals wanted to leave the promenade crowd, and perhaps the first instance of substantial buildings on the body of a pier and an embryonic form of the larger pavilions subsequently characteristic of fully fledged pleasure piers. A small minaret surrounded by ornate railings topped the roof of each kiosk. Inside was 'a spiral staircase leading to the roof, whence a magnificent panoramic view of the town, east and west, is obtained'. Together with the cast-iron gas lamp standards entwined by serpents that ringed the edge of the pier, the kiosks gave a distinctive Oriental feel to the structure.

The West Pier, then, was architecture and engineering designed to use, consume, relegate and dominate nature, allowing society access to a separate, distinctive world above the sea. The new pier quickly became an important part of seaside Brighton. But it was not a complete success.

The one potentially ruinous flaw in the early years, despite the claims made on the pier's opening, was the instability of the structure. In early August 1868, for example, panic broke out among the crowd on the pier-head who feared the structure would collapse. One letter writer to *The Times* explained that there were

> Several thousand present at the head of the pier, many seated round, while others were standing and promenading during the performance of a band. There was a sudden commotion among the company, who endeavoured *en masse* to make for the shore end of the pier, ladies fainting and children screaming, some trodden upon, many of whom, I fear, must have been seriously injured. The cry having been raised that the pier was giving way was the cause of what might have proved a great calamity.[34]

In illustrating the weaknesses of devising a new architecture and built form using cutting-edge technology, the incident threatened to undermine public confidence in the pier as a place of pleasure and business. Repeated remedial work to rectify the problem occurred over the following two decades.

For some critics the pier promenade experience was staid and tedious. In the early 1880s Richard Jefferies commented on how 'Most people who go on the West Pier at Brighton walk at once straight to the farthest part. This is the order and custom of pier promenading; you are to stalk along the deck until you reach the end, and there you go round and round the band in a circle like a horse tethered to an iron pin, or else sit down and admire those who do go round and round.'[35] Jefferies himself was more interested in using the pier as a voyeurs' platform, looking down to the breaking waves where young female bathers, 'brave womanhood', were rolled and tossed about in the sea.

Aware of the need to make the pier more attractive, the company sought to enliven the visitor experience by providing spectacles using the sea. The pier became a place for visitors to marvel at human ingenuity in conquering the watery elements, most typically through watching spectacles involving swimming and diving in the sea. Both were presented to and seen by visitors as unique and exceptional activities that defied the accepted existing boundaries between society and nature.

Soon after the pier's opening, Brighton Swimming Club with a membership of local people provided 'aquatic entertainment' for the West Pier Company. The theatrical performances on 3 August 1868 included 'Captain Camp, the one-legged Swimmer [who] will prepare and partake of breakfast on the water', and a member of the swimming Club who 'will perform Airs upon the Concertina, and read the Daily Paper whilst lying on the water'. By 1875 the Swimming Club's West Pier swimming matches 'attracted a large crowd of spectators . . . Swimming in Brighton is comparatively a new thing, for it dates from 1860 when the Swimming Club was established. Since then, the healthy, useful, and delightful exercise has flourished well.'

The new Marine Palace and Pier *c.* 1903.

The Chain Pier immediately before its destruction, illustrating the structure's technology and the pier-head promenading space. Arthur Elliot, *Brighton Chain Pier*, 1896, pencil and watercolour.

The Old Chain Pier, Brighton

A souvenir postcard sent in 1909, thirteen years after the Old Chain Pier's destruction.

Human ingenuity in and under the water was also brought on to the pier itself. In 1889 visitors could pay to witness 'the model undine', Miss Louie Webb, in 'her unique, scientific, and graceful under-water performance in the glass tank' in one of the pier kiosks. While submerged in 3 feet of water Miss Webb performed a variety of feats, including eating sponge cake, drinking milk from a bottle, 'opening and closing the eyes', 'attitude of prayer' and sewing and writing.

The high point of the pier's visitor numbers of 845,000 in 1880 fell to 591,000 eight years later. Even this figure was threatened by the prospect of a new purpose-built pier to be constructed a short distance to the east by the Brighton

Marine Palace and Pier Company, the ordering of the words indicating the company's intent on building not so much a pier but a people's palace above the sea. The West Pier could not survive as a promenade with a few added attractions. Radical action was needed and over the quarter of century from 1890 the passive and sedate promenade pier was transformed into a spectacle- and performance-based pleasure pier through the addition of large new entertainment buildings. A pier-head pavilion, with an exterior echoing the Oriental design of the earlier kiosks, was completed in 1893, in sight of the emerging Palace Pier. Once the Palace Pier opened in 1901, the two piers entered a period when they raced neck and neck for the position as Brighton's premier seaside attraction.

'Professor Reddish's Bicycle Dive from the West Pier, Brighton' on a postcard of c. 1904.

'Walter Tong, Diver, Life Saving Champion' and spectators, on a postcard of c. 1915.

As Brighton, its visitors and its seafront architecture changed, so the Chain Pier became increasingly antiquated and redundant. By the mid-1860s it was sometimes 'given up to a boisterous crowd of unwashed or overwashed excursionists', something never intended for the genteel structure.[36] On the approach to the Chain Pier by the mid-

1870s, the new Brighton Aquarium was not just a place to look at marine life but provided a plethora of modern entertainments. The old pier could not compete; it was closed as unsafe in October 1896 and destroyed in a storm in early December. In its death throes the Chain Pier seemed eager to take its younger competitor with it, the wreckage destroy-

'Zoe Brigden West Pier. Aquatic entertainer, Brighton', on a postcard of *c.* 1912–25.

ing a 100-foot section of the West Pier above the beach, stranding a clerk and waitresses. Even a century after its destruction, publications and an exhibition in Brighton celebrated the significance of the pier.[37]

Although the West Pier's new pavilion was praised in the local press as being 'like another Aphrodite emerging from the sea',[38] the plans were contested by Brighton Corporation, which objected to the proposal for an imposing Oriental dome, echoing those on the Royal Pavilion. Instead, the pier owners 'were compelled to adopt the "flattened, dish-cover roof"'.[39] The Pavilion was designed as a flexible space for entertainment with an emphasis on music and reportedly seating up to 1,700 people. The *Daily Telegraph* acclaimed the building as providing 'Brighton

with an establishment which surpasses all its rivals, and may be made to correspond in every desirable detail with the attractive casinos of continental resorts'.[40] The varied musical entertainments were supplemented with other acts, including, for example, a female impersonator and a 'wonderful talking and calculating horse', and attractions including a dog show and a temporary art gallery. In 1903 the Pavilion was converted into a theatre and hosted a vast array of theatrical plays and stage entertainments from Shakespeare and 'Russian Ballet', through romances, comedies and thrillers, to opera, musicals and the occasional concert party.

New landing stages running out from the pier-head also allowed further exploitation of the sea through the development of public swimming using new bathing facilities, displays of professional diving and aquatic entertainments, and the extension of the paddle steamer excursion business. The steamers provided pleasure trips to nearby resorts or ventured on longer voyages to the Isle of Wight or across the Channel to Boulogne, Dieppe and Trouville. With the new landing-stage bathing station the company decided that 'in right appreciation of public feeling' bathing costumes should be worn after 9 o'clock.

A new breed of professional marine entertainers also used the new pier-head. Professional diving and associated aquatic entertainment were spectacles that, like swimming, combined demonstrations of physical prowess and skill pitted against nature with elements of theatre. Two noted early West Pier divers were Professor Reddish and Professor Cyril, the latter making the ultimate spectacular sacrifice during his 'sensational bicycle dive' in May 1912. He was killed when, attempting his frequently accomplished exploit, he 'had a side-slip and was thrown heavily on to the deck of the pier, fracturing his skull'.[41] Other West Pier

The new Winter Garden, Palace Pier, on a postcard of *c.* 1910.

The completed West Pier in its heyday, with Concert Hall and pier-head Theatre, *c.* 1920s.

The beginnings of the funfair pier: the West Pier after the installation of the miniature race track in 1927.

divers used diving boards, some towering 80 feet into the sky. Walter Tong's special feats included his famous 'Mole-berg' and 50 feet dives, while Zoe Brigden was renowned for her 'wooden soldier' dive, involving plunging head first into the sea with arms at her sides.

The success of the Theatre, and the opening of the Palace Pier's central winter gardens in 1910, led the pier company to build a low eight-sided oval concert hall, opening in 1916, for musical performances and other events. The exterior decoration included 'Brighton dolphins on shields, set off with heavy festoons. At due intervals on the parapet of the roof arise graceful urns' that 'suggest champagne rather than ashes'. The interior of the building was unbroken by pillars or balconies, the sweep of the iron roof trusses praised for resembling 'the delicate fan lines of a

Late Gothic roof'. Commentators, though, were unsure just what to make of the building, describing its 'certain individuality of design' and 'architecture in a holiday mood'.[42] The opening concert both evidenced the war being fought across the Channel and celebrated the pleasurable purpose of the structure, with the romantic and patriotic musical programme provided by the King's Royal Rifles silver band of 'wounded soldiers or men invalided out of the Army'.

Its transformation into a pleasure pier complete, in 1919–20 the pier achieved its highest recorded figure of 2,074,000 paying visitors. Seemingly well attuned to holiday fashions and tastes, the West Pier became a major symbol of seaside Brighton entwined with the image and sense of the resort. It was a perpetual subject for visual artists[43] and, more significantly, it featured on endless post-

BRIGHTON
BY BEVERLEY NICHOLS

H. G. GAWTHORN

THE OFFICIAL HANDBOOK OF
THE CORPORATION OF BRIGHTON

The West Pier used to promote Brighton as a resort, 1934–5 guidebook cover.

cards and, particularly during the inter-war years, on guidebook covers and posters promoting images of seaside modernity, fashion and high status.[44] But it was a chimera to believe that a successful place-promotion strategy could use the pier as a symbol of the resort. From the early 1920s the pier began a relatively rapid and bumpy descent, in less than twenty years the annual number of visitors falling by almost two-thirds. Part of the problem was the changing nature of holidaymaking and the increasing enchantment with the pleasures of the sun and sea and, ideally, sand. Brighton as a resort, thrown into intense competition from newer rivals, was also changing and, despite the image being promoted, moved downmarket. For the West Pier there was increased local competition, not only from the Palace Pier but also from the resort's new seaside attractions.

As the pleasure-pier enterprise began to fail the pier company turned to funfair attractions and new mechanical games and amusements to entice back the lost visitors. From April 1927 part of the broad root end of the pier was given over to an 'auto-motor track', described disparagingly by one commentator as a 'toy motor track, which is anything but an ornament to the pier'.[45] New sun terraces and sunshine shelters opened in 1935, a radical change from what the original Victorian promenaders had wanted and expected of the pier. But these new facilities were poorly patronized, holidaymakers preferring the beach or lured to the delights of the resort's new open-air swimming pools and lido.

The Palace Pier took to the funfair business more readily than the West Pier, and the newer structure was a critical location in Graham Greene's 1938 novel *Brighton Rock*.[46] Treating the pier and its visitors with remoteness and distaste, Greene's portrayal of Brighton caused consternation at Brighton Corporation, not least because it undermined the official promotion of the town as an elite quality resort. The early post-war film version of the novel returned to the Palace Pier, using the ghost train for the murder of Fred Hale and the landing stages for the death of Pinkie: this was the seaside and its architecture revealed as a fearful and murderous site, unseen and unsuspected by the jolly holidaymaking crowd.

In the late 1940s the West Pier's evolution into a funfair pier was completed. Remnants of the nautical entertainments from the past survived, at least for a while, and aquatic entertainers continued to perform from the pier-head: as late as 1970 The Great Omani, hooded and locked in chains, successfully repeated Houdini's famous 'death dive' from the end of the pier.[47] Otherwise, however, and

The funfair pier: West Pier dodgems, *c.* 1949.

An undated postcard of the Palace Pier by night, the 'Finest pier in the world'.

although it looked much the same on the outside, a different pier experience was offered to post-war visitors. The former theatre was divided into two, the ground floor becoming the Games Pavilion, later renamed as 'Laughterland', housing an indoor funfair. Upstairs, the relics of Victorian and Edwardian decoration disappeared and the space was given a plain 'Festival of Britain' make-over, becoming the Ocean Restaurant advertised with the slogan 'lunch and tea over the sea'. The Concert Hall was converted to a café with small-scale musical entertainments, while the root end of the pier was transformed into a funfair with helter-skelter, dodgems, a ghost train and amusement arcades.

The changes were not enough to secure a prosperous future. By 1950 more than twice as many people were visiting the rival Palace Pier, by then proclaimed as 'the brightest jewel in Brighton's crown' and, as before the war, 'the finest pier in the world'. At the same time the novelist Patrick Hamilton was writing one of the most alluring of alternative representations of the West Pier, describing it as 'resembling in the sea a sort of amiable, crouching, weird battleship – a sex-battleship', the object and arena for young people to 'get off' with each other.[48]

By 1956, and drawing on the success of holiday camps, the West Pier was presented as 'a completely self-contained holiday unit on which the visitor to Brighton can spend a first-class holiday without stepping ashore . . . except to sleep'. Despite the upbeat presentation of the pier's attractions, the West Pier spiralled into a decline of failing attractions, falling visitor numbers, declining income and under-investment. A similar story could be told for other English piers during this

The West Pier officially photographed before listing as architecturally significant, c. 1970.

period, and by the 1970s even the Palace Pier was increasingly unkempt. The resort's official guidebook was unsurprisingly blind to the problems, in 1968 representing the pier as an exotic cruise liner: 'The West Pier is as brilliant by day as it is by night. To laze in the sun on its many sun decks is like a luxury cruise in the tropics.'[49] But at the same time Richard Attenborough, making the film *Oh! What a Lovely War*, used the pier as another form of transportation, this time to the horror and tragedy of the First World War.[50]

The Palace Pier viewed from the pier-head of the closed and derelict West Pier, late 1980s.

From the late 1960s, amid threats to close and demolish the pier, its architectural and heritage value suddenly came to the fore. A vocal and popular 'We Want the West Pier' campaign sought to save the structure; it was listed by the Government as a building of historic and architectural interest; and in 1974 a Brighton Council report emphasized 'its immeasurable architectural and historical importance', arguing that it was second only to the Royal Pavilion among internationally famous buildings in Brighton and Sussex. This acclaim was in great contrast to the contemptuous comments less than a decade before from the doyen of architectural historians, Nikolaus Pevsner, who in 30 closely packed pages on the architecture of Brighton dismissed the West Pier in just two lines.[51]

The pier closed at the end of the 1975 summer season. In 1978 the charitable West Pier Trust became the owner, with the objective of saving the pier and returning it to use. Four years later the pier's architectural listing was raised to Grade I, the only English pier then to have received this highest classification of architectural importance.

With closure, dereliction and ruination, the pier increasingly engaged the public imagination and, in turn,

was featured in a vast array of imaginative and factual representations. For the English Tourist Board in 1983, for instance, it was a 'monument of dereliction';[52] a year later the architect, artist and writer Hugh Casson described 'the magnificent West Pier' as 'a tragic site, still just about exists';[53] in 1991 Helen Zahavi used the 'gaunt and gutted' structure for the denouement in her novel *Dirty Weekend*;[54] and it was the location for the murderous endgame in Lynda La Plante's 1998 TV series *Killer Net*. The West Pier, as with many other piers, was again represented as a place of narrow escape or no return; in this case, however, the combination of elements – danger, violence and death, a fear of nature and the derelict pier, eerie and ghostly architecture where the present confronts the past, the remoteness from safety and society – provided a particularly compelling atmosphere.

The derelict island pier could conjure powerful and sometimes conflicting responses in individuals. For some people it was romantic and picturesque, perhaps invoking wistful memories of holiday pleasures long ago; for others the pier was decrepit and ruined, an emphatic symbol of the decline of Brighton, the English seaside resort and perhaps Britain more generally; for still more others, it was a national architectural jewel to be saved and restored. There could be astonishment at the impact of nature on the pier combined with outrage that it had been allowed to happen, or the structure could be anthropomorphized into a defiant old lady in desperate need of help.

The pier also generated complex emotional feelings, more difficult to comprehend than openly expressed responses, but to do with the relationships between society

The pier-head at low tide in 1997, a quarter of a century after it was sealed off.

A relic of the 1866 West Pier: a derelict kiosk in 1999.

top: The collapse of West Pier Concert Hall, December 2002.

left: Scavenging for the remains of the Concert Hall.

top right: The fire in March 2003.

right: The ravaged pier before a further arson attack and continued storm damage.

and nature, the past and present. Although writing almost a century ago, Georg Simmel's interpretation was that in 'the ruin' – and the West Pier had become a seaside ruin par excellence – 'with its extreme intensification and fulfillment of the present form of the past, such profound and comprehensive energies of our soul are brought into play that there is no longer any sharp division between perception and thought'.[55] By the start of the twenty-first century, the structure originally designed to consume and dominate nature had largely been remade into a natural site and sight. The pier began to fulfil the requirements of an ideal type natural attraction, 'unmarked' and not 'tampered with for touristic purposes'.[56] With the exception of the lifejacket- and hard-hat-clad intrepid explorers joining the West Pier tour parties, the pier was an unobtainable natural spectacle, available only to view from a distance.

Caught up in Britain's burgeoning heritage industry and visited and acclaimed by government ministers and members of the British royal family, the pier was increasingly represented as national heritage with popular appeal and significance. For the town council, the restored pier was also an important element in the regeneration of Brighton's seafront. The advent of the National Lottery Heritage Fund appeared at last to solve the funding problem, particularly when the organization sought more popular recipients in response to the widespread criticism of the elitist character of its first awards.[57] In 1998 the Lottery Fund agreed 'in principle' to grant the West Pier Trust £14.5 million for the restoration. Into the new century, however, society and nature continued to frustrate the realization of the restoration plans. Proposals for new buildings at either side of the root end, required to match the Lottery money, proved controversial with some groups of local people, while the owners of the Palace Pier were virulently opposed to the proposed Lottery Fund award to the old rival.

The restoration scheme was dragged into a quagmire of bureaucratic dithering, private sector self-interest, legal challenges, political lobbying, planning inquires and public protest.[58] Ten thousand seafront visitors signed a petition against the actions of the Palace Pier. Designs were put forward for new twenty-first-century piers. Then, in an eighteen-month period ending in June 2004, the pier's Pavilion and Concert Hall were spectacularly destroyed in two violent storms and two carefully planned arson attacks by untraced perpetrators. The visually dramatic images received international media coverage, while locally each event drew hundreds of spectators to gaze, record and scavenge for remnants of the structure.[59]

The two most significant national bodies for the historic environment then locked horns to contest the future of the pier. English Heritage, responsible for protecting the historic environment, remained fully supportive of the restoration, arguing: 'The West Pier was the most important pleasure pier ever built in terms of its climactic and seminal engineering design, its architectural ambition and as an enduring social symbol of Brighton as the acme of seaside resorts.'[60] The Heritage Lottery Fund, though, took the alternative view, perhaps demonstrating its inability to be weaned from an elitist high culture perspective on the arts and heritage. It withdrew its financial support, saying that in the context of the intense competition for its funds the project was too risky and uncertain.[61] Further storm damage and six months later, English Heritage abruptly withdrew from the contest, saying the restoration project no longer possessed 'historic credibility'.[62] A scathing *Daily Telegraph* editorial on the 'tragedy' saw the fate of the West Pier as 'a parable for everything that is wrong with Britain'.[63]

Away from Brighton, many other British piers have experienced similar traumatic upheavals.[64] Nationally the number of piers has halved since the peak a century ago, the structures destroyed through fire and storm or demolished following stagnation and decline. Of those that survive, some are closed with uncertain fates, some have been repackaged as heritage piers and restored as part of the process, while in other resorts piers continue as commercial ventures, nowadays most often centred on the seaside amusement business. Individual piers have both reflected the more general character and purpose of the British seaside, while also absorbing the qualities and circumstances of a specific resort. Conversely, though, if the nineteenth-century proponents are to be believed, a pier had a seminal influence on the character and standing of a resort. Today, however, amid debates about the social and economic regeneration of older seaside resorts, there is ambivalence about whether British piers are part of the problem to be addressed or whether their rehabilitation can contribute to the solution to a more general seaside regeneration problem.[65]

In one perspective, in the twenty-first century British piers are a redundant and archaic architectural form. The decline of piers, Urry argued, is symptomatic of the transformation of British resorts from once extraordinary places to very ordinary ones upon which a decreasing number of tourists wish to gaze.[66] Parris, certainly, found nothing enchanting about them, asserting 'piers are not beautiful, novel or architecturally interesting' and rather than having public money spent on them should be 'allowed to slip beneath the waves'.[67] More sympathetically, Walton has suggested the pier 'symbolizes the demise of a cohesive culture and its replacement by storm-ridden diversity . . . Its past has vitality and social resonance: its future, sadly, may belong in the world of the museum, the preservation society and the professional purveyor of nostalgia.'[68]

And yet in full view of the skeletal West Pier, by 2004 the Palace Pier was remarkably different from the stagnating structure of two decades before. Rebranded and renamed as 'the world famous Brighton Pier', it had been transformed into Britain's commercially most successful pier, high in the national rankings for the most popular free tourist attractions with 3.5 million visits a year, and a curious English seaside version of Disneyland dominated by amusement arcades – 'family entertainment centres' – and modern funfair rides.[69] In the process, the original exotic pier-head theatre had been removed and replaced with a plain prefabricated 'Pleasuredome' for an amusement arcade, the pier-head enlarged and strengthened to take the funfair, and the remaining older pier buildings restored but re-clad in plastic. An illustration of the symbiotic relationship between pier and resort and a warning against reading the decline of either as inevitable, the brash modern Brighton Pier was part of a larger rejuvenation of the Brighton seafront over the last two decades, both in turn bound up in the reinvention of Brighton into a fashionable twenty-first century seaside city.[70]

CONTRASTS AND COMPARISONS

Although initially a British architectural response to the seaside, other Western countries also took to the business of building for pleasure not simply beside but in the sea. In the United States from the late nineteenth century, many established resorts developed distinctive amusement piers. Although perhaps also used as landing stages and promenades, the primary purpose of amusement piers was simply that of entertaining visitors to the seaside while ensuring

above and right: The Brighton Palace Pier as a funfair in 1999.

The 1935 Nautical Moderne-styled pier-head pavilion,
Worthing Pier, Sussex, photographed in 1999.

top: The truncated Cleethorpes Pier, Lincolnshire, 2001.

above: The 1903 Art Nouveau-inspired pavilion on the Wellington Pier, Great Yarmouth, Norfolk, 2000.

right: Herne Bay Pier, Kent, with its detached pier-head 1999.

Blackpool Central Pier, 2000.

Cromer Pier, Norfolk, 2000.

they paid for the pleasure. Especially in resorts with more than one pier or with land-based amusement parks, the competition to attract and keep visitors led to spectacular architectural responses and equally spectacular and distinctive entertainments. As places of spectacle, piers vied to provide the most extreme, impressive, unique and innovative attractions. Size – of a ride, a dance hall or theatre – and fame – of the entertainers or entertainments – mattered, and piers often represented modernity, technology, excess and pleasure at the seaside.

Atlantic City, at the beginning of the twentieth century the East coast's most successful resort, took amusement pier building to an extreme not seen elsewhere: Applegate's Pier opened in 1884, followed by the Iron Pier, the Ocean Pier (the Applegate transformed), the Steel Pier, the Million Dollar Pier and the Steeplechase Pier of 1908. The largest and most successful of the piers proclaimed a diverse range of attractions, including rides, amusement arcades and live performances from nationally popular entertainers. As if to show what modernity could do with nature, many of the piers featured extreme entertainments over the sea: one of the most outlandish and long-lasting was the Steel Pier's High Diving Horse, involving a horse and rider jumping from a 60-feet-high platform into a 10-feet-deep pool. At night the piers were marked out by the use of electric lights and large advertising signs. Atlantic City's market was varied and huge enough for piers to specialize. In 1898 the Iron Pier was remade as the Heinz Pier as a marketing device for the food company, including a museum exhibiting the Heinz art collection and an early sun parlour. The Garden Pier of 1913 was intended for the resort's most respectable visitors, its Spanish Renaissance architecture and landscaped gardens including a theatre and ballroom, although four

decades later it was purchased by the city and subsequently used as an art gallery and museum.[71]

The fate of the other Atlantic City piers followed that of the resort: prolonged success followed by deep decline, and then from the 1970s, the transformation of Atlantic City into a casino town,[72] a remaking of the resort and the surviving piers. By the early twenty-first century the reconstructed Steel Pier alone carried traditional seaside rides and arcades, while the Central Pier focused on electronic arcade games. Ocean One Pier, a 1983 structure on the site of the Million Dollar Pier, took the form of an ocean liner, although it housed a mundane shopping mall, and in 2004 was again being remade into 'The Pier at Caesars', a 'luxurious' retail-dining-entertainment complex linked to one of Atlantic City's largest casinos and drawing on design and retailing ideas from Las Vegas.

If the Atlantic City contemporary pier experience is dislocated from the resort's amusement piers of a century ago, south along the New Jersey coastline at Wildwood is the most sustained twenty-first-century version of the American amusement pier, proclaimed as the 'largest seaside amusement center in the Western Hemisphere'. A group of what in origin were early twentieth-century piers has, since the 1970s, been continually redeveloped and remodelled into a modern amusement park complex.[73] Morey's Piers, with 90 rides and two pier-based waterparks, aims to provide 'a spectacular family recreation experience in an exceptionally safe, clean, friendly and unique environment'. Wildwood is 'safe danger' using a seaside location to rival inland theme parks.

On the West Coast the post-war theme-park challenge had contrasting, devastating, consequences for California's amusement piers. As Santa Monica Bay emerged as the seaside playground for the ever-growing Los Angeles, there

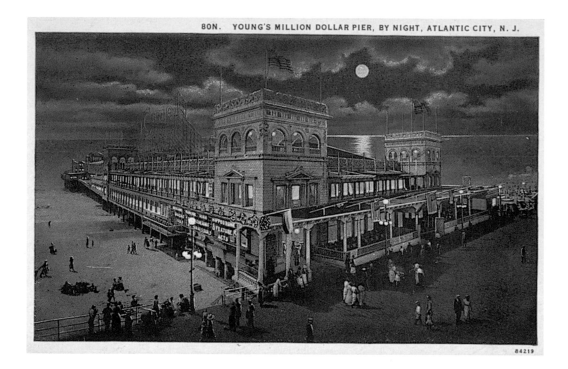

An undated postcard of Young's Million Dollar Pier, by night, Atlantic City, New Jersey.

A postcard, perhaps 1920s, of the 'garden pier showing flower beds' at the entrance, Atlantic City.

A postcard of 'Young's residence on Million Dollar Pier, Atlantic City', *c.* 1912.

A postcard of the 'Interior, Heinz Ocean Pier, Atlantic City', *c.* 1910.

The Steel Pier's High Diving Horses, *c.* 1940.

fantastic, copying styles from across the centuries and often inventing new ones. Separated by just a short stretch of beach, there was intense competition between the two piers. The newest and most innovative rides were quickly erected. In their 1920s heyday, both piers had Giant Dipper roller coasters; Venice Pier featured a Some Kick roller coaster and Flying Circus, Dragon Slide and Coal Mine rides; and Ocean Park Pier countered with the Hi-Boy roller coaster, Lighthouse slide, the Whip and The Chutes.[74]

Like so many piers elsewhere, both the Venice amusement piers, and others in Santa Monica Bay, were ravaged by storm and fire. Venice Pier burnt down in 1920, Ocean Park Pier in 1924. Both, though, were quickly rebuilt. Despite post-war optimism that the pier business would prosper, the Los Angeles seaside was rapidly changing and the municipal authorities were antagonistic. The City of Los Angeles' decision to reconstruct the Venice seafront led to the closure of Venice Pier and its demolition in 1947. More important still, the remaining Bay amusement piers were to face the challenge of Disneyland, opening at nearby Anaheim in 1955, and other inland theme parks seemingly better able to capture the public's imagination in the second half of the century. The first theme park was initially belittled as no more than an amusement park in new clothes. And yet the creation of Disneyland with its focus on the contemporary family as consumer and participant, and the development of an 'architecture of reassurance' built around the meticulous

was a concentrated period of pier building during the early years of the twentieth century. At one point there were five amusement piers within sight of each other on Santa Monica and Venice Beach, and each dominated by funfairs, theatres and dance halls.

Copying freely from its Italian namesake, Venice Beach was planned and developed at the turn of the last century as 'the Coney Island of the Pacific'. To the canals, a lagoon, a replica St Mark's Square and gondolas were added two un-Venetian amusement piers, Venice Pier and Ocean Park Pier. The architecture of individual attractions was often

A postcard of the Steel Pier diving bell, *c.* 1950s.

Steel Pier's Music Hall theatre, early 1950s.

theming of a confusion of real and imagined worlds, to relegate the amusement piers into relic entertainments of an earlier age.[75] In response to the Disney offensive, in 1957 Ocean Park Pier was remodelled into a 28-acre nautical theme park and renamed as Pacific Ocean Park. Among its attractions were the Sea Serpent roller coaster, Neptune's Kingdom, Mystery Island and the Super Sea Circus. The attempt to emulate Disney failed and the pier closed in 1967; the rides were auctioned off, and the empty and derelict pier was finally demolished in 1973.[76]

A similar fate overtook the Bay's other amusement piers, with the one exception of Santa Monica Pier. In early twentieth-century origin a long municipal pier, partly designed to carry a sewage outfall pipe, and joined with a shorter, squarer amusement pier, between the wars Santa Monica Pier was famous for the Whirlwind Dipper and the La Monica Ballroom, a dance palace advertised as the largest in the world.[77] Following major storm damage and reconstruction, the pier's Pacific Park amusement park opened in 1996.[78] By then the public appetite for entertainment over the sea had at least in part returned. Ironically, within a few years Disney launched its new California Adventure at Anaheim, which featured Paradise Pier as a 'land' providing traditional Californian beach and amusement-pier entertainments. It was as though Disney, having destroyed its coastal competition, then set about claiming for its own the essence of the Californian seaside of the past.

But a new Californian pleasure-pier form emerged in the last decades of the twentieth century. Echoing the early nineteenth-century use of breakwaters and harbour arms as promenades, former commercial shipping or fishing wharves – essentially maritime commercial structures from the past – were rejuvenated and transformed into major tourist destinations, often advertised as heritage sites, but in practice dominated by retail outlets, eating places and visitor attractions.

Santa Barbara's Stearns Wharf, the oldest surviving timber wharf in California, was built in 1872 to unload the timber used to build the expanding town. In the period before the arrival of the railroad, the wharf quickly became important as the only practical way to move goods, agricultural produce and visitors in and out of the area. Redundant as a shipping wharf, since the early, 1980s the structure has been transformed into Santa Barbara's major tourist attraction with shops, restaurants, a marine life centre and fishing from the pier-head. Further north along the Californian coast, Monterey has been remade from the sardine town captured in John Steinbeck's novel *Cannery Row* (1945) into a major tourist destination built around the seaside heritage industry. Along with a spectacular aquarium and cannery buildings converted into shopping centres, Monterey's Fisherman's Wharf, a wooden pier originally constructed for fishing vessels, nowadays carries craft and gift shops, seafood restaurants and kiosks selling boat trips. San Francisco has another even more touristy Fisherman's Wharf, in the heart of what was the city's great harbour and waterfront industrial area. A crucial feature of the transformed wharf area is Pier 39, partly built from timbers salvaged from demolished piers, and advertised as San Francisco's 'Number One Attraction'. Pier 39 is based around the re-creation of a supposed street scene from a century ago. It also includes an Underwater World, Cinemax Theatre showing 'The Great San Francisco Adventure', restaurants, 110 shops and 'postcard views' of Alcatraz Island with its infamous federal prison.

At first sight San Francisco's Pier 39 has little in common with seaside pleasure piers elsewhere, and yet the

Santa Monica Pier, California, 1998.

Disney's inland Paradise Pier, Anaheim, California, in 2002.

The new Venice Pier, California, in 1998.

essence, a seaside attraction built into the sea and designed to make money out of holidaymakers, is the same. The pier as a form of seaside architecture in the United States has also evolved in other ways. Some carry a single restaurant, hotel or home. Across the Golden Gate Bridge from San Francisco, the small resort of Sausalito has a clutch of tiny piers, each supporting just a single building over San Francisco Bay. At the northern edge of Santa Monica Bay, Malibu Pier has a more European look with buildings at the root end and pier-head, linked by the narrow neck of the pier. Originally built in 1903 as a wealthy family's yacht mooring, the chequered history of the pier included continual battering by storms and long periods of closure, although by 2004 it had been partially reopened and represented as an iconic symbol of a famously exclusive and stylish enclave of Los Angeles.

On mainland Europe a late-nineteenth-century bout of pier building reflected the British pier influence. In the French resort of Trouville, on the Channel coast due south of Brighton, the 1892 pier was designed by a British engi-

neer, prefabricated in Britain, and initially owned by a London-based company and controlled by an English businessman. The innovative arched cast-iron structure was part landing stage bringing visitors to the resort, particularly from the otherwise inaccessible Le Havre on the other side of the Seine estuary, part a promenade extension to the slightly earlier seafront esplanade, and part pleasure pier with a concert hall and a café restaurant on the pier-head.[79]

On the French Riviera coast, the 1880s Nice pier jutted out from the Promenade des Anglais, appropriately enough, given that the pier was designed by James Brunlees, a prolific Victorian engineer, and erected by a British company. The pier's primary purpose was as a casino, and the broad pier-head just a short distance from the shore carried one of the earliest and largest pier buildings in an elaborate ornamental design. A fire destroyed the building a few days before its inauguration. The replacement Casino de la Jetée,[80] opened in 1891, was both taller and more explicitly Oriental in design, with minarets and a large dome topped by a trident-carrying siren plated in gold. This

Stearns Wharf, Santa Barbara, California, in 1998.

Monterey's Fisherman's Wharf, California, in 1998.

much disputed pier – unwanted by the municipal authorities, criticized by some local people for obstructing the view of the bay, and abhorred by some architectural commentators – was one of the most extreme of the resort's *belle époque* buildings. By the inter-war period it was an established feature of the Nice seafront, much painted by Raoul Dufy and a symbol of the resort continually represented on postcards and posters. The German occupying forces destroyed both Trouville and Nice piers in the later stages of the Second World War.

There was also a spate of late-nineteenth-century pier building on the German Baltic coast islands of Rügen and Usedom following the emergence of a unified German state in the 1870s and the rapid development of mostly small-scale and respectable seaside resorts. As the name *Seebrücke* ('sea

A Sausalito pier, California, in 1998.

Pier 39, San Francisco, California, in 1998.

bridge') suggests, many German piers functioned primarily as promenades and as landing stages for pleasure steamers, and were open-deck structures. A few carried substantial buildings, including the 1891 pier at Heringsdorf, which featured a large and elaborate root-end building of ornate woodwork and tall, slender, tiled spires. At Sellin, the pier included restaurants, dance halls, shops, a casino and a 'Kursaal', originally a word used to described a spa building but transformed into a term for a seaside leisure building and particularly popular in English resorts before the First World War. These Baltic piers were mostly wooden structures, resting on pointed timbers driven into the seabed. While the engineering challenge was reduced because of the minimal tidal rise and fall of the land-locked sea, the Baltic provided an alternative natural hazard in the form of sea ice threatening to crush a pier to destruction.[81]

Malibu's closed pier, in 1998.

By the early 1900 piers had become an essential attraction of most Baltic resorts, along with tree-lined promenades, band shelters and open-air dance arenas, casinos and spas. Most piers endured at least to the early part of the Nazi era. With the Second World War and the subsequent communist regime, however, the existing piers declined and eventually vanished from the seaside landscape. Sometimes the immediate reasons were traumatic events such as fire or adverse weather, but the political and economic complexion of East Germany had no place for piers, a seaside architectural form from a rejected past.

And yet in the last decade of the twentieth century they were miraculously to reappear. Following the fall of the Berlin Wall and German reunification, a remarkable pier-building mania occurred, with seventeen new piers constructed between 1989 and 2000. It was as though the wheel had turned full circle back to the original enthusiasm

for pier building of a century earlier. Part of the wholesale rejuvenation of the Baltic seaside resorts, the new piers were used as the focal point of the seafront and important resort attractions, and given an economic and political significance and even symbolic value. New piers and their renewed resorts were an act of faith that, after two wars and two totalitarian states, the seaside should be an integral part of a modern democratic society.

The new piers depended on substantial regional and federal state funding. Although decked in wood, to withstand the Baltic winter ice they were constructed with huge steel tubes thumped into the seabed and filled with concrete. On or close to the sites of the first generation of piers, most are open-decked with no significant buildings. The exceptions include the piers at Sellin and Ahlbeck, both with a pastiche of the original pier buildings, while at Heringsdorf the new structure, the longest in continental

103 TROUVILLE. — *La Jetée Promenade.* — *The Promenade Jetty.* — LL.

4 Nice   *Casino de la Jetée*

An early postcard of the Promenade Jetty, Trouville.

'Nice – Casino de la Jetée', in a postcard of *c.* 1906.

Heringsdorf Pier, Usedom, in 2000.

Ahlbeck Pier, 2000.

Sellin Pier, 2000.

Europe and built just metres from the skeleton remains of the earlier pier, has a substantial root-end building drawing on the style of the first pier and a modern circular pier-head restaurant.

In contrast to the use of piers on the Baltic coast as a vehicle of regeneration, in contemporary Britain there are ambivalence and dithering towards piers and, indeed, the seaside more generally. But in both countries, and in the United States with the burgeoning conversion of redundant wharfs and landing stages into heritage piers, the recurring theme represents piers as an architecture of the past. In Germany the seaside reconstruction project looks to the past to make the future; in the United States the maritime industrial past is reused and reinvented for modern amusement purposes; while in Britain the best that can done with the remains of the seaside past is to reinterpret it as heritage.

Against this dominant motif, however, there are inklings that an original twenty-first-century architecture for pleasure building in the sea may materialize. In Britain, for example, imaginative new buildings have been added to some existing piers and innovative, although unrealized, designs have been proposed for new piers in Brighton and other resorts. But the present-day jostling of conflicting representations and interpretations of piers as the past, as nostalgia, as heritage or as the future, has marginalized and ignored in public debate the abiding pier pleasures. These include the excitement, first learned in the nineteenth century and equally accessible to the contemporary seaside visitor, of walking on water or peering through the gaps in the deck to the surging and perhaps still mysterious sea below.

Proposal for a new pier, Brighton, 2003, designed by Nick Readett-Bayley and Jovan Colic, AROS.

Proposal for a new pier on the site of Brighton's West Pier, 2003, designed by Foreign Office Architects.

CHAPTER 9
PAVILIONS AND AMUSEMENT PARKS

The embryonic seaside resorts of the mid-eighteenth century copied an established pattern of entertainment buildings from the inland spas of assembly rooms, with their master of ceremonies as the animateur of a resort's social life, theatres and circulating libraries. All were directed at the aristocratic visitor, and in design and style remarkably similar to, and indeed sometimes copied from, their inland counterparts. In Britain, the broadening in the visitor market from the mid-nineteenth century was accompanied by the flowering of speculative new seaside entertainment buildings; in addition to those built on the new pleasure piers, many others had their foundations more solidly rooted in dry land.[1] Sometimes ideas, styles and uses found in the large inland towns and cities, for example, for theatres and concert halls and later on cinemas, were taken to the coast. But, especially from late on in the century, there were some distinctive seaside themes. Across the Channel and around the coast of mainland Europe there were alternative architectural expressions of buildings for seaside pleasure, most notably the casino, with the name if not the purpose – at least not until relatively late in the twentieth century – occasionally imported into Britain.

Resort entertainment buildings were often constructed as near the sea as possible and, in the largest of resorts especially, the absolute number in close proximity to each other and the relationship to the seafront made for a distinctive and specialized urban form. The competition for visitors, especially where the market was expanding and thought

(sometimes wrongly) to be profitable, had various results. The need for buildings to stand out from each other led to the production of conspicuous exterior façades perhaps Orientalized, or in another eye-catching style, or at night-time brightly illuminated. Interiors were typically opulently decorated and luxuriously themed in a mood-enhancing style, perhaps with design detail featuring Oriental, marine or mythical themes. In the most competitive environments, buildings were repeatedly refurbished or new additions made, and there was a continual quest to capitalize on the latest entertainment fashions. At the Victorian and Edwardian seaside, the winter garden and floral hall and the implications they suggested for the taming of nature provided particularly compelling themes, whatever the actual mix of entertainment offered.

Often, too, seaside entertainment buildings were multi-purpose. Brighton's innovative Aquarium, for instance, not only exploited the fascination with the natural world under the sea through its exhibition of marine life, but, within four years of its 1872 opening, also included a reading room, restaurant, café, a winter-garden conservatory with a rockery and cascade, roller-skating rink, terrace garden, smoking room and music conservatory. Scarborough's Spa provided for respectable and rational entertainments. Blackpool's Winter Gardens of 1878 initially featured a pavilion theatre with enclosed glass promenading area, but less than two decades later, and in a riot of theming and opulence, also boasted a grand Opera House, Indian Lounge and Empress Ballroom. The largest popular resorts were also able to

A postcard of the Casino at Menton.

Trouville's Casino in a *c.* 1947 postcard.

A postcard of Miami Beach Casino, Florida.

And one of the Casino Blankenberghe, Belgium.

A postcard of The Spa, Scarborough, *c.* 1928.

sustain specialized forms of entertainment that had few if any comparisons inland. Examples include the late nineteenth- and early twentieth-century circuses in Blackpool, Great Yarmouth and Lowestoft, some including circus rings that could be flooded to provide water spectacles; aquaria – a particularly appropriate seaside entertainment – such as those in Brighton, Scarborough and Blackpool; and the fixed funfairs and amusement parks that had few sustained inland competitors until the development of theme parks in the later twentieth century.

But just as seaside entertainment buildings could come, so they could go. Sometimes they were destroyed by fire. Sometimes they were demolished as uneconomic, perhaps to make way for a new innovation. Occasionally they were dismantled to be reused elsewhere, as with Torquay's late-1870s Winter Gardens building that early in the new century was taken down and re-erected in Great Yarmouth. This and many other nineteenth-century resort entertainment buildings survived in Great Yarmouth to the present day, although many had been reused for other purposes or disguised through the addition of later facades.

The increasing municipal involvement and direct intervention in many aspects of the resort entertainment business in the first half of the twentieth century led to some private-sector operations coming into council ownership. Architectural transformations were often involved in the process, as with the late-1920s remodelling of the by then local-authority-owned Brighton Aquarium, its exterior remade with a plainer Empire style with white stonework, kiosks with pagoda roofs, sun terraces and a bandstand.[2] A new breed of municipal pavilion also emerged, ranging from Bournemouth's monolithic Italianate structure of 1929 – 'the most ambitious municipal undertaking of its kind in Britain'[3] – to Southend's Pavilion, originally begun in the 1930s but completed only in 1964 and then remodelled three decades later.[4] Sometimes there were unique engineering and architectural challenges, as with Margate's 1911 Winter Gardens sited in a hollowed-out chalk cliff-top.[5] The classically-referenced Leas Cliff Hall of 1927 in Folkestone, seemingly clinging to the cliff face, was presented soon after the war as 'probably the finest concert hall on the south coast' and 'a building of imposing design with wide balconies from which one can look almost straight down upon the waters of the Channel',[6] although it was disdained by modernist architects as 'a particularly unsuitable use of classical ornamentation'.[7] Municipal enterprise was also associated with other sorts of rational entertainment. There was increasing provision of museums and art galleries, sometimes based around donated privately owned collections and making use of seaside buildings constructed for some other purpose, and of indoor sports facilities for traditional resort activities such as bowls.

In the second half of the twentieth century there were immense challenges to many seaside entertainment businesses, both private and public sector, and the associated buildings. For example, live entertainment and amusement parks in many resorts faltered and faded, eroding the economics of the business and leading to the demolition or re use of seaside buildings. Some resorts sought salvation in the conference industry, building often undignified and inward-looking new complexes such as the Brighton Centre of 1977. But into the twenty-first century there were also revivals and new initiatives. A range of new imposing buildings for rational entertainment in the south-west of England, for instance, reinterpreted some traditional themes such as the aquarium (Plymouth's 1998 National Marine Aquarium), winter garden (the Eden Project in Cornwall, opening in 2001), art gallery (the 1993

The Winter Gardens, Blackpool, in 2000.

Tate St Ives) and museum (Falmouth's National Maritime Museum of 2002). Some resorts – Blackpool, Bournemouth and Brighton among them – could boast vibrant club scenes, sometimes reusing much older seaside entertainment buildings and centred on particular market segments from gays and lesbians to students. And there was the uncertain and unfulfilled lure of a Las Vegas and Atlantic City-style new architecture of casinos with its promise of a radical and Americanized remaking of at least some English resorts.

Hippodrome, Great Yarmouth, in 1999.

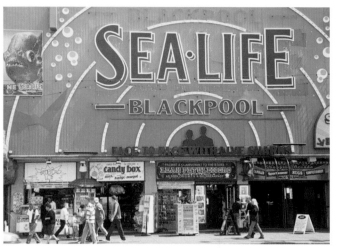

The present-day commercial aquarium, Blackpool, photographed in 2004.

A postcard of the Winter Gardens, Great Yarmouth. Commercially unsuccessful in its original Torquay location, it became an enduring feature of Great Yarmouth's seafront.

An early purpose-built English seaside cinema, The Gem of 1908, Great Yarmouth, 2000.

A local authority building for seaside entertainment, the Bournemouth Pavilion, 1929, in a detail from an illustration by Eustace Nash from the *Souvenir Programme* celebrating the building's opening.

Twenty-first-century seaside casinos are one example of an established tradition of translating and implanting ideas and styles from elsewhere in the entertainment architecture of the English resort. There are fascinating comparisons and contrasts to be made in exploring the histories and representation of iconic seaside buildings, and the following section sets the late nineteenth-century Blackpool Tower, for more than a century Britain's most famous seaside entertainment building, against Bexhill's inter-war modernist De La Warr Pavilion. We then turn to seaside amusement parks, tracing the formative influence of the American amusement park industry in Coney Island on the British seaside, and contrasting Margate's Dreamland with Blackpool's Pleasure Beach. Each of these entertainment architectures – and the two amusement parks each contain a host of different built structures – have been enduring and iconic architectural features of their resort landscapes and are examples of particular designs for seaside entertainment being taken to an extreme form. Three of the four (the Blackpool Tower is the exception) also involved the construction in the 1930s of architecturally outstanding modernist buildings designed to realize alternative contemporary visions of seaside entertainment and recreation.

TOWER AND PAVILION

Blackpool's Tower and Bexhill's Pavilion illustrate the complex relationships between a resort and its emblematic entertainment architecture, and the iconography of both, and also present fascinating contrasts in how iconic status is developed and maintained, the use of architecture from the

The 1911 Winter Gardens at Margate, carved into a chalk cliff, shown in a postcard sent in 1957.

Interior of the sedate and respectable The Leas at Folkestone, Kent, *c.* 1930.

The Leas as pictured in a Folkestone poster, 1947, artwork by Verney L. Danvers.

Torquay Pavilion, Devon, c. 2001, put to new use as a specialist shopping arcade.

past in the present and for the future, and the transformation of what was once modern into heritage or tradition.

The Blackpool Tower of 1894 was the apotheosis of late Victorian seaside entertainment building for a mass market. It was a product, among other things, of the booming northern resort establishing itself as the most successful working-class seaside town in the country, a thriving demand for 'artificial' entertainments and popular amusements, and a speculative enterprise with considerable local appeal. Derivative of the modern and extreme 1889 Eiffel Tower, for four decades the highest building in the world, the Blackpool Tower, designed by the Manchester architects Maxwell and Tukes, was the only enduringly successful of a number of otherwise ephemeral 1890s and 1900s tower projects in British resorts.[8] At Blackpool the inspiration from

France was adapted to the requirements of the late Victorian British seaside: apart from being topped by an intricate Oriental crown, at its base the tower included a large building housing a plethora of what by then were classic seaside entertainments. A tower such as the one at Blackpool, when completed the tallest building in Britain, was perhaps the ultimate means of standing out from the seaside competition, looming over the seafront and structuring the resort's geography and sense of place. But there was no guarantee of success or that such a structure would be the making of a resort: the slightly later and taller New Brighton Tower survived for just two decades before demolition.

Writing in the mid-1930s of a booming seaside Blackpool, James Laver described the Tower as the 'noblest of all human erections' (later commentators were more explicit in

Blackpool Tower in 2004.

A postcard of a moonlit New Brighton on the Wirral, Merseyside, with its unsuccessful rival to the Blackpool Tower.

their references to its priapic symbolism). Apart from the delights of being at the top, including the uniqueness of the environment and the views of both society and nature at the seaside, in the basement were 'an aquarium, cunningly contrived in the niches of artificial rocks' and an amusement arcade of 'fantastic machines, mechanical theatres', while above these attractions was 'a kind of palace, piled storey upon storey and containing within its walls restaurants and cafés, roof-gardens, shops, an immense ballroom and the finest circus in the world'.[9]

And yet in the same period the Tower, along with much of the rest of seaside Blackpool, could already be seen as old-fashioned: 'The great main parade with its building, tower, winter gardens, piers, boarding houses, and bathing-vans is just as it was in the palmy days of Queen Victoria. The Tower building with its wild-beast show, its souvenir shops, and its red plush upholstery is quite a period piece.'[10] A similar opinion was expressed almost six decades

later, on the Tower's centenary, with the argument that its cultural meaning had evolved from an appeal to modernity, when it opened, to tradition and heritage 100 years later.[11] In another view, just two years later, the Tower was 'proletarian tat', representative of all that was wrong with a vulgar and debased resort.[12]

The present-day Blackpool Tower is not the tower as built in 1894. The exterior steel forming the Tower has been continually renewed through the maintenance process, and the internal spaces have also in part been remade. For example, following a fire, the Ballroom is a 1950s recreation of an 1898 room that, in turn, had replaced the Tower's original Grand Pavilion. The entertainments provided have also been repeatedly reinvigorated: most obviously, animals no longer perform in the circus and the Menagerie is no more. But despite – indeed because of – these changes the Tower appears unchanged, both as an enduring symbol of Blackpool as a resort and as an emblem of the seaside past and

The Tower Ballroom, Blackpool, *c.* 1930.

traditional seaside present. Unloved by many architectural commentators, because it is seen as a derivative and old-fashioned structure, the centrepiece of an unfashionable and working-class resort, the Tower's iconic status is derived from the role it performs for the resort and the esteem it is held in by many holidaymakers to the town. The Tower dominates the iconography of the resort: it is Blackpool if the front covers of the municipal guides and postcard images are to be believed. It also literally towers above the resort, the first structure to be seen from miles away when travelling across the flat coastal plain towards Blackpool and also endlessly on view from the promenade and the piers.

In the 1930s, and at the same time as the Blackpool Tower and its entertainments were already being represented by some commentators as old-fashioned, on the south coast of England an alternative and forward-looking vision of building for seaside entertainment was being realized. In the context of the inter-war municipal enterprise of

British seaside authorities, Bexhill-on-Sea had fallen behind its competitors. The resort had developed an uncertain place in the hierarchy and positioning of seaside towns: designed for wealthy holidaymakers, it represented itself as modern and progressive, and yet it was increasingly attractive to wealthy residents, many of whom had retired from service in the empire, and had a strong conservative element in its politics.[13] In 1932 the aristocratic but socialist Earl De La Warr was elected unopposed as mayor of the town. The Earl not only played a significant role in national politics, but was also the dominant local land and property owner.[14]

By 1933 Earl De La Warr was the driving force behind Bexhill Corporation's architectural competition for a new pavilion in the resort. He believed that recreation and architecture should be a significant force in local and national regeneration, with the Bexhill Pavilion intended to perform both a local role as a centre for entertainment

Bexhill-on-Sea, a railway publicity poster for a modernized Edwardian resort.

and the community and as an exemplar to other resorts of what the future should hold. The competition brief made clear that:

> The building should be simple in design, and suitable for a Holiday Resort in the South of England. Character in design can be obtained by the use of large window spaces, terraces and canopies. No restrictions as to style of architecture will be imposed but buildings must be simple, light in appearance and attractive, suitable for a Holiday Resort. Heavy stonework is not desirable.[15]

The winners of the competition, the recently established German/Russian partnership of Erich Mendelsohn and Serge Chermayeff, made a radical break from the resort entertainment pavilions constructed in the 1920s whose lineage could be traced to earlier decades. With the southern side presenting large expanses of sheet glass on three levels to the sea and sun, Mendelsohn and Chermayeff's Bexhill building responded to the rising passion for an architecture for the sun and open air and, like many subsequent 1930s buildings, made use of nautical symbolism. It was the first public building in Britain to be designed and built on International Style principles. Running parallel to the coast, the Pavilion included a large flexible theatre, restaurant, library, conference room and lounge. Outside there were terraces for sunbathing and listening to music and a rooftop sundeck for sports and games popular on ocean liners. The architects were concerned with the total design of the Pavilion, extending to the details of the flooring, interior colour scheme, fabrics, door furniture and the furniture used in the principal rooms. Apart from its startling appearance, innovative, modern construction techniques were also used, it being the first large building in Britain with a welded steel-frame structure. The Pavilion was conceived as the centrepiece of a larger scheme to include hotel, cinema, swimming pool and a slender double-storey pier reaching into the sea, although for reasons of cost none of these additional elements survived into the design as executed.

De La Warr, at the laying of the foundation stone of the building, argued that the Pavilion was the means of achieving a new form of cultural and social provision:

> How better could we dedicate ourselves today than by gathering round this new venture of ours, a venture which is going to lead to the growth, the prosperity and the greater culture of this our town; a venture also which is part of a great national movement, virtually to found a new industry – the industry of giving that relaxation, that pleasure, that culture, which hitherto the gloom and dreariness of British resorts have driven our fellow countrymen to seek in foreign lands. We are rightly proud of ourselves today. In no other sphere of human activity do a people display their calibre, or impress their inner selves, more than in their architecture. Great people leave behind them great memorials to themselves which they have erected in brick and stone.[16]

Providing a radical architecture for social experimentation, for the most part the Pavilion was praised by architectural critics and the national press. John Summerson, an influential architectural historian of the Regency period, identified two special qualities: 'One is the sense of "open-ness" of the building; one has the sense of walking within enclosed space rather than in a structure. The other is the exquisite finish of the design, so far as structural details are concerned.'[17] In the *Manchester Guardian* Sir Charles Reilly, professor of architecture at Liverpool University, described it as 'a revelation from another planet in the rococo redness of that terrible town',[18] while the architectural correspondent of *The Times* commented that it was 'by far the most civilized thing that has been done on the south coast since the days of the Regency'.[19] George Bernard Shaw believed the opening of the Pavilion signified that 'Bexhill had emerged from barbarism'.[20]

Despite the acclamation, there was also vociferous local and national opposition to the Pavilion and its architects. Locally the medley of concerns ranged from the quality and appropriateness of the design, the costs falling on ratepayers and unease at the use of foreign architects. The last argument was fuelled by a national antagonism orchestrated by the British Union of Fascists and voiced both in the specialist architectural and more popular press. The Fascist view was opposed to the use of 'foreign' architects, arguing: 'The planning of our future towns and homes lies before us as an immense and glorious opportunity. Britons, not aliens, shall carry out the task.'[21] Six decades later the opposition was seen as 'one of the nastiest episodes in our architectural history'.[22]

Rather cautiously and not without a little duplicity, the town council, in its official guide, prepared visitors for the building being constructed. The 'large and attractive

De La Warr Pavilion, Bexhill-on-Sea, postcard, c. 1930s.

building' promised 'a new standard in seaside amusement pavilions', but the design, the guide was concerned to point out, was 'not too daringly modernistic in character and appearance'.[23] The guide also quoted one of the building's architectural advocates who argued both that 'there is no aggressive "modernism" in the design' and that: 'No part of England has suffered more from indiscriminate building than have the sea fronts of popular resorts, and it is gratifying to see a problem of this kind tackled in an intelligent manner with full appreciation of "that holiday feeling", and still a care for the amenities, both natural and architectural.'[24]

Although writing under the pseudonym 'Peter Maitland', Serge Chermayeff used the *Architectural Review* to reply to his critics. His derogatory description of an unspecified 1930s resort revealed his contempt for the existing architecture and politics of Bexhill-on-Sea:

The Parade, with restriction notices – iron railings, the breakwater, the uniform pattern running away in both directions from the ingenious bandstand into the middle distance of desirable modern residences, mainly Tudorbethan, a sprinkling of pseudo-Georgian with bulging builders' bays, and occasionally – the cherry in the contemporary speculative fruit salad – a 'modernistic' villa.[25]

Part of the problem, as he saw it, were the political protests and obstructions from local residents – 'the retired empire builders, whose gardens and brasses are the pride of all the little Poonahs-on-Sea' – fearing increases in local taxes. It was exactly this group that two years earlier had helped force a public inquiry into the Bexhill scheme. Chermayeff's own plea was for a 'new seaside synthesis' with a 'new architectural expression' in the form of modern buildings constructed for 'the airy, unrestricted life that people come to the seaside to enjoy'. The author went on to make the audacious claim, given that he was writing about his own building, that the most notable

English example of modern seaside architecture was the new Bexhill Pavilion. Bexhill Corporation extolled the completed Pavilion's virtues, describing the 'pleasing suggestions of the yacht, the pier and the lighthouse' and 'the elegance derived from simplicity and the soft colouring which reveals the spirit of beauty'.[26]

Over the following decades Bexhill evolved from a resort into a residential town by the sea, with one of the highest proportions of retired people in Britain. For the comedian Spike Milligan the town was 'God's waiting room', and others saw it as part of the Costa Geriatrica. The Pavilion, rather than functioning to regenerate the town and as engine of the 'new industry' of relaxation, pleasure and culture, took on the character of post-war Bexhill. By the early 1960s there were increasing concerns about the building's physical fabric, the quality of post-war refurbishments and other inappropriate changes.[27] The rooftop deck terrace was sealed off as unsafe, the library abandoned and converted into a meeting room, the original modern furniture replaced by 1960s easy chairs, and the original colour scheme and flooring hidden by flock wallpaper and patterned carpet.

Visiting critics were unsure what to make of the building in the context of Bexhill itself. For one reviewer the Pavilion was 'perched incongruously on the seafront, with the uneasy pride of a camp teenager waiting in the wings at the school play'.[28] In Stephen Bayley's view,

The De La Warr Pavilion in 2003 immediately before restoration.

Bexhill was the most unlikely place to build a 'socialist palace by the sea',[29] while in the early 1980s Paul Theroux saw the town and Pavilion as the epitome of the elderly English middle class:

And there was the De la Warr Pavilion, where on the various decks and verandas, the very old people sat in chairs with blankets in their laps staring out to sea, like people on a cruise, resting between meals. They drank tea, rattling their china cups on trembling saucers . . . If Bexhill-on-Sea was a résumé of one English class, the De La Warr Pavilion – moored there on the seafront like an ocean liner – was a résumé of Bexhill-on-Sea . . . It seemed clear to me that once an English person had reached Bexhill-on-Sea he had no intention of going any farther. This was, so to speak, the edge of the cliff.[30]

However, there was also increasing local and national interest in the architectural quality and heritage of the Pavilion, and in the early years of the twenty-first century it was variously eulogized as 'one of the most famous modernist buildings in Europe', a 'modernist masterpiece looking out over the sea [with] a sinuous elegance that has rarely been surpassed',[31] 'arguably the most beautiful 20th century building in Britain',[32] and 'the most beautiful work of art in Britain'.[33] Commentators have praised its 'sun-washed spiral staircase pirouetting round a neon chandelier . . . [and] . . . the building's astonishing sensitivity to light'.[34] The Pavilion, in the minds of cultural commentators and architectural critics, had become an iconic building.

There was still, though, a struggle over the future of the Pavilion. In 2000 the local-authority owners, desperate to control council spending on the structure, proposed leasing the building to a national pub chain for 125 years. Local and national opposition defeated the 'pure vandalism' of the privatization proposal from the 'philistine local council'. In 2002 the Arts Council and Heritage Lottery Fund awarded a new charitable trust £6 million to restore the building.

The restoration plans, including new gallery and education spaces and a new bar, café and restaurant, were intended to 'help to serve as a catalyst towards the wider ambitions for Bexhill, as the town becomes an important centre for cultural tourism and is the focus for sustainable economic regeneration'.[35] Although the language had changed, these early twenty-first-century aspirations were curiously reminiscent of the original thinking behind the building. Stripping back the accretions of the previous seven decades, the restored Pavilion was to have an internationally significant new role as a centre for contemporary art, architecture and live performance. These grand ambitions ignored the past history of the building, its failure to provide a model for seaside entertainment buildings elsewhere in England, its slow post-war decline and sponge-like ability to soak up the essence of Bexhill rather than being a catalyst for change in the town. In 1990 Stevens and Willis argued: 'The pavilion now stands in even greater isolation, apparently awaiting the arrival of a world that will never come.'[36] In 2004 the Pavilion was closed to the public, undergoing restoration. With its reopening in the autumn of 2005, its role in the new millennium, and perhaps a new world, remains to be established.

ARCHITECTURE FOR CARNIVAL

A dramatic new form of seaside entertainment and architecture, the fixed, enclosed and fee-charging amusement park, developed at Coney Island, New York's vibrant and chaotic seaside resort, at the turn of the nineteenth into the twentieth century. Coney Island and its 'honky-tonk' reflected and responded to New York, America's great melting pot on the eastern seaboard. In turn, the Coney Island amusement parks were to be an important influence on seaside entertainment in many Western mass-market resorts. Although by the late nineteenth century Coney Island already provided a vast range of attractions, the critical development in the seven years from 1897 was of three amusement parks – Steeplechase, Luna Park and Dreamland.[37] Steeplechase Park dating from 1897 copied and developed on a lavish scale the Sea Lion Park of 1895, a short-lived enterprise but nonetheless Coney Island's and the world's first enclosed and fee-charging amusement park.

The new parks provided extreme entertainments, focused on mechanical amusement rides and complemented by sideshows featuring unbelievable or exotic attractions, all set in a newly invented and outlandish architecture. The parks assailed the senses. The spectacular and incredible entrances through the enclosed park boundaries provided the sense of entering another and separate world. Once within a park, the carefully planned entertainment sites employed extravagantly themed and make-believe architecture drawing on the past, and other and imagined places. Visually, fantasy was enhanced at night through the innovative use of vivid and intensive electric illuminations. A cacophony of sounds came from music, the rides, sideshows

'Coney's enchanted city in all its brilliancy': the electric wonderland of Luna Park, c. 1922.

left: A Dreamland sideshow, Coney Island, c. 1905.

Coney Island's Luna Park, early 1900s.

Gateway to another world: a postcard of the entrance to Luna Park, Coney Island.

The Cyclone from the Astroland Tower, Coney Island, in 2004.

The Wonder Wheel, Astroland Park, in 2004.

and from the crowd itself. The mechanical rides, using modern technologies, moved people in unexpected, bizarre and often alarming ways. The principles of the amusement park business, according to the estate promoter of Luna Park, were to 'manufacture' a spirit of carnival with fast-moving rides – 'elaborated child's play' in an environment that was respectable – unlike much that lay elsewhere in Coney Island outside the boundaries of the park – but out of the ordinary and enticing.[38] Respecting the nature of Coney Island and its customers, there was no attempt to educate, unlike the vision of other entertainment. Many commentators have seen amusement parks as respites from the real world, perhaps as a release valve from the pressures of the everyday and perhaps as a place where conventional modes of behaviour, especially between the sexes, could be disregarded. The parks and their rides would sometimes literally throw people together and there was pleasure to be had from watching the confusion and humiliation of others and even from experiencing it oneself.

The Coney Island parks were a product of a particular time and place and, although hugely influential for the development of seaside entertainment and architecture elsewhere, their heyday was surprisingly short lived. Dreamland survived for just seven years before it was engulfed by fire, beginning in the apocalyptically named Hell Gate ride, in 1911. The 1903 Luna Park floundered during the 1930s, was destroyed in a series of fires in the 1940s and became the site for post-war high-rise apartments. The earliest of the parks, the Steeplechase of 1897, was largely reconstructed following a fire a decade later; it then survived for half a century before eventually closing in 1964. The parks and their sites, and Coney Island more generally, became a contested landscape, the former architecture of amusement gradually eroded, destroyed and transformed into a combination of dereliction, high-rise housing and urban regeneration.[39] There was one 1960s reincarnation, although a shadow of the parks that had gone before, with the development of Astroland Park on a Coney Island seafront site. By the early twenty-first century, the original parks were nostalgically mourned for their important role in New York's past, and the few physical relics valued and preserved as heritage, while Astroland Park, with its Wonder Wheel, Astrotower and Cyclone roller coaster, featured in the iconography of present-day New York.

Although the original three great Coney Island amusement parks did not endure at the New York seaside, they did have a formative influence beyond America, as revealed in the development of two of the most significant British seaside amusement parks, Margate's Dreamland and Blackpool's Pleasure Beach. Although by the late nineteenth century there were various mechanical amusement attractions in British resorts as diverse as Blackpool and Folkestone, both of which could boast of primitive switch-back railways by 1891, it was not until early in the twentieth century that the most popular and mass-market British resorts began to copy avidly from Coney Island and that amusement parks proper started to be developed.

Turning a disused railway terminal into a seaside entertainment centre, Margate's 'The Hall by the Sea' opened in 1864 as a venue for respectable concerts and dances. Relatively unsuccessful in its first incarnation, from the mid-1870s it was owned by the Victorian showman 'Lord' George Sanger. The use of the old station building changed from being a restaurant by day to a music hall by night, while the derelict railway land at the rear was transformed into pleasure gardens, including a ruined abbey folly doubling as a bandstand and a menagerie for Sanger's

The relics of New York's Coney Island amusement parks, the present-day Astroland, and the boardwalk and beach in 2004.

animals. The innovation represented a break with the past and a shift in the resort's entertainment focus from the respectable visitor to the popular mass market. In the late 1890s the station was replaced by a purpose-built entertainment structure functioning as a music hall by day and dance hall for up to 3,000 people by night. A new owner in 1919 – John Henry Iles, an amusement-park pioneer who had installed Britain's first switchback railway on Blackpool Pleasure Beach in 1907 – began a further transformation into a multi-purpose entertainment complex and amusement park.

Apart from using American technology, Iles also drew on leisure-industry ideas and iconography from across the Atlantic. The Margate venue became Dreamland, named after the ill-fated Coney Island amusement park. The commercially and symbolically most important innovation at Margate's own Dreamland, although eventually just one of many different rides, was the Scenic

Railway of 1920.[40] There followed innovative rides, frequently imported from the USA, and, as the park became more successful and permanent, original wooden buildings were remade in brick and concrete. In the first two years there was a miniature railway, Cake Walk, Joy Wheel, Helter Skelter, Lunar Ball, The Whip and The Tumbler. Other rides in subsequent years included a smaller scenic railway soon to be called the Roller Coaster, The Caterpillar and The River Caves.

In the early 1930s Dreamland, with 'all the fun of the fair', was where Margate was 'at its merriest'.[41] The success of the park and the need to respond to new entertainments led to a radical remaking of Dreamland's seafront between 1933 and 1935 and the construction in modernist style of new entertainment buildings to the design of Iles, Leathart and Granger. The aim at Margate was 'the erection of one of

The low-technology and gravity-powered Switchback Railway, Folkestone, Kent, c. 1900.

The late 1890s Hall by the Sea, Margate, following its 1919 renaming as Dreamland and remaking into a Coney Island-style amusement park.

building of which the whole town can be justly proud. One cannot even estimate the benefit which this will give to the Company's existing enterprises both in revenue and prestige.[43]

The transformation of the complex included a new wider entrance from the promenade, a de-luxe cinema with 2,200 seats, a ballroom for 1,500 people, the Sunshine Café, 'with big windows overlooking the sea, and seating for 500 people', four restaurants with seating for 3,500 and saloon and public bars 'decorated in a modern version of the Tudor style'.[44] By 1948 Dreamland, with its 20-acre amusement park, eight different restaurants including six for large-scale 'beanfeasts', 70 sideshows, cinema, skating rink and gardens, could be represented as 'the be-all and end-all of Margate', with more than 40,000 visitors on a busy day.[45]

the finest and most comprehensive entertainment buildings in the country'.[42] In addition:

> The main front, which is at present low and unimpressive, will be replaced by the striking elevation . . . the tower of which is over 80 feet high. These reconstructions will make Dreamland the most up-to-date entertainment centre in the south, and will provide a

In classic amusement-park manner, up to about 1970 there was a repeated make-over, replacement and reinvention of rides. In 1950 the Dreamland gardens were illuminated, automated and reinvented as the Magic Garden; the magic was to fade and the Safari Wild Animal Park took its place at the end of the following decade. In 1951 a replica of the ocean liner the *Queen Mary* was installed to function as an amusement arcade. But even in the mid-1950s Dreamland began to look to the past for its future. The Sunshine Café was closed in 1955, the space redecorated in Edwardian style and reopened as an Old Time Music Hall; by 1969 that too had

The iconic Scenic Railway, Dreamland, Margate, *c.* 1950s.

Dreamland's Sunshine Café, shortly after opening in the mid-1930s.

top: The synthetic attractions of the Dreamland amusement park, Margate, *c.* 1973.

above: The fairytale Magic Gardens, Dreamland, 1956.

right: Promoting Dreamland's new Safari Park, 1969.

The 1930s entrance building to Dreamland, Margate, in 1999.

The 80-year-old scenic railway at Dreamland in 1999.

Dreamland, 'Fun for all ages', 2004.

given way to the space being used for bingo.

From the 1970s, however, despite investment in refurbishing and changing the use of the entertainment buildings and the installation of modern rides, Dreamland slowly if erratically declined as Margate's iconic amusement centre, the fall from grace shadowing the worsening fortunes of holiday Margate more generally. Visitor numbers fell and by the late twentieth century there were threats of closure and the redevelopment of the site for retail uses. As if to emphasize that Dreamland was more past than future, the park's emblematic Scenic Railway

wooden roller coaster was listed as architecturally important in 2002, the first amusement park ride in Britain recognized officially for the significance of its architectural heritage. Although partly inspired by nostalgia for previous decades, the Save Dreamland Campaign continued to assert the value of the park for contemporary Margate's economic and cultural landscape.[46]

Unlike Dreamland's geographical location and cultural role at the heart of seaside Margate, Blackpool's Pleasure Beach is on the edge of the holidaymaking town, distant from the Tower, the 'Golden Mile' and the resort's other

top: The South Beach at the margin of Blackpool. Tobias Boswell's encampment, 1905.

above: New machines for a new century: Maxim's Flying Machine opened in Blackpool in 1904; it survives into the twenty-first century.

top: The developing Pleasure Beach at Blackpool, 1912.

above: On the edge: the insecure boundary with the sea. The Pleasure Beach, 1913.

The thrills of the Switchback in Blackpool, a postcard of *c.* 1908.

attractions. The Pleasure Beach is both part of Blackpool as a resort and yet distinct and separate from it.

What was to become the Pleasure Beach began in the late nineteenth century on marginal South Shore land, close to the sea and on the edge of the resort. Around a long-established Gypsy encampment providing fortune-telling and other services to the nearby resort, gradually the core elements of a funfair were established. From 1905 the Pleasure Beach name and amusement-park character and role were ever more firmly defined and operationalized.[47] By 1909 it was the largest and most modern amusement park in the country, a status maintained up to the following century. A visual history of the park reveals its varied and evolving attractions and use by holidaymakers. The park's entrance was made more alluring with the construction in ferro-concrete in 1913 of the Casino (despite its name, the building housed a 700-seat cinema, billiards room and restaurant) in a medley of Oriental and classical styles and, illuminated at night, a beacon to visitors. The park's boundaries were also made more substantial and permanent, particularly following the building of a new sea wall and promenade by 1930 that at last separated the Pleasure Beach from the natural beach.

Increasingly, from the 1930s, commentators emphasized the modernity and distinctiveness of the Pleasure Beach in contrast to the tradition of the larger resort.[48]

The contemporary Pleasure Beach, 2004.

CHAPTER 10
SLEEPING BY THE SEA

As two of the first holidaymakers to Brighton, visiting the coastal town in the summer of 1736, the Reverend William Clarke and his wife needed somewhere to sleep. In a period before the development of any purpose-built architecture for visitors, they lodged in an older pre-resort Brighton building. Urging a friend to come and visit, Clarke described his accommodation:

> I assure you we live here *almost under ground*. I fancy the architects here usually take the altitude of the inhabitants, and lose not an inch between the head and the ceiling, and then dropping a step or two below the surface, the second story is finished something under 12 feet. I suppose this was a necessary precaution against storms, that a man should not be blown out of his bed into New England, Barbary, or God knows where. But as the lodgings are *low* they are cheap; we have *two parlours, two bed chambers, pantry &c.* for 5s. per week; and if you will really come down you need not fear a bed of proper dimensions. And then the coast is safe; the canons all covered with rust and grass; the ships moored, and no enemy apprehended. Come and see.[1]

The appropriation of pre-resort buildings and the homes of local people run through the history of many seaside places. In *Tender is the Night*, F. Scott Fitzgerald describes the French Mediterranean home of the Drivers, a young American couple: their 'villa and its grounds were made out of a row of peasant dwellings that abutted on the cliff – five small houses had been combined to make the house and four destroyed to make the garden'.[2] Just as the Clarkes were pioneers in the making of modern Brighton, so the impact of the Drivers on the mid-1920s Riviera went further. They had 'invented' the summer season of the nearby 'large, proud rose-colored hotel . . . and its bright tan prayer rug of a beach', by persuading the hotel to remain open after the English clientele had gone north in April.

The influence of the Clarkes and Drivers was not unique. During the twentieth century, many long-established coastal towns and villages throughout Europe were 'discovered' as holiday places. Sometimes to the anguish of local people priced out of the housing market, visitors acquired fishing community cottages and other dwellings and turned them into holiday homes.

More typically, though, sleeping by the sea has involved purpose-built architecture whether for a temporary holiday-making visit or in the form of permanent homes of seaside residents. The boundaries between the two are not watertight. The Clarkes lodged in what had been the home of local people, and in the most popular of English resorts there was a long tradition of local families taking in visitors in the busy summer season. In other cases, the allure of the sea has led people to settle on the coast with holiday homes becoming permanent residences. Alternatively, if the resort business is in decline, a hotel might be converted into apartments. The major examples used here are of the seaside bungalow, the makeshift and marginal holiday homes of people eager to be free of the constraints of the large resorts, the development of the 'complete resort' with the focus on holiday camps, and the seaside hotel and guesthouse.

The architecture of sleeping by the sea accommodates a diversity of styles and forms in response to shifting patterns of holidaymaking, social relations and attitudes to nature. And yet individual resorts often have a particular architectural feel and design character because of the place-specific dimensions of building for sleeping by the sea. Often seaside holiday homes were essentially local responses, perhaps because of the influence of a specific landowner, development process, local tradition or sustained architectural style. Similarly, individual resorts might respond to meet the demands of an insistent and powerful group of visitors. The result, combined with a specific landscape and topography, was to give a particular and frequently enduring feel and character to particular seaside places. A century after their construction, the Regency terraces of Brighton and Hove, built to capitalize on the early nineteenth-century success of the fashionable resort, were eulogized by John Piper, when describing how 'The wave of Brighton washes up through the town towards the front, and breaks on the promenade in the wonderful efflorescence to meet and dominate the incoming channel breakers.'[3] On another south coast, that of France, the invention of the Riviera was associated with the creation of an aristocratic villa-clad seaside landscape, despite a diversity of individual styles.[4] Trouville and Deauville, on the Channel coast of France, also developed a distinctive nineteenth-century Second Empire villa architecture, on occasion a curious blend of vernacular Normandy meeting Gothic.[5] The emergence and growth in the late nineteenth and early twentieth centuries of a string of resorts along the German Baltic coast in much the same manner produced a particular resort built form of solid and imposing villas embellished with a variety of architectural references.[6]

Similarly, Sidmouth, in the south-west of England, partly built its long-lasting reputation as a unique and respectable resort around a distinctive Regency-period architecture of both rustic Cottage Orné, blending a local tradition of thatched roofs with considerable ornamentation, and Strawberry Hill Gothic, with castellated battlements, Gothicized windows and associated design detail. Guides to the resort have consistently emphasized the quality of the townscape. A 1950s guide describes how

When the fashionable people came here in search of a more rustic watering place than Brighton, they found

Brighton's Decimus Burton-designed Adelaide Crescent, began in 1830 and completed in the 1850s, photographed in 2004.

Trouville seafront villas in 2002.

Restored villa on the German Baltic coast, Heringsdorf, in 2000.

top and left: Restored villas, Heringsdorf, 2000.

right: Unrestored seaside housing, Binz, German Baltic coast, 2000.

Marine Court, Hastings, in 2001.

an almost virgin valley. Fortunately for us, they were cultured, aristocratic and rich: the houses which they built are beautiful and wonderfully matched to the country . . . the result is happier than any deliberate town-planning.[7]

From the mid-nineteenth century and on the other side of the Atlantic, a few intrepid Americans with time and money to spare became pioneers not of the West but of the closer-to-home seaside, increasingly deserting the burgeoning and hot cities to spend summer by the sea. One commentator, writing in 1880, noted how:

About thirty years ago, the first private cottage was erected at Long Beach, by the late Commodore Stockton; and it was long the only one. Now, at almost all these places, the great majority of buildings are of this class. Cottage life at the sea-shore has, indeed, become a very marked phase of our social system.[8]

Over the next century cottage life developed, spread along the Long Island coast and evolved around a distinctive and idiosyncratic architecture in places such as the Hamptons to become an enduring symbol of rich New Yorkers at summer play.[9]

At another remove from Sidmouth, but still a response to particular times and a specific place, are the modernist inter-war Californian beach houses, viewed by some of their architects 'as agents to nurture the physical and psychological health of a liberated and egalitarian society'.[10] Designed for a specific social context and to capitalize on sunshine and seaside nature, the Californian beach house is revered by many present-day architectural critics. Similarly, the renovated or reproduced Art Deco of Miami Beach in Florida provides a specific built form redolent with meaning of a stylish, sometimes corrupt and often reinvented resort.

In some resorts an imported style may intrude in an otherwise uniform townscape. On the south coast of England, the architecturally innovative and Wells Coates-designed Embassy Court apartment building of 1935 was ill-placed next to the neo-Classical glories of Hove's earlier Regency-period Brunswick Town. Constructed in reinforced concrete, Embassy Court proposed a futuristic 'new design for living' in mansion flats, including the first penthouse flats in England, making much of the sun and sea views. Despite the initial argument over the appropriateness of the building, its subsequent decline in the late twentieth century led to national publicity and pressure for its preservation and restoration. Thirty-five miles to the east, the nautically themed Marine Court of 1938 at Hastings was in one authoritative view 'the first modernistic affront to the English seaside'.[11] Looming over the early nineteenth-century planned resort of St Leonards, Marine Court became known locally as the 'Queen Mary' after the mid-1930s ocean liner.

The real ship was, of course, eventually to become a major seaside tourist attraction at Long Beach, California.

BUNGALOWS AND PLOTLANDS

One English predecessor to the Californian beach house, the bungalow, was also designed for physical and psychological health, although not in the context of an egalitarian society. The bungalow is a classic example of a building for staying in by the sea that has echoed ideas from elsewhere, only, in turn, to be replicated in other places.[12] A Western import from India, the bungalow had originally described a peasant's hut in seventeenth-century rural Bengal; it then came to mean a house for Europeans in India and evolved into an architectural symbol of the power of the British empire. Relocated to the late-nineteenth-century English seaside, its form, purpose and meaning were transformed in ways that were bound up with the contemporary nature and use of the seaside, although it continued to be associated with status and power, albeit in a manner much removed from its Indian standing.

The first bungalows in the West were built from 1869 to the 1880s at Birchington-on-Sea and Westgate-on-Sea, close by each other on the coast of Kent and both emerging as exclusive and modern small resorts in contrast to Margate, their excursionist-packed and rowdy older neighbour. Westgate offered an alternative seaside experience centred on 'the peace and quiet of those who desire rest of mind and freedom from irritating noises, together with bracing air and sea-bathing',[13] while Birchington provided 'the jaded professional man . . . the most invigorating tranquility, for the perfect repose of the place is unruffled by the usual noisy sea-side attractions', making it 'an uncontaminated play-ground for large families, and a secluded sanitorium for invalids.'[14]

As a fundamental departure from what had gone before, the innovative bungalows were detached, low-rise, light and airy, and surrounded by gardens. They were a new type of holiday home, designed for a wealthy, family-based and healthy leisure in privacy, for an innovative seaside holiday with a stress on the summer and where rest and relaxation and sea air, bathing and views of the ocean were central. The Birchington bungalows were variously described as 'isolated, cosy, rural looking', as 'modified Indian country-houses', and as 'commodious cottages by the sea'. The designer, John Taylor, was acclaimed for his 'inventive genius and construction skill', and the bungalows admired for 'the quietness of design . . . the airiness of their open verandahs and corridors, and continuous suites of rooms on the ground floor'.[15] The sitting of the bungalows on the edge of the private cliff top with tunnels leading from each to the beach below were a means to deliver on the most fashionable elements of the seaside. The tunnels to the essentially private beaches, for example, in making the bathing machine redundant, promised a new use of the sea.

The distinctive private steps leading from each of Taylor's first bungalows to the beach were used by John Buchan as the mystery to be unravelled and the denouement in *The Thirty-Nine Steps*, published in 1915, with Birchington becoming Ruff: 'It's a very high-toned sort of place, and the residents there like to keep by themselves.'[16] In truth, by the time Buchan's adventure story was published Birchington was already losing its elusive character, with gentle fun being poked at the idiosyncratic bungalows by the author of a local guide: 'Was it some sunburnt Anglo-Indian, with refreshing memories of Simla, who conceived the idea of building the first bungalow, or was it merely a sore-kneed housemaid? Stairs or no stairs, the bungalows are most captivating residences.'[17] Over the following decades Birchington became more ordinary, and by the early twenty-first century was a suburban 'satellite village' to Margate; none of the original first-phase bungalows survived, although some of the later ones were still to be seen.

Despite the very specific character and purpose of the first English seaside bungalows, from the start of the twentieth century the term was applied to a broader range of building styles and locations. The bungalow came to represent not a specific dwelling type but an idea of leisure and 'getting away from it all'. In varied forms, the bungalow became ubiquitous in many Western countries, both inland and on the coast, although in Britain there was also an increasing belittling of the bungalow as uninspiring and suburban, with its occupants derided as narrow-minded and unexciting.[18]

At the English seaside in the first half of the twentieth century, the bungalow also developed an alternative niche role as an accessible home by the sea, cheaply built on marginal or low-cost 'plotlands', sometimes literally on the beach or cliff top, and 'a makeshift world of shacks and shanties, scattered unevenly in plots of varying size and shape, with unmade roads and little in the way of services'.[19] Architecturally, they were very different from the professionally designed Birchington structures, and their owners typically had a major role in the design process, making use of readily available materials from redundant railway carriages to old army huts. Socially, too, they appealed to a more diverse range of people united by their attraction to an alternative vision of the seaside as an arcadia of freedom, health and nature.

But there was another contradictory representation, forcefully made by establishment architectural and planning commentators and public authorities, of the plotlands desecrating the landscape and the users failing to respect the proper demands of society. The editor of a 1937 guide to seaside houses and bungalows, for example, lamented 'the shoddy camping sites or wastes of hut and railway carriage that disfigure so many miles of English coast'.[20] This strain is just one dimension of the enduring and complicated stress in so many aspects of designing the seaside between regulation and freedom and between the public good and private interests. As far as the original English seaside plotlands were concerned, by the 1970s many had either been erased from the coast or remade as more ordinary, regular and controlled seaside places.

The paradox of the plotlands is that their success contained the seeds of their own destruction. An unconventional and primitive life was difficult to sustain if shared by countless other people, while the environment, initially so attractive, was changed and even harmed by their very presence. In the tangled web of argument it is a simple matter to identify a number of demons that make easy if inconsistent targets. For example, both the establishment and officialdom wrecking individual freedoms and selfish private interests despoiling the environment are, in their own ways, equally fulfilling criticisms to adopt. Behind the difficulty is the ambiguous nature of the seaside and the continual struggle to assert and balance alternative visions of how the seaside should be designed.

Although united by the marginal character of their location and the desire for freedom by the sea, the plotlands took varied forms. Some resulted from an almost organic process of the individual decisions of people establishing their own holiday homes by the sea, while others evolved following the initial vision of a speculative developer.

Pagham Beach, on the Sussex coast south of London, began as a summer camping place in 1908 for tent pioneers

A railway home made respectable. West Sussex in 2003.

'Perfick', the Fitties, Lincolnshire, in 2001.

Pagham Beach railway home, West Sussex, in 1989.

which exists nowhere else in England' and that 'the name of the genius who first . . . realized the holiday possibilities of this sterile "No Man's Land" is unknown to fame'.

The anonymous author continued:

> The charm of life here is its absolute simplicity. One can dress, and do, or not do, as one pleases. The morning dip is taken within a dozen yards of bed, and all one's meals are eaten within sight and hearing of the sea.[22]

wishing to be as close to the sea and as remote from existing resorts as possible. The first more permanent structure, a bungalow made by its owner and erected in 1910, was followed by a variety of other seaside homes. Within two decades, the pioneers had been joined by a throng of other plotlanders, leading one novelist to reflect on how the beach had changed:

> Where it had been bordered on the shoreward side by a great broad strip of open land, rough with tussocks of grass, sea poppies and a hedge of tamarisk separating it from cornfields, stood, in a medley of confusion, two score or more of dwelling places. Old railway carriages converted into 'bungalows', wooden erections of all shapes and sizes, refreshment huts and a row of bathing cabins.[21]

Twenty-five miles to the east, Shoreham Beach's Bungalow Town developed from the 1880s on a shingle spit. Unlike many other plotlands, contemporary representations often applauded Bungalow Town, an early 1930s guide, for example, noting that although it had lost its early individuality, it was still 'a settlement the like of

The 'unconventional holiday resort' gained a reputation as a bohemian, even risqué place, in part because from 1900 it attracted many people working in the music-hall and subsequently film industries.[23] Following the demolition of many of the holiday homes as a defensive measure during the Second World War, a turbulent struggle took place between the plot-holders and, the ultimate victors, the seaside authorities. Today a few brightly varnished remains of railway carriages are still to be seen embedded in what look to be otherwise quite ordinary homes. But on the nearby tidal river mudflats – still more marginal than the beach – a motley collection of houseboats, including a motor torpedo boat from the Second World War, provide a last vestige of unplanned idiosyncratic seaside homes.

The most notorious of the grander speculative plotland developments was at Peacehaven on open downland to the east of Brighton, where a developer sold plots of land and images of an unfettered and healthy life in a garden city by

The joy of the plotlands: holidaymakers on Jaywick Sands near Clacton, Essex, June 1932. The plotlands' development was entwined with a back-to-nature idealism and the quest for health and fitness out-of-doors.

the sea.[24] Peacehaven was greeted by a storm of establishment vile, described as a 'poison'[25] and 'a monstrous blot on the national conscience'.[26] Although Peacehaven subsequently developed as a more ordinary seaside place, in the mid-1960s it could still draw the ire of England's most respected establishment architectural critics: 'What is one to say? Peacehaven has been called a rash on the countryside. It is that, and there is no worse in England . . . Whose haven was it? Whose haven is it?'[27]

At Jaywick Sands, on the coast of Essex east of London, tidal land close to the resort of Clacton-on-Sea was developed with a layout supposedly based on the design of a Bentley radiator grill and narrow avenues named after English cars. Like many other plotland places, Jaywick evolved in a grudging, argumentative manner. Repeated local-authority attempts were made to control, then demolish and then regenerate Jaywick, with all the while the estate was gradually transforming from a holiday site to a place of permanent residence. Seven decades after it was started, professional architects and planners at last got to work on the serious business of remaking Jaywick Sands. In

the late 1990s, 40 new prefabricated houses, 'reflecting the timber-clad nature of many of the original estate properties',[28] were built on the adjacent site of a former holiday camp. The intention was to rehouse the occupants of the older 'worst properties', which would then be replaced by new houses or open spaces. Despite winning architectural awards and being proclaimed by government bodies, there was considerable resistance from local people and in the event only five original properties were demolished.

The same desire to make a holiday home of one's own on the margin between land and sea helped create makeshift settlements on other parts of the West.

The New Zealand 'baches' reveal a similar yearning to be close to the water's edge, idiosyncratic personal architecture, and a history of battling against regulation and at times removal. Some baches began in the late nineteenth century as no more than human adaptations – a front wall or roofed extension – to existing seaside caves. The subsequent history is often presented as one of a 'creative bach culture' developing from the appeal and challenge of isolation and inaccessibility bordering the sea, but also of increasing

At The Mount. Tauranga. F.G.R.6165.

The Blake family outside their bache at Mount Maunganui, New Zealand, *c.* 1950s.

Baches, Mount Maunganui, *c.* 1920.

threat from municipal authorities wishing to regularize and remove the structures. An alternative view argues that private baches, enjoyed by a small minority, are the problem, despoiling the natural environment and reducing public access, while civic authorities equivocate in their duty to ensure the greater environmental and public good. Amid

this conflicting set of representations, popular design magazines have also featured baches 'going from shack to chic',[29] while a few of the original structures have been officially recognized and designated as worth preserving as part of the country's built heritage.

Makeshift buildings for staying by the sea can be represented as extraordinary locations, separate from the everyday concerns and regulation of work and domesticity where powerful personal and social relationships can be isolated, explored and unravelled. The 2001 film *Rain*, by Christine Jeffs, portrays family and sexual relationships on the edge, played out in a New Zealand bache summer community, itself on a geographical boundary.

Although a different seaside place – Florida – a similar theme of makeshift settlements by the sea providing a sphere where people step outside their normal lives is explored in the 2002 film *Sunshine State* by John Sayles. Here, though, the fictional Lincoln Beach, a community of African Americans, is both in a marginal location and positioned on the periphery of a dominant white society, eager to 'modernize' the seaside and transform the remaining natural coastal environment into a land of country clubs, golf courses and luxury dwellings. The fiction of the film mirrored a real-life controversy at the same time over plans to develop part of American Beach (used as a location in the film) on Amelia Island. The real American Beach, established in the 1930s, was the state's only African American beach resort, the architectural and leisure product of a formally segregated society.[30] As desegregation opened other seaside places to African Americans it changed from a

A postcard of the first holiday camp, on Douglas, Isle of Man, showing its Oriental architecture and bell tents.

thriving resort into what today is described as a 'quiet beachfront community' with a hundred of the original small individual houses surviving, and a new role as a crucial part of Florida's Black Heritage Trail. American Beach, though, sits uncomfortably on present-day Amelia Island, 'a 13.5-mile-long slice of heaven to visitors and to year-round residents',[31] with huge residential growth and demand for real estate.

HOLIDAYS FOR THE MASSES

The developing interest in physical fitness and the pleasures of life out of doors combined with the rapid broadening of the demand for seaside holidays led to another alternative to sleeping and staying by the sea – the holiday camp. In origin the first camps, late Victorian camping holidays for disadvantaged children, had a strong philanthropic and moralistic philosophy. The holiday camp required an architecture for a shared communal holiday for large numbers of people. By the early years of the twentieth century, the first holiday camp proper – Cunningham's, on the Isle of Man – provided bell tents lit by candle as sleeping accommodation.[32] But Cunningham's more permanent buildings included features to become common in later camps: communal dining room, a concert hall and a heated swimming pool with some exterior design following the seaside tradition of functional purpose veiled by extraordinary fantastic architecture – one building was in Indian style with verandas and domed washrooms while a toilet block was disguised as a castle. On the east coast of mainland Britain, J. Fletcher Dodd had established the 'Caister

Socialist Holiday Camp' by 1906. It soon lost its socialist tag, with canvas replaced by wooden chalets and huts.[33]

Despite their temporary nature, the pioneer camps pointed the way to the subsequent holiday-camp development of permanent, complete and planned resorts.[34] Although the essence of communal healthy holidays remained, increasingly the philanthropic or political purpose behind the pioneering camps succumbed to commercialization. The competitive holiday-camp business boomed and both the small-scale independent camps and large-scale enterprises added a significant new dimension to the landscape and architecture of the seaside. On the Isle of Wight, for instance, the first holiday camp was established in 1935; despite the wartime hiatus, by 1949 'at least a dozen camps now cater for holidaymakers'.[35] Architecturally, the holiday camps varied. Some with tented pioneer origins were remade with brick and timber into durable camps. Others were redundant military camps reused for holiday purposes. But the quintessential holiday-camp design and architecture was of larger purpose-built and sometimes architect-designed camps.

At Skegness, on the east coast of England, Billy Butlin,

Club Room, Caister Camp.

Double Hut, Caister Camp.

The 'Club Room' at the embryonic holiday camp, Caister Camp, near Great Yarmouth, Norfolk, c. 1910.

The 'Double Hut' at Caister Camp, c. 1910.

makers.[37] The entrance welcomed campers with the slogan, in huge letters, 'Our True Intent Is All For Your Delight'. The architecture, from the decorated facades of the modernist communal buildings to the manicured lawns and gardens and iconic pools with imposing fountains, provided a unique environment for a participatory holiday compared with what was offered in the old seaside resorts.

The professionally most applauded holiday-camp design and architecture was the Prestatyn camp of 1938 in North Wales. The venture was portrayed as progressive and modern and an 'endeavour which turned a bare, featureless site on the north coast of Wales into a magnet for holiday-makers, all within a period of 26 weeks'. Designed by the railway architect William Hamlyn, Prestatyn was 'based on sound architectural precepts': 'There was to be no piecemeal building, no sprinkling of chalets to destroy the symmetry of the camp plan'.[38] Making much of the fashionable nautical style, the spectacular centre of the camp was the Sun Court, a large landscaped square with swimming pool and 60-feet-high observation tower, both for judging beauty and other competitions and viewing the sea. Close by, the Prestatyn Clipper 'gives the impression of a ship on land, which indeed it is! . . . You can sit in one of the quaint barrel seats and imagine yourself on the high seas in the bar of a luxury liner.'[39] The Clipper experience is one example of how theming, particularly of interiors, was used to evoke other exotic and luxurious places and times.[40]

Although enlivened by grand architectural gestures and facades, in the large modern camps the communal halls

the most famous of the camp builders and entrepreneurs, opened his first holiday camp in 1936.[36] Designed by Butlin himself, within a year the camp accommodated 2,000 people and eventually five-fold that number. The Butlins enterprise, replicated around the coast, proved immensely attractive and made a considerable impact on holiday

A 1940 LNER poster, artwork by J. Greenup.

for eating, drinking, entertainment and leisure were in structure monolithic, constructed using modern industrial building techniques, and the chalets for sleeping were usually set in serried rows. From the air the overall design layout was more reminiscent of the light industrial factory estate or military barracks and parade ground than the traditional seaside.

Eager to reach a broad market, the commercial holiday-camp movement presented itself as classless: 'in the vehicle park stand the shining limousines, nearby them the travel stained tandem'.[41] Apart from providing the usual resort attractions from funfairs to pools, the camps avidly

A postcard of the holiday camp at Prestatyn, Wales.

promoted the distinctive variety of participatory activities and competitions from communal open-air games to beauty contests, including a nationally organized League of Lovelies Trophy. In establishing its place at the seaside, the holiday-camp lobby eagerly denigrated traditional seaside accommodation, arguing that the 'seaside landladies are doomed', and the old-style resorts, many of which resisted the coming of the camps.

By the middle of the century, the holiday camp had become part of the national consciousness. Godfrey Winn, the author of the screenplay of the 1947 film *Holiday Camp* (with location scenes in Prestatyn), believed these 'playgrounds of the man-in-the-street' would solve the 'holiday problems of literally thousands of human beings . . . in the healthiest and happiest kind of manner'.[42] However, there were other middle-class voices criticizing holiday camps for commercialization, their attack on individuality, and for cultural, moral and spiritual decline.[43] Writing shortly after the Second World War and arguing that 'much of what goes by the name of pleasure is simply an effort to destroy consciousness', George Orwell was withering of the holiday-camp-like modern pleasure spots.[44]

The 1930s British holiday camps as complete and planned resorts had noteworthy Italian and German counterparts. In Italy the existing well-established children's Colonie movement was seized upon by the Fascist government and developed into a centrepiece of its

Two views of Butlins at Skegness, *c.* 1964, postcards.

MIDDLETON TOWER HOLIDAY CAMP

The nautical style at Middleton Tower near Morecambe,
Lancashire, in a postcard of c. 1949.

plans to instil fascism into children and to transform
society.[45] In the 1920s and '30s newly constructed and
architecturally distinctive Colonie scattered the Italian
coastline, mostly, like the British holiday camps, in isolated
coastal locations on the edge of existing settlements or in
previously unexploited stretches of the coast. In the Italian
context, though, the physical isolation had other benefits,
allowing an institutionalized segregation, separating the
Colonie from the outside world, from ordinary holidaymakers and the children from their families. Although
initially drawing on a variety of architectural styles, including neo-classical designs, a modern 'rationalist' style
became dominant. Monumental building forms made a
stark statement within the surrounding landscape with, for
example, 'the height of their towers or the sheer size of the
facades, acting as advertisements of the social policies of
the government'.[46] There was an associated concern to
provide a totally designed environment that would have a
significant impact on the colonists.

Post-war, the original Colonie tradition was initially re-
established but then faded as Italian society and economy
evolved, living standards increased and a multiplicity of
alternative holidays became available. Of the surviving
Fascist Colonie buildings, some stood derelict, others were
restored as Colonie for other holiday purposes or used in
alternative ways. Among architectural historians there was
a growing fascination with rediscovering and interpreting
the Fascist architecture for children by the sea.

At Prora on Germany's Baltic shore, the architect
Clemens Klotz designed a unique complete resort development for National Socialism, including an astounding 4.5
kilometres linear structure of holiday flats gently curving
around the sandy beaches of a broad bay and perhaps the
longest habitable building in Europe.[47] Understood by
Hasso Spode as a Fordist-inspired summer holiday machine
for the masses, architectural commentators have floundered
when defining the design, sometimes portraying it as neo-
classical, sometimes as inspired by the International
Movement. The resort, for 20,000 German workers, was
constructed between 1936 and 1939 and designed to make a

top: Built at Marina di Massa in 1938 as the Colonia Marina XXVIII Ottobre and designed by Ettore Sottsass and Alfio Guaitoli, by 2005 its conversion into a hostel was almost complete.

above: The derelict Prora resort complex on the Baltic island of Rügen in 2000.

Germany there are continuing debates about how to understand and what to do with the astonishing, and mostly derelict, buildings.[48]

Comparisons of the British, Italian and German versions of these 1930s architectures for mass holidaymaking, in the context of fundamental differences in political systems, reveal a common context of a dominant Western interest in the sun, health and exercise out of doors, a rapidly expanding demand for seaside holidays from previously excluded sections of the population and the production of new forms of seaside architecture in self-contained and often isolated developments. The varied architectural responses in all three countries included some monumental modernist structures often drawing on nautical themes and ideas. And in all three cases, post-war, the resultant architectural edifices were either abandoned or transformed and remade.

reality of the National Socialist concept of 'strength through joy'. The Second World War and the following Communist political system meant that this seaside place was left untouched by holidaymakers; subsequently, in unified

As to the British vision of holidays for all, increasing individualism, rising standards of living, the magnet of overseas package holidays and the cheaper British self-catering coastal caravan parks all undermined the holiday-camp ideal. Some proprietors responded by developing an overseas product, most famously with Fred Pontin's Pontinental venture with purpose-built Mediterranean

top left: Coping with the English weather: a Butlins Skyline Pavilion.

middle left: Impression of Butlins Shoreline Hotel, opened in 2005 at Bognor Regis, Sussex.

top right: New England village life meets England's Lincolnshire coast at Butlins Skegness resort.

right: Caravan site overlooking Cromer, Norfolk, in 2001.

A postcard of camping on the south-west coast of France: 'Arcachon-Les Abatilles (Gironde) Camping en Forêt'.

Campsite, French Mediterranean coast, 2004.

being duped by the architecture and artificiality of the holiday-camp experience, an alternative approach, developed by Hardy and Ward, emphasized the holidaymakers' 'sense of personal involvement in the experience, and the part which ordinary people play in their own history'.[51]

But there were also remarkable survivals and transformations. At Caister in Norfolk, John Fletcher Dodd's 1906 camp, a product of 'guild socialism',[52] had by 2004 become Haven Caister Holiday Park. Following numerous changes of ownership, in 2004 Butlins survived at three sites. Reimagined as 'beach resorts' rather than holiday camps, there were also significant architectural innovations, including 'indoor Splash Waterworlds' with 'a wonderful sub-tropical climate' and white-tented 'Skyline Pavilions' visually dominating the local landscape and providing an atmosphere that 'is truly electric – whatever the weather outside'.[53] Images of other fashionable Western seaside places were used in the Ocean Drive and Coral Beach restaurants, while the newest accommodation included New England village styles and, at Bognor, a seafront resort hotel in a twenty-first-century version of Nautical Moderne so prevalent in 1930s seaside buildings. Both Haven and Butlins formed part of the privately owned Bourne Leisure group, the market leader with 40 parks containing tens of thousands of 'pitches' and perhaps 200,000 bed spaces around the United Kingdom.

hotels, the first, the Pineta Beach Hotel at Platamona, Sardinia.[49] Towards the end of the century, many of the most prominent British holiday camps closed, the sites sometimes remaining derelict and the decaying architecture a wistful reminder of previous holiday times.[50] With decline came increasing nostalgia for the former camps and a reappraisal of their impact. Rather than holidaymakers

And yet despite the decline of the iconic holiday camps of the mid-twentieth century, one of the remarkable architectural developments at the recent British seaside has been the static caravan park. On the shoreline of Lincolnshire, for example, the 20-mile coast between Skegness – known to its aficionados as 'Skeggy' – and Mablethorpe has Europe's largest concentration of caravans. Each of the numerous sites has its own separate geography composed of rectangular and flat-roofed boxes made out of plastic and aluminium in varied pastel shades, with the parks in total forming a disjointed and hidden linear city held together by the closeness to the sea and a web of private roads and clusters of commercial facilities from shops to amusement arcades.[54] Often termed holiday parks or holiday villages and the caravans re-branded as holiday homes, such seaside sites form a significant part of the estimated 3,500 caravan parks in Britain and a sizeable resource for the 17.3 million camping and caravanning holidays taken in 2002.[55] The largest of the holiday parks have many of the facilities and attractions of the former holiday camps, including the remnants of seaside live entertainment. Despite the regimented rows of caravans being screened from public view, planning authorities have been anxious to concentrate and control park sites and limit their visual impact. This largely unnoticed and hidden modern seaside holiday world meets the demands of holidaymakers eager for their own private spaces, however temporary, to stay by the sea.[56] If the original holiday camp was architecture for communal staying by the sea, the present-day holiday park is a mass architecture for the private family seaside.

Camping under canvas also proved far more resilient than the holiday camps it spawned; after the Second World War seaside camping flowered to become a major and sustained feature of the European holiday industry. Here, though, the designed campsite layout with its pitches, route-ways, facilities blocks and, on the grander sites, entertainment centres and pools, hosts an idiosyncratic, makeshift and jostling architecture of tents and mobile caravans. The holiday camp of the past also had a more distant and successful relative in the form of present-day Club Mediterranée villages. Like the original holiday camps, Club Mediterranée also began under canvas – although in the late 1940s. Over half a century later it had become Club Med, with holiday villages in 40 countries, each offering a curiously reminiscent menu of architecturally distinctive and all-inclusive complete holidays, with an early twenty-first-century version of hedonism, health and pleasure.[57]

LODGING HOUSE TO GRAND HOTEL

The holiday camp and caravan park and the makeshift landscape of self-made plotlands were an escape from the traditional forms of seaside accommodation in the established resorts. At the British seaside until the middle of the nineteenth century most visitors stayed in lodging-houses. There were graduations in lodging-house status and quality: the most affluent families would rent a grand house for a complete season, others perhaps a suite of rooms, while for the working class the lodgings, for a much shorter period of time, might be a single and perhaps shared room.[58] The wealthiest families would staff their temporary seaside home with their own servants; in other lodging houses landladies – the profession of seaside lodging-house keeper was gendered, and there were few landlords – would either prepare food bought by their guests or provide a more expensive 'full board' alternative. In a resort such as Brighton, there were just a few older inns and, from the early part of the nineteenth century, purpose-built hotels,

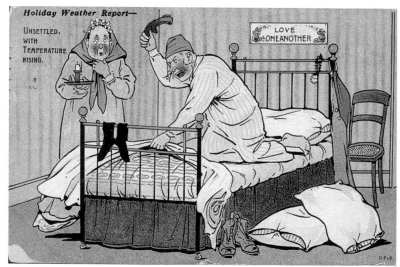

The delights of a private hotel, south coast of England, mid-twentieth century.

Bed bugs as a problem in seaside accommodation. Postcard, c. 1917.

although even in these a suite of rooms or an apartment would be hired and meals eaten in privacy.[59]

As the market for sleeping by the sea broadened, there was a flowering of both the boarding house and of the large architect-designed seaside hotel. Although it ranged from the domestic dwelling functioning as a guesthouse with just one or two rooms to rent through graduations to much larger and more hotel-like establishments with a dining room and other communal facilities, the boarding house and its more elite cousin the private hotel became a mainstay of resorts, dominating the advertising sections of municipal guide-books.[60] But despite its economic importance, the boarding-house experience, like that of the earlier lodging houses, was widely lampooned for the petty restrictions, low quality of food, excessive charges and poor hygiene.[61] Representations of the boarding house as the ridiculed epitome of the British seaside and the landlady as a tartar figure to be derided appeared in media as diverse as comic postcards and respectable poetry.[62] An intensively competitive business, in many resorts guest-houses and small boarding houses were externally decorated with idiosyncratic names, notices displaying prices and facilities, and brightly painted walls perhaps embellished with hanging baskets of flowers and garden ornaments.

In contrast, from the mid-nineteenth century, the largest and most successful of the respectable British resorts also experienced a burgeoning of the purpose-built and architect-designed 'grand' hotel.[63] Illustrative examples are, in Brighton, the Grand Hotel of 1864, an entirely rebuilt Norfolk Hotel of 1865 and the Metropole Hotel of 1890; Scarborough's Grand Hotel opened in 1867, Eastbourne's Grand in 1875 and Torquay's Imperial in 1866; at the close of the century Folkestone acquired an adjacent pair of imposing new hotels, the Grand and the Metropole.[64] The magnitude and significance of the projects drew some of the period's most distinguished architects. The French-style Brighton Grand was the work of John Whichcord; Scarborough's Second Empire-styled Grand

Entrance foyer and staircase, Grand Hotel, Scarborough.

below: Scarborough's Grand Hotel in 1994, looking much as it did when built, although the hotel experience had radically changed.

was designed by Cuthbert Brodrick; and Brighton's Metropole by Alfred Waterhouse. Architecturally, such hotels followed no single style, although they were all visually dominant, marked out by their huge size, monumental design and occupation of significant seafront sites. The location provided hotel guests, especially those renting the most expensive rooms, with unparalleled and private sea views.[65] Often, too, they were designed in styles and built of imported materials that intruded on to existing resort townscapes, marking them out as exclusive buildings somehow separate from the rest of the resort. Inside, the generic grand hotel – and the uniformity of their names suggests the uniformity of product and clientele – offered an opulent array of ballrooms, restaurants, smoking rooms, baths and waiting areas, luxuriously decorated and often exotically themed. The unwelcome were excluded from the experience by price, by the daunting architecture of wide entrances and grand lobbies, and by the uniformed doorman. Into the twentieth century, new grand hotels appeared in modernist guise, most notably with Morecambe's Midland Hotel of

Brighton's Metropole, as represented on a postcard sent in 1909.

1933 and the Ocean Hotel at Saltdean near Brighton of 1938.

The grand hotel concept was replicated and developed with variations in many other fashionable Western seaside resorts, including, for instance, Trouville on the French Channel coast,[66] the French Riviera,[67] Venice Lido and American resorts such as Atlantic City.[68]

In the second half of the twentieth century the development of the package holiday heralded an array of new ways to sleep by the sea. Where people stay while on a package holiday has evolved and developed with the industry, its marketing strategies and building technologies. In Mediterranean Europe it included basic holiday camps in the 1950s, copying from the contemporary British camps, the increasing domination from the 1970s of modern balconied tower hotels to, more recently, low-rise holiday villages and villas often designed and decorated in a supposed vernacular southern European style. The seaside package-holiday hotel became the supreme architectural symbol of the Mediterranean resort, crowding out and replacing what was there before – whether an existing coastal settlement or the undeveloped seaside – and framing the beach and sea.

As an ever-greater proportion of British holidaymakers spent their summers in warmer and sunnier seaside places, the concomitant decline of many British resorts had significant consequences for the use of seaside hotels and guesthouses. In some resorts a vicious cycle of decline set in of empty rooms, increasing competition for fewer visitors, falling prices, under-investment and quality driven ever lower. Once vibrant and successful hotels and guesthouses deteriorated, the owners searching for ways of attracting visitors. In the least successful resorts, marginalized and mobile people on state benefits replaced traditional holidaymakers. Among

ENGLAND'S LATEST SEASIDE HOTEL

MIDLAND HOTEL MORECAMBE

AN LMS HOTEL

A 1933 LMS poster for the Midland Hotel.

these new visitors to the British seaside were the homeless and unemployed, people released from prisons and psychiatric hospitals, refugees and economic migrants illegally entering the country. A national and local media frenzy reported the situation in varied ways: resorts could be represented as havens for 'scroungers' holidaying on the state; hoteliers exposed for exploiting the socially excluded (and taxpayers) through high rents and overcrowded and appallingly bad accommodation; and government bodies or inland local authorities criticized for 'dumping' the unwanted at the seaside. The most aggressive media and political arguments surrounded illegal economic migrants and refugees, spilling out to demonstrations by local people against the housing of migrants at the

MIDLAND HOTEL, MORECAMBE.   222059

The Midland.

CANNES. — Hôtel Beaurivage

seaside and physical conflict between groups of newcomers and residents.

Other hotels closed and were converted to some other use, most often as apartments and flats. Demolition was the most ignominious fate, with the previously prime seafront site perhaps being used as a temporary car park or for building retirement homes.

Even the formerly exclusive nineteenth-century grand hotels and the fashionable modernist constructions of the inter-war years have not all been immune from the quest to find substitutes for their absent former visitors. Name and architecture remain, but the original grand hotel use has ceased, perhaps replaced by budget coach parties and November 'turkey and tinsel' breaks, the housing of refugees and migrants, or conversion into apartments for permanent residents.

Elsewhere, though, in resorts like Eastbourne, Brighton and Bournemouth, the grand hotel concept has proved more resilient, nowadays trading on promises of lavish service, modern facilities, fine cuisine, tradition, heritage

Hotels in Cannes, past . . .

. . . and present: The Carlton Inter-Continental.

Excelsior Hotel, Venice Lido, in 2004.

The monolithic Traymore Hotel, Atlantic City, as it looked *c.* 1960s.

and architecture. Although a relatively rare feature of the early twenty-first-century British seaside, such hotels have many counterparts in other Western resorts attracting affluent holidaymakers. Usually part of national or international hotel chains and despite the similarity of the product and experience being sold, each of these modern-day corporate grand hotels is presented as a place of individuality, personal service and exclusivity. A 300-room hotel on the busiest part of the Cannes seafront, for example, becomes a secluded haven protected by a landscaped, flower-filled garden. Staying in another hotel of the same chain supposedly delivers a memorable experience made more exclusive by access to the hotel's private beach – although in reality one of a dozen hotel private beaches close by each other and each with 200 sun loungers. The promise is still more exclusive and personal in one of Monte Carlo's 'hotels of exception which one day cease being an address to become a legend'.[69]

Perhaps in reaction to the corporate luxury hotels, there is a growing niche market for smaller 'chic' or 'boutique' hotels, providing 'a contemporary, comfortable and laid-back place to stay'.[70] Many of these hotels are modern-day versions of the classic seaside small business, marked out, however, by significant recent investment, idiosyncratic buildings close to the sea, themed or eclectic interior design and relatively high prices to match. In Britain at least they are represented as stylish and informal, sometimes 'quirky' or 'funky', and associated with the rediscovery of the seaside as 'a cool place to be' by younger, affluent people. In 2003 the refurbished Hell Bay Hotel on the Isles of

Invented vernacular architecture for the visitor to southern
Europe, Menorca, 1995.

right: Invented vernacular for southern Europe, Portugal, 2001.

Clifftop grand hotel architecture: the Headland Hotel, Newquay, 2005.

A 1960s publicity postcard for the Cavendish at Eastbourne.

Scilly was described as 'New England and the Caribbean meet Cornwall' and included 'palm trees, human-sized chessboard and bold steel *bas-reliefs*'.[71] In Brighton, the Hotel du Vin, using a mock Tudor former public house and nightclub, featured a new block with rooms resembling beach huts, while the revamped bar was 'a cross between a buzzing Paris bar and a medieval dining hall'[72] with wooden seagulls dangling from the ceiling.

Increasingly, the interior design for places to sleep by the sea, whether boutique hotel, former fishing cottage or beach house, is achieved through decoration in a seaside or nautical style.[73] Designers typically turn to an idealized and romanticized seaside, referencing the past, vernacular architecture, other coastal places or nature. One example, from Britain in 2003, was described as 'New England meets the beach hut'.[74] In a desperate urge for the artificial to be as authentic and natural as possible, design details and furnishing might use the debris of the working seaside, including driftwood and broken fishing nets or raw material from the beach, including shells and pebbles. The return to the seemingly authentic, vernacular and natural seaside is also apparent in many luxurious new hotels and holiday villages on tropical shores. The intrusive modern world is likely to be hidden from view with holidaymakers provided with minimalist and close-to-nature waterside villas, perhaps disguised in some traditional style, and structures close to the sea carefully designed to look like makeshift beach shacks built by local people. There is an uncertainty here about the seaside and its architecture that is surprisingly reminiscent of the hesitation with which the first resort builders searched for their own designs for the seaside.

FINIS!
(THE END OF THE SEASON)

A cartoon by du Maurier.

REFERENCES

INTRODUCTION

1 David Cannadine, *Ornamentalism: How the British Saw Their Empire* (London, 2001), p. 3.

2 The point is made by a number of commentators, including Ken Worpole in *Here Comes the Sun: Architecture and Public Space in Twentieth-century European Culture* (London, 2000), p. 11.

3 Miriam Akhtar and Steve Humphries, *Some Liked It Hot: The British on Holiday at Home and Abroad* (London, 2000).

4 John K. Walton, 'The Seaside Resorts of Western Europe. 1750–1939', in *Recreation and the Sea*, ed. Stephen Fisher (Exeter, 1997), pp. 36–56.

5 Colin Ward and Dennis Hardy, *Goodnight Campers! The History of the British Holiday Camp* (London, 1986).

6 Anthony D. King, *The Bungalow: The Production of a Global Culture* (New York, 1995).

7 Alain Corbin, *The Lure of the Sea: The Discovery of the Seaside in the Western World, 1750–1840* (Cambridge, 1994).

8 John K. Walton, *The English Seaside Resort: A Social History, 1750–1914* (Leicester, 1983) and John K. Walton, *The British Seaside: Holidays and Resorts in the Twentieth Century* (Manchester, 2000).

9 See, for example, the seaside-focused contributions to Susan C. Anderson and Bruce H. Tabb, eds, *Water, Leisure and Culture: European Historical Perspectives* (Oxford, 2002).

10 King, *The Bungalow*, p. xiv.

11 John Lowerson, 'Review Article: Starting from Your Own Past? The Serious Business of Leisure History', *Journal of Contemporary History*, XXXVI/3 (2001), pp. 517–18.

12 John K. Walton, 'British Tourism between Industrialization and Globalization', in *The Making of Modern Tourism: The Cultural History of the British Experience, 1600–2000*, ed. Hartmut Berghoff, Barbara Korte, Ralf Schneider and Christopher Harvie (Basingstoke, 2002), p. 111.

13 John Urry, 'Cultural Change and the Seaside Resort', in *The Rise and Fall of British Coastal Resorts*, ed. Gareth Shaw and Allan Williams (London, 1997), p. 112.

14 Illustrative accounts of local histories of individual English resorts are the early Edmund M. Gilbert, *Brighton: Old Ocean's Bauble* (London, 1954) and the recent Ken Fines, *A History of Brighton and Hove* (Chichester, 2002). For two American examples, see Fred E. Basten, *Santa Monica Bay* (Los Angeles, CA, 1997) and Michael Immerso, *Coney Island: The People's Playground* (New Brunswick, NJ, 2002).

15 Mary Blume, *Côte d'Azur: Inventing the French Riviera* (London, 1992).

16 For instance, Nick Evans, *Dreamland Remembered: 140 Years of Seaside Fun in Margate* (Whitstable, 2003), Bill Curtis, *Blackpool Tower* (Lavenham, 1988) and Peter Bennett, *Blackpool Pleasure Beach: A Century of Fun* (Blackpool, 1996).

17 Simon Adamson, *Seaside Piers* (London, 1977) and Lynn F. Pearson, *The People's Palaces: Britain's Seaside Pleasure Buildings of 1870–1914* (Buckingham, 1991).

18 A catalogue of English seaside social histories ranges from the early post-war H. G. Stokes, *The English Seaside* (London, 1947) and Ruth Manning-Sanders, *Seaside England* (London, 1951) to, half a century later, Joseph Connolly, *Beside the Seaside* (London, 1999) and John Hannavy, *The English Seaside in Victorian and Edwardian Times* (Princes Risborough, 2003).

19 Lena Lencek and Gideon Bosker, *The Beach: The History of Paradise on Earth* (London, 1998).

20 Thomas A. P. van Leeuwen, *The Springboard in the Pond: An Intimate History of the Swimming Pool* (Cambridge, MA, 1999).

21 Charles Sprawson, *Haunts of the Black Masseur* (London, 1992).

CHAPTER ONE: NATURE AND SEASIDE ARCHITECTURE

1 Quoted in Charles Wright, *The Brighton Ambulator* (London, 1818), pp. 24–5.

2 Alain Corbin, *The Lure of the Sea: The Discovery of the Seaside in the Western World, 1750–1840* (Cambridge, 1994), pp. 82–6, and John K Walton, *The English Seaside Resort: A Social History, 1750–1914* (Leicester, 1983), pp. 10–11.

3 Corbin, *The Lure of the Sea*, p. 78.

4 John Hassan, *The Seaside, Health and the Environment in England and Wales since 1800* (Aldershot, 2003).

5 Edmund M. Gilbert, *Brighton: Old Ocean's Bauble* (London, 1954), p. 18.

6 Corbin, *The Lure of the Sea*.

7 Corbin, *The Lure of the Sea*, p. 62.

8 Richard Russell, *A Dissertation on the Use of Sea-Water in the Diseases of the Glands*, 3rd edn (London, 1755), p. vi.

9 Michael H. Fisher, *The First Indian Author in English: Dean Mahomed (1759–1851) in India, Ireland and England* (Delhi, 1996), pp. 267–8.

10 Russell, *Dissertation*, p. 128.

11 Martin Stanton, 'Sea Bathing at Margate', *History Today* (July 1983), p. 21.

12 An early example of a seafront resort building was East Cliff House in

Hastings of *c.* 1761: J. Manwaring Baines, *Historic Hastings* (St Leonards on Sea, 1986), p. 335. For a discussion of the early development of Brighton, see Sue Farrant, *Georgian Brighton, 1740 to 1820* (Brighton, 1980).

13 Corbin, *The Lure of the Sea*, p. 266.

14 Kate Flint, *The Victorians and the Visual Imagination* (Cambridge, 2000), pp. 285–6. See also Orvar Löfgren, *On Holiday: A History of Vacationing* (Berkeley, CA, 1999), pp. 41–8.

15 Anthony Dale, *Fashionable Brighton, 1820–1860* (London, 1947).

16 Gilbert, *Brighton*, p. 21.

17 Gilbert, *Brighton*, p 27.

18 Philip Henry Gosse, *Tenby: A Sea-Side Holiday* (London, 1856), p. 34.

19 Gosse, *Tenby*, p. 218.

20 Gosse, *Tenby*, p. 289.

21 Gosse, *Tenby*, p. 290.

22 J. E. Taylor, *Half-Hours at the Sea-Side; or, Recreations with Marine Objects* (London, 1890), p. 260. On the religious motivation to Victorian seaside natural history, see Christiana Payne, 'Seaside Visitors: Idlers, Thinkers and Patriots in Mid-Nineteenth-century Britain', in *Water, Leisure and Culture: European Historical Perspectives*, ed. Susan C. Anderson and Bruce H. Tabb (Oxford, 2002), pp. 87–104.

23 Robert W. Fraser, *The Seaside Naturalist: Out-door Studies in Marine Zoology and Botany, and Maritime Geology* (London, 1868), p. 21.

24 Allen Stanley and Christopher Newall, *Pre-Raphaelite Vision: Truth to Nature*, exh. cat., Tate Britain, London (2004), pp. 188–9.

25 Payne, 'Seaside Visitors'.

26 J. G. Wood, *The Common Objects of the Sea-Shore Including Hints for an Aquarium* (London, 1857).

27 Philip Henry Gosse, *A Naturalist's Rambles on the Devonshire Coast* (London, 1855).

28 Gosse, *Tenby*, p. vi.

29 John Jeremiah Bigsby, *The Sea-side Manual for Invalids and Bathers* (London, 1841).

30 Bigsby, *Sea-side Manual*, p. 18.

31 George Moseley, *Eastbourne as a Residence for Invalids and Winter Resort* (London, 1882), p. 9.

32 John Hooker Packard, *Sea-Air and Sea-Bathing* (Philadelphia, PA, 1880), p. 19.

33 Packard, *Sea-Air and Sea-Bathing*, p. 22.

34 Hassan, *The Seaside*, pp. 76–8.

35 Anthony Dale, *The History and Architecture of Brighton* (Brighton, 1950), p. 21.

36 Corbin, *The Lure of the Sea*, p. 76.

37 Bigsby, *Sea-side Manual*, pp. 109–10.

38 Charles Sprawson, *Haunts of the Black Masseur* (London, 1992).

39 Fred Gray, *Walking on Water: The West Pier Story* (Brighton, 1998).

40 A history of the swimming pool, concentrating on mainland Europe and the United States and having little detail of public seaside baths and pools, is provided by Thomas A. P. van Leeuwen, *The Springboard in the Pond: An Intimate History of the Swimming Pool* (Cambridge, MA, 1999).

41 Avril Lansdell, *Seaside Fashions, 1860–1939* (Princes Risborough, 1990), Marie-Christine Grasse, *Coups de Soleil & Bikinis* (Toulouse, 1997) and Lena Lencek and Gideon Bosker, *Making Waves: Swimsuits and the Undressing of America* (San Francisco, CA, 1989),

42 Hassan, *The Seaside*, pp. 78–90.

43 George Ryley Scott, *The Story of Baths and Bathing* (London, 1939), p. 216.

44 Lencek and Bosker, *Making Waves*, quotation p. 68.

45 Scott, *Baths and Bathing*, p. 218.

46 Grasse, *Coups de Soleil*, p. 43.

47 Grasse, *Coups de Soleil*, p. 63.

48 Ken Worpole, *Here Comes the Sun: Architecture and Public Space in Twentieth-century European Culture* (London, 2000), p. 14.

49 *Health and Efficiency*, VI/8 (1936).

50 Scott, *Baths and Bathing*, p. 272.

51 Worpole, *Here Comes the Sun*, p. 45.

52 Scott, *Baths and Bathing*, p. 222.

53 *France Soir*, 18 August 2003. See also *Midi Libre*, 5 August 2004.

54 Timothy T. De La Vega, ed., *200 Years of Surfing Literature: An Annotated Bibliography* (Hawaii, 2004).

55 See, for example, Peter Dickens, *Society and Nature: Changing Our Environment, Changing Ourselves* (Cambridge, 2004); Adrian Franklin, *Nature and Social Theory* (London, 2002); 'What is Nature Now?', *Harvard Design Magazine* (Winter–Spring 2000).

56 John Urry's work includes *The Tourist Gaze: Leisure and Travel in Contemporary Societies* (London, 1990, 2nd edn 2002); *Consuming Places* (London, 1995); 'Cultural Change and the Seaside Resort', in *The Rise and Fall of British Coastal Resorts*, ed. Gareth Shaw and Allan Williams (London, 1997), pp. 102–13; and with Phil Macnaghten, *Contested Nature* (London, 1998).

57 Macnaghten and Urry, *Contested Nature*, p. 113.

58 Urry, *Consuming Places*, p. 136.

59 Macnaghten and Urry, *Contested Nature*, p. 13.

60 Urry, *The Tourist Gaze*, p. 18.

61 Urry, 'Cultural Change', p. 103.

62 The influence of Urry's work is seen, for example, in David Crouch and

Nina Lübbren, eds, *Visual Culture and Tourism* (Oxford, 2003).

63 John K. Walton, 'British Tourism between Industrialization and Globalization', in *The Making of Modern Tourism: The Cultural History of the British Experience, 1600–2000*, ed. Hartmut Berghoff, Barbara Korte, Ralf Schneider and Christopher Harvie (Basingstoke, 2002), pp. 109–31, p. 115.

64 Franklin, *Nature and Social Theory*, p. 186. For a discussion of the range of 'sensual experiences' involved in tourism, see Löfgren, *On Holiday*.

65 Edmund Gosse, *Father and Son: A Study of Two Temperaments* (London, 1974), p. 78.

66 Gosse, *Father and Son*, pp. 57–8.

67 R. M. Lockley, 'The Sea Coast', in *Britain and the Beast*, ed. Clough Williams-Ellis (London, 1937), p. 232.

68 Poole Borough Council, *Official Guide to Poole* (Poole, 1939).

69 GESAMP and Advisory Committee on the Protection of the Sea, *A Sea of Trouble* (New York, 2001), p. 23.

70 *Daily Telegraph*, 2 September 2004.

71 Hassan, *The Seaside*, p. 244.

72 A. M. Rowland and T. P. Hudson, *The Victoria History of the County of Sussex* (London, 1980), vol. VI, pt 1, pp. 94–5.

73 John Lowerson, *Victorian Sussex* (London, 1972), p. 31.

74 Lowerson, *Victorian Sussex*, p. 31.

75 Miriam Akhtar and Steve Humphries, *Some Liked It Hot: The British on Holiday at Home and Abroad* (London, 2000), pp. 24–5.

76 Hassan, *The Seaside*.

77 Marine Conservation Society, *Good Beach Guide, 2001* (Ross-on-Wye, 2001); *The Guardian*, 20 March 2001.

78 GESAMP, *A Sea of Trouble*, p. 6.

79 Scott, *Baths and Bathing*, p. 226.

80 Grasse, *Coups de Soleil*, p. 71.

81 *The Guardian*, 21 February 2004.

82 *The Guardian*, 31 March 2004.

83 *The Guardian*, 21 February 2004.

84 *The Observer*, 11 May 2003.

85 Eric R. Delderfield, *The Lynmouth Flood Disaster* (Exeter, 1953).

86 Dennis Hardy and Colin Ward, *Arcadia for All: The Legacy of a Makeshift Landscape* (London, 1984), pp. 127 and 154–5.

87 *The Guardian*, 16 February 2005.

CHAPTER TWO: BUILDING THE SEASIDE

1 Quoted in Felicity Stafford and Nigel Yates, *The Later Kentish Seaside* (Gloucester, 1985), p. 24.

2 Peter Jackson and Nigel Thrift, 'Geographies of Consumption', in *Acknowledging Consumption: A Review of New Studies*, ed. Daniel Miller (London, 1995), pp. 204–37.

3 Jules Michelet, *La Mer* (Paris, 1983), p. 279, quoted in Alain Corbin, *The Lure of the Sea: The Discovery of the Seaside in the Western World, 1750–1840* (Cambridge, 1994), p. 64.

4 Sarah Howell, *The Seaside* (London, 1974), pp. 13–14.

5 Lena Lencek and Gideon Bosker, *The Beach: The History of Paradise on Earth* (London, 1998), p. 77.

6 Gerard Young, *A History of Bognor Regis* (Chichester, 1983).

7 J. Manwaring Baines, *Burton's St Leonards* (Hastings, 1956).

8 Anthony Dale, *Fashionable Brighton, 1820–1860* (London, 1947).

9 David Cannadine, *Lords and Landlords: The Aristocracy and the Towns, 1774–1967* (Leicester, 1980).

10 L. J. Bartley, *The Story of Bexhill* (Bexhill-on-Sea, 1971).

11 Jane Austen, *Sanditon* (Harmondsworth, 1974).

12 Ivor Brown, 'Marine Parade: New Look', in *A Book of England*, ed. Ivor Brown (London, 1958), p. 386.

13 In the case of Britain see, for example, John K. Walton, *The English Seaside Resort: A Social History, 1750–1914* (Leicester, 1983), John K. Walton, *The British Seaside: Holidays and Resorts in the Twentieth Century* (Manchester, 2000), and H. Cunningham, 'Leisure and Culture', in *The Cambridge Social History of Britain, 1750–1950*, vol. II: *People and their Environment*, ed F.M.L. Thompson (Cambridge, 1990), pp. 279–339.

14 A useful summary of the class and gender changes in the use of the British seaside is provided by John Benson, *The Rise of Consumer Society in Britain, 1880–1980* (London, 1994).

15 J. Whyman, 'Water Communications to Margate and Gravesend as Coastal Resorts before 1840', *Southern History*, III (1981), pp. 111–38.

16 Walton, *The English Seaside Resort*.

17 E. Graeme Robertson and Joan Robertson, *Cast Iron Decoration: A World Survey* (London, 1977).

18 Simon H. Adamson, *Seaside Piers* (London, 1977) and Cyril Bainbridge, *Pavilions on the Sea: A History of the Seaside Pleasure Pier* (London, 1986).

19 John Hooker Packard, *Sea-Air and Sea-Bathing* (Philadelphia, PA, 1880), p. 117.

20 Cindy S. Aron, *Working At Play: A History of Vacations in the United States* (New York, 1999), pp. 212–14.

21 A comprehensive account of late nineteenth- and early twentieth-century British resort entertainment buildings is Lynn F. Pearson, *The People's Palaces: The Story of the Seaside Pleasure Buildings of 1870–1914* (Buckingham, 1991).

22 Little's Hastings work can be rediscovered in the 1930s issues of the

Municipal Review. See, for example, the January 1932 and July 1933 issues for reports on his underground car park and open-air pool.

23 John F. Travis, *The Rise of the Devon Seaside Resorts, 1750–1900* (Exeter, 1993) and Nigel J. Morgan and Annette Pritchard, *Power and Politics at the Seaside: The Development of Devon's Resorts in the Twentieth Century* (Exeter, 1999).

24 C. H. Bishop, *Folkestone: The Story of a Town* (Folkestone, 1973), pp. 110–20.

25 John K. Walton, 'British Tourism between Industrialization and Globalization', in *The Making of Modern Tourism: The Cultural History of the British Experience, 1600–2000*, ed. Hartmut Berghoff, Barbara Korte, Ralf Schneider and Christopher Harvie (Basingstoke, 2002), pp. 109–31.

26 Quoted in Stafford and Yates, *The Later Kentish Seaside*, p. 86.

27 Kenneth Young, *Music's Great Days in the Spas and Watering-Places* (London, 1968).

28 Orvar Löfgren, *On Holiday: A History of Vacationing* (Berkeley, CA, 1999), pp. 216–19.

29 Packard, *Sea-Air and Sea-Bathing*, p. 27.

30 For the example of Newlyn, Cornwall, see Catherine Wallace, *Under the Open Sky* (Truro, 2002) and for Provincetown, Cape Cod, see James C. O'Connell, *Becoming Cape Cod: Creating a Seaside Resort* (Lebanon, NH, 2003), pp. 80–93.

31 Nina Lübbren, 'North to South: Paradigm Shifts in European Art and Tourism, 1880–1920', in *Visual Culture and Tourism*, ed. David Crouch and Nina Lübbren (Oxford, 2003), pp. 125–46. For an alternative perspective on the development of the French Mediterranean seaside, see Marie-Christine Grasse, *Coups de Soleil & Bikinis* (Toulouse, 1997).

32 For a related if somewhat contradictory study of Sweden, see Michelle Facos, 'A Sound Mind in a Sound Body: Bathing in Sweden', in *Water, Leisure and Culture: European Historical Perspectives*, ed. Susan C. Anderson and Bruce H. Tabb (Oxford, 2002), pp. 105–17.

33 Aron, *Working At Play*, pp. 214–16.

34 Mary Blume, *Côte d'Azur: Inventing the French Riviera* (London, 1992).

35 Löfgren, *On Holiday*, pp. 163–71.

36 Illustrations of such nostalgic publications are Shirley Johnson, *The Villas of the Riviera: Magnificence and Majesty on the Côte d'Azur* (London, 1998) and Philippe Collas and Eric Villedary, *Edith Wharton's French Riviera* (Paris, 2002).

37 The remaking of the Riviera is represented in both academic studies and fiction: for the former, see André Rauch, 'Vacationing on France's Côte d'Azur, 1950–2000', in *Water, Leisure and Culture*, pp. 223–38, and J.V.N. Soane, *Fashionable Resorts Regions: Their Evolution and Transformation* (Wallingford, Oxon, 1993); for the latter, J. G. Ballard, *Super-Cannes* (London, 2000).

38 Vicki Gold Levi and Lee Eisenberg, *Atlantic City: 125 Years of Ocean Madness* (New York, 1979).

39 The process as it relates to package holidays in Europe is described in Löfgren, *On Holiday*, pp. 155–209.

40 For the example of the remaking of Benidorm, see Sue Wright, 'Sun, Sea, Sand and Self–Expression: Mass Tourism as an Individual Experience', in *The Making of Modern Tourism*, pp. 182–202. An analogous account of the development of beach resorts in Thailand is provided by Erik Cohen, *Thai Tourism: Hill Tribes, Islands and Open-Ended Prostitution* (Bangkok, 1996), part 2.

41 Ellen Furlough and Rosemary Wakeman, 'La Grande Motte: French Regional Development, Tourism, and the State', in *Being Elsewhere: Tourism, Consumer Culture, and Identity in Modern Europe and Northern America*, ed. Shelley Baranowski and Ellen Furlough (Ann Arbor, MI, 2001), pp. 348–72.

42 David Mohney and Keller Easterling, eds, *Seaside: Making a Town in America* (New York, 1991) and Karen Falconer Al–Hindi and Caedmon Staddon, 'The Hidden Histories and Geographies of Neotraditional Town Planning: The Case of Seaside, Florida', *Environment and Planning D: Society and Space*, XV (1997), pp. 349–72.

43 See chapter Four: 'The Seaside as Another Place'.

44 Edmund Vale, *North Country* (London, 1937), p. 49.

45 Wesley Dougill, 'The British Coast and its Holiday Resorts', *Town Planning Review*, XVI/4 (1935), pp. 265–78.

46 'Leisure at the Seaside', *Architectural Review*, LXXX (1936), pp. 7–27.

47 'Leisure at the Seaside', *Architectural Review*, p. 18.

48 John Piper, 'The Nautical Style', *Architectural Review*, LXXXIII (1938), pp. 1–14.

49 Quoted in Stafford and Yates, *The Later Kentish Seaside*, pp. 169–71.

50 English Tourist Board, *The Future Marketing and Development of English Seaside Tourism* (London, 1974).

51 James Walvin, *Besides the Seaside* (London, 1978), pp. 152–3.

52 Chris Cooper, 'Parameters and Indicators of the Decline of the British Seaside Resort', in *The Rise and Fall of British Coastal Resorts: Cultural and Economic Perspectives*, ed. Gareth Shaw and Allan Williams (London, 1997). p. 87. See also Ian Gordon and Brian Goodall, 'Resort Cycles and Development Processes', *Built Environment*, XVIII/1 (1992), pp. 41–56.

53 John K. Walton, 'British Tourism between Industrialization and Globalization', in *The Making of Modern Tourism*, pp. 109–31, p. 119.

54 Christina Beatty and Stephen Fothergill, *The Seaside Economy: The Final*

Report of the Seaside Towns Research Project (Sheffield, 2003), pp. 105–6.

55 *The Guardian*, 26 July 1993.

56 English Tourist Board, *Turning the Tide: A Heritage and Environment Strategy for a Seaside Resort* (London, 1993), English Tourism Council, *Sea Changes: Creating World-Class Resorts in England* (London, 2001), and English Heritage and Commission for Architecture and the Built Environment, *Shifting Sands: Design and the Changing Image of English Seaside Towns* (London, 2003).

57 *The Observer*, 5 August 2001.

58 *The Daily Telegraph*, 27 April 2002.

CHAPTER THREE: REPRESENTING THE EDGE

1 Stephen V. Ward, *Selling Places: The Marketing and Promotion of Towns and Cities, 1850–2000* (London, 1998), p. 1.

2 John K. Walton, 'Municipal Government and the Holiday Industry in Blackpool, 1876–1914', in *Leisure in Britain, 1780–1939*, ed., John K. Walton and James Walvin (Manchester, 1983), pp. 160–85.

3 Quoted in Felicity Stafford and Nigel Yates, *The Later Kentish Seaside* (Gloucester, 1985), pp. 44–5.

4 Patricia J. Anderson and Jonathan Rose, eds, *British Literary Publishing Houses, 1820–1880* (Detroit, MI, 1991), p. 326. For a discussion of the significance of guidebooks, using those for London as a case study, see David Gilbert, '"London in all its glory – or how to enjoy London": Guidebook Representations of Imperial London', *Journal of Historical Geography*, XXV/3 (1999), pp. 279–97.

5 A comprehensive account of the place promotion of the seaside is Ward, *Selling Places*. Railway posters are discussed in Beverley Cole and Richard Durack, *Happy as a Sand-Boy: Early Railway Posters* (York, 1990), Beverley Cole and Richard Durack, *Railway Posters, 1923–1947* (London, 1992), Julia Wigg, *Bon Voyage! Travel Posters of the Edwardian Era* (London, 1996), and Tony Hillman and Beverley Cole, *South for Sunshine: Southern Railway Publicity and Posters, 1923 to 1947* (Harrow Weald, 1999).

6 John Beckerson, 'Marketing British Tourism: Government Approaches to the Stimulation of a Service Sector, 1880–1950', in *The Making of Modern Tourism: The Cultural History of the British Experience, 1600–2000*, ed. Hartmut Berghoff, Barbara Korte, Ralf Schneider and Christopher Harvie (Basingstoke, 2002), pp. 133–57.

7 Ward, *Selling Places*, p. 71.

8 Quoted in Ward, *Selling Places*, p. 70.

9 Bexhill Corporation, *Bexhill-on-Sea. For . . . Health & Happiness, Holidays and Homes: The Official Guide of the Corporation* (Bexhill, 1935), p. 105.

10 Southport Corporation, *Sunny Southport: Official Guide, 1938–39* (Southport, 1938).

11 Southport Corporation, *Southport Official Guide 1957* (Southport, 1957).

12 Thomas Richards, *The Commodity Culture of Victorian England: Advertising and Spectacle, 1851–1914* (London, 1991), p. 228.

13 Quoted in Lena Lencek and Gideon Bosker, *Making Waves: Swimsuits and the Undressing of America* (San Francisco, CA, 1989), p. 38.

14 Elwood Watson and Darcy Martin, 'The Miss America Pageant: Pluralism, Femininity, and Cinderella All in One', *Journal of Popular Culture*, XXXIV/1 (2000), p. 107. See also Sarah Banet-Weiser, *The Most Beautiful Girls in the World: Beauty Pageants and National Identity* (Berkeley, CA, 1999).

15 British Health Resorts Association, *British Spas and Seaside Resorts: An Appreciation of Their Medical Values and Uses in the Prevention and Cure of Disease* (London, 1936), p. 8.

16 British Health Resorts Association, *British Spas*, p. 20.

17 Bexhill Corporation, *Bexhill-on-Sea*, p. 19.

18 John Hassan, *The Seaside, Health and the Environment in England and Wales since 1800* (Aldershot, 2003), pp. 96–8.

19 John Betjeman, *Collected Poems* (London, 1979), p.125.

20 J. B. Priestley, *Postscripts* (London, 1940), pp. 30–31.

21 Priestley, *Postscripts*, p. 33.

22 *Daily Telegraph*, 30 May 1998.

23 Blackpool Borough Council, *Blackpool: The Official Holiday Journal* (Blackpool, 1964), quotations pp. 3–4.

24 Blackpool Borough Council, *Blackpool: The Big One!* (Blackpool, 1982).

25 Blackpool Borough Council, *Costa Notta Lotta* (Blackpool, 1985).

26 Blackpool Borough Council, *Blackpool: Where the Family Fun Never Stops* (Blackpool, 1993).

27 Blackpool Borough Council, *Blackpool: So Much Fun You Can Taste It* (Blackpool, 1994).

28 Sue Wright, 'Sun, Sea, Sand and Self–Expression: Mass Tourism as an Individual Experience', in *The Making of Modern Tourism*, pp. 186–7.

29 Orvar Löfgren, *On Holiday: A History of Vacationing* (Berkeley, CA, 1999), pp. 193–4.

30 Wright, 'Sun, Sea, Sand and Self–Expression'.

31 Nigel J. Morgan and Annette Pritchard, *Power and Politics at the Seaside: The Development of Devon's Resorts in the Twentieth Century* (Exeter, 1999).

32 S.P.B. Mais, *Glorious Devon* (London, 1934), p. 1.

33 Mais, *Glorious Devon*, p. 7.

34 Catherine Wallace, *Under the Open Sky* (Truro, 2002).

35 Daphne du Maurier, *Vanishing Cornwall* (London, 1967), p. 197.

36 Rosamunde Pilcher, *The Shell Seekers* (London, 1987), p. 518.

37 See, for example, *The Times*, 31 July 2004, and *Daily Telegraph*, 31 July 2004.

38 Hartmut Berghoff, 'From Privilege to Commodity? Modern Tourism and the Rise of the Consumer Society', in *The Making of Modern Tourism*, pp. 159–79, p. 171.

39 Frederick Treves, *The Riviera of the Corniche Road* (London, 1921), pp. 15–16.

40 Gary Cross, ed., *Worktowners at Blackpool: Mass-Observation and Popular Leisure in the 1930s* (London, 1990).

41 The partiality of the research is discussed in John K. Walton, 'Afterword: Mass-Observation's Blackpool and Some Alternatives', in *Worktowners at Blackpool: Mass-Observation and Popular Leisure in the 1930s*, ed. Gary Cross (London, 1990), pp. 229–39.

42 *Daily Telegraph*, 29 June 2002, and *The Guardian*, 23 August 2003.

43 *Sunday Telegraph*, 10 June 2001.

44 *The Observer*, 27 July 2003.

45 *Sunday Telegraph*, 10 June 2001.

46 Philippe Garner, *A Seaside Album: Photographs and Memory* (London, 2003).

47 Royal Pavilion, Libraries and Museums, Brighton and Hove, *Kiss and Kill: Film Visions of Brighton* (Brighton, 2002).

48 Fred Gray, 'Learning from the Seaside', *Journal of Access, Policy and Practice*, II/1 (2004), pp. 83–92.

49 *The Sun*, 15 July 2002, and *The Times*, 15 July 2002.

50 Edmund M. Gilbert, *Brighton: Old Ocean's Bauble* (London, 1954), pp. 195–6.

51 John Fowles, *The French Lieutenant's Woman* (London, 1969).

52 Robert Tressell, *The Ragged Trousered Philanthropists* (London, 1965), p. 585.

53 Stephen Reynolds, *A Poor Man's House* (Oxford, 1982), p. 10.

54 Graham Greene, *Brighton Rock* (London, 1959), pp. 186–7. From another part of the world, Carl Hiaasen provides a contemporary satirical version of such revealing fiction in his novels about the Florida tourist industry: see, for example, the *Tourist Season* (New York, 1986) and *Strip Tease* (London, 1993).

55 Examples of this approach from Sussex seaside towns are Fred Gray, ed., *Bexhill Voices* (Falmer, Sussex, 1994), Hastings Modern History Workshop, *Hastings Childhoods* (Falmer, Sussex, 1987), Daisy Noakes, *The Town Beehive – A Young Girl's Lot in Brighton, 1910–1934* (Brighton, 1975) and Arthur Thickett, *Deckhand, West Pier* (Brighton, 1993).

56 Office of the Deputy Prime Minister, *The English Indices of Deprivation 2004* (London, 2004), p. 71.

57 Gray, 'Learning from the Seaside'.

58 V. A. Karn, *Retiring to the Seaside* (London, 1977).

59 Jo Bell et al., *Living on the Edge: Sexual Behaviour and Young Parenthood in Seaside and Rural Areas* (Hull, 2004), p. 14.

60 For a selection of postcard images from the late nineteenth- and early twentieth-century British seaside, see John Hannavy, *The English Seaside in Victorian and Edwardian Times* (Princes Risborough, 2003).

61 *Daily Telegraph*, 27 August 1994.

62 Elfreda Buckland, *The World of Donald McGill* (Poole, 1984), p. 171.

63 Löfgren, *On Holiday*, pp. 88–91.

64 A richly illustrated account of twentieth-century postcards and their message writers is Tom Phillips, *The Postcard Century: 2000 Cards and Their Messages* (London, 2000).

65 A discussion of the John Hinde image-making process is in John Hinde, *Our True Intent is All for Your Delight: The John Hinde Butlin's Photographs* (London, 2002), pp. 121–7.

66 Martin Parr, *Boring Postcards* (London, 1999).

67 Buckland, *Donald McGill*.

68 George Orwell, 'The Art of Donald McGill', in *The Collected Essays, Journalism and Letters of George Orwell*, vol. II: *My Country Right or Left, 1940–1943*, ed. Sonia Orwell and Ian Angus (London, 1968), pp. 155–65, p. 164.

69 Five decades before, conservative publics and seaside authorities in British resorts such as Rhyl, Southport and Folkestone had similarly stopped the showing of erotic films: Alison Smith, ed., *Exposed: The Victorian Nude* (London, 2001), p. 179. In Rhyl in 1899 mutoscopes showing titillating images were placed in male public toilets; as a result the revenue from toilet admission charges increased by seven times the previous rate.

70 Elizabeth Edwards, 'Little Theatres of Self: Thinking about the Social', National Portrait Gallery, *We Are The People: Postcards from the Collection of Tom Phillips* (London, 2004), pp. 26–37.

71 Edwards, 'Little Theatres', p. 29.

72 Doug Sandle, 'Joe's Bar, Douglas, Isle of Man: Photographic Representations of Holidaymakers in the 1950s', in *Visual Culture and Tourism*, ed. David Crouch and Nina Lübbren (Oxford, 2003), p. 191.

73 Edwards, 'Little Theatres', p. 36.

74 Mary Blume and Martine D'Astier, *Lartigue's Riviera* (Paris, 1997).

75 Reproduced., for example, in Robert Kee, *The Picture Post Album* (London, 1989), Gavin Weightman, *The Seaside* (Devizes, Wilts., 1993) and Joseph Connolly, *Beside the Seaside* (London, 1999).

76 Russell Roberts, ed., *Tony Ray-Jones* (London, 2004). Examples of Ray-Jones's Brighton photographs are in Philippe Garner, *A Seaside Album:*

Photographs and Memory (London, 2003), pp. 133, 115 and 117.

77 Martin Parr, *The Last Resort: Photographs of New Brighton* (Wallasey, Cheshire, 1986).

78 Garner, *A Seaside Album*, pp. 136–7.

79 Phillips, *The Postcard Century*, and Parr, *Boring Postcards*.

80 *The Guardian*, 27 August 2001 and 24 July 2003.

CHAPTER FOUR: THE SEASIDE AS ANOTHER PLACE

1 Charles Wright, *The Brighton Ambulator* (London, 1818), p. 41.

2 The architect's own portrayal of the Pavilion is provided by John Nash, *Views of the Royal Pavilion, Brighton, 1826* (published in 1827) and reprinted with a commentary in Gervase Jackson-Stops, *Views of the Royal Pavilion* (London, 1991). The design and building of the Pavilion are described in Clifford Musgrave, *Royal Pavilion: An Episode in the Romantic* (London, 1959), John Dinkel, *The Royal Pavilion Brighton* (London, 1983), and Jessica Rutherford, *A Prince's Passion: The Life of the Royal Pavilion* (Brighton, 2003).

3 Wright, *The Brighton Ambulator*, p. 44.

4 Wright, *The Brighton Ambulator*, p. 46.

5 Musgrave, *Royal Pavilion*, p. 53.

6 Dinkel, *The Royal Pavilion Brighton*, p. 61.

7 Robert Venturi, Denise Scott Brown and Steven Izenour, *Learning from Las Vegas* (Cambridge, MA, 1977), p. 107.

8 John M. MacKenzie, *Orientalism: History, Theory and the Arts* (Manchester, 1995), p. 71.

9 Anthony Dale, 'The Architecture of Amusement', in *Seaside Piers*, ed. Simon H. Adamson (London, 1977), p. 80. For a discussion of decorative cast iron, see E. Graeme Robertson and Joan Robertson, *Cast Iron Decoration: A World Survey* (London, 1977).

10 The use of seaside Orientalism and other styles on piers is discussed in Lynn F. Pearson, *The People's Palaces: The Story of the Seaside Pleasure Buildings of 1870–1914* (Buckingham, 1991), pp. 23–8.

11 MacKenzie, *Orientalism*, p. 71.

12 Thomas A. P. van Leeuwen, *The Springboard in the Pond: An Intimate History of the Swimming Pool* (Cambridge, MA, 1999), p. 205.

13 Raymond Lister, *Decorative Cast Ironwork in Great Britain* (London, 1960), pp. 191–2.

14 Quoted in Robertson and Robertson, *Cast Iron*, p. 18.

15 Wesley Dougill, 'The British Coast and its Holiday Resorts', *Town Planning Review*, XVI/4 (1935), pp. 265–78.

16 Frederick Treves, *The Riviera of the Corniche Road* (London, 1921), pp. 15–16.

17 Quoted in Vicki Gold Levi and Lee Eisenberg, *Atlantic City: 125 Years of Ocean Madness* (New York, 1979), p. 48.

18 George Orwell, 'Pleasure Spots', in *Collected Essays*, vol. IV (Harmondsworth, 1970), p. 103.

19 The broader Orientalism debate is represented by the analysis of Edward W. Said, *Orientalism* (London, 1978); one response is in David Cannadine, *Ornamentalism: How the British Saw Their Empire* (London, 2001) and varied viewpoints are provided in A. L. Macfie, ed., *Orientalism: A Reader* (Edinburgh, 2000). The architectural issues are examined in Patrick Conner, *Oriental Architecture in the West* (London, 1979), Raymond Head, *The Indian Style* (Chicago, 1986); MacKenzie, *Orientalism*, and Mark Crinson, *Empire Building: Orientalism and Victorian Architecture* (London, 1996).

20 Said, *Orientalism*, p. 3.

21 Cannadine, *Ornamentalism*.

22 MacKenzie, *Orientalism*, p. 94.

23 Michael Paris, *Warrior Nation: Images of War in British Popular Culture, 1850–2000* (London, 2002).

24 Christiana Payne, 'Seaside Visitors: Idlers, Thinkers and Patriots in Mid-Nineteenth-Century Britain', in *Water, Leisure and Culture: European Historical Perspectives*, ed. Susan C. Anderson and Bruce H. Tabb (Oxford, 2002), p. 92.

25 Stephen V. Ward, *Selling Places: The Marketing and Promotion of Towns and Cities, 1850–2000* (London, 1998), p. 60.

26 Van Leeuwen, *The Springboard in the Pond*, p. 235.

27 Jeffrey Stanton, *Venice California: 'Coney Island of the Pacific'* (Los Angeles, CA, 1993).

28 Van Leeuwen, *The Springboard in the Pond*, p. 237.

29 Southport Corporation, *Sunny Southport: Official Guide, 1938–39* (Southport, 1938), p. 18.

30 Philippe Garner, *A Seaside Album: Photographs and Memory* (London, 2003).

31 Edmund M. Gilbert, *Brighton: Old Ocean's Bauble* (London, 1954), p. 107.

32 *Illustrated Times*, 15 April 1865.

33 Joyce Collins, *Dr Brighton's Indian Patients December 1914–January 1916* (Brighton, 1997).

34 Gilbert, *Brighton: Old Ocean's Bauble*, p. 91.

35 Ward, Lock & Co., *A Pictorial and Descriptive Guide to Brighton and Hove* (London, c. 1913), p. 34.

36 Osbert Sitwell and Margaret Barton, *Brighton* (London, 1935), p. 183.

37 Rutherford, *A Prince's Passion*, p. 179.

38 Michael Turner, *Osborne House* (London, 2001), p. 32.

39 Head, *The Indian Style*, pp. 115–18.

40 Nancy E. Loe, *Hearst Castle: An Interpretive History of W. R. Hearst's San Simeon Estate* (Santa Barbara, CA, 1994).

41 Anthony Dale, *Fashionable Brighton, 1820–1860* (London, 1947), p. 153.

42 Ward, Lock & Co., *A Pictorial and Descriptive Guide to Torquay, Paignton, Dartmouth* (London, c. 1919), pp. 23–4.

43 Percival H. W. Almy, *Torquay with its Surroundings* (London, 1925), p. 58.

44 Nigel J. Morgan, 'Seaside Resort Strategies: The Case of Inter-War Torquay', in *Recreation and the Sea*, ed. Stephen Fisher (Exeter, 1997), p. 94.

45 Michel Racine, Ernest J.-P. Boursier-Mougenot and Françoise Binet, *The Gardens of Provence and the French Riviera* (Cambridge, MA, 1987).

46 Orvar Löfgren, *On Holiday: A History of Vacationing* (Berkeley, CA, 1999), p. 219.

47 *United Arab Emirates Yearbook 2005* (London, 2005), p. 162.

48 *The Guardian*, 18 July 2003.

CHAPTER FIVE: DESIGNING RESORT OPEN SPACES

1 John Fiske, *Reading the Popular* (London, 1989), pp. 43–76.

2 Quoted in Michael Jacobs and Malcolm Warner, *Art in the South-East* (London, 1980), p. 25.

3 Christiana Payne, 'Seaside Visitors: Idlers, Thinkers and Patriots in Mid-Nineteenth-Century Britain', in *Water, Leisure and Culture: European Historical Perspectives*, ed. Susan C. Anderson and Bruce H. Tabb (Oxford, 2002), pp. 87–104.

4 Quoted in Sarah Howell, *The Seaside* (London, 1974), pp. 78–9.

5 Avril Lansdell, *Seaside Fashions, 1860–1939* (Princes Risborough, 1990), p. 58.

6 Kaye Webb, 'By the Sea', *Leader Magazine*, X/29 (1948), pp. 20–21.

7 *Daily Mirror*, 17 May 2004, *The Sun*, 18 May 2004, *The Guardian*, 18 May 2004, *The Guardian*, 19 May 2004, *The Times*, 18 May 2004,

8 Sylvia M. Tunstall and Edmund C. Penning-Rowsell, 'The English Beach: Experiences and Values', *Geographical Journal*, CLXIV 3 (1998), pp. 319–32.

9 This perspective has been most thoroughly developed by Rob Shields, *Places on the Margin: Alternative Geographies of Modernity* (London, 1991). See also Chris Rojek, *Ways of Escape: Modern Transformations in Leisure and Travel* (London, 1993).

10 Jack D. Douglas and Paul K. Rasmussen with Carol Ann Flanagan, *The Nude Beach* (Beverly Hills, CA, 1977).

11 Donald Horne, *The Education of Young Donald* (Sydney, 1967), p. 12, quoted in Geoffrey Dutton, *Sun, Sea, Surf and Sand – The Myth of the Beach* (Melbourne, 1985).

12 Douglas and Rasmussen, *The Nude Beach*.

13 Mandalay Bay Resort and Casino, 'Welcome' booklet (c. 2002).

14 *The Guardian*, 22 July 2003, *The Times*, 10 July 2003.

15 Marcel Smets, 'Promenade, Past and Present', *Topos*, XLI (2002), p. 6.

16 Charles Wright, *The Brighton Ambulator* (London, 1818), p, 47.

17 Wright, *The Brighton Ambulator*, pp. 47–8.

18 Steve Peak, *Fishermen of Hastings: 200 Years of the Hastings Fishing Community* (St Leonards on Sea, 1985), p. 32. Peak's book describes the two centuries of struggle between the fishing community and seaside authorities over the use of the beach.

19 Sue Berry, 'Pleasure Gardens in Georgian and Regency Seaside Resorts: Brighton, 1750–1840', *Garden History*, XXVIII/2 (2000), pp. 222–30.

20 John K. Walton, *The British Seaside: Holidays and Resorts in the Twentieth Century* (Manchester, 2000), especially pp. 102–4.

21 Chandra Mukerji, 'Reading and Writing with Nature: Social Claims and the French Formal Garden', *Theory and Society*, XIX (1990), p. 657.

22 Sophie Chevalier, 'From Woollen Carpet to Grass Carpet: Bridging House and Garden in an English Suburb', in *Material Cultures: Why Some Things Matter*, ed. Daniel Miller (London, 1998), p. 60.

23 John M. MacKenzie, *Orientalism: History, Theory and the Arts* (Manchester, 1995), p. 77.

24 For the example of Brighton, see Timothy Carden, *The Encyclopedia of Brighton* (Lewes, 1990), entry 43.

25 Christopher Somerville, *Britain beside the Sea* (London, 1989), p. 207.

26 Quoted in John K. Walton, 'Municipal Government and the Holiday Industry in Blackpool, 1876–1914', in *Leisure in Britain, 1780–1939*, ed. John K. Walton and James Walvin (Manchester, 1983), p. 172.

27 Vicki Gold Levi and Lee Eisenberg, *Atlantic City: 125 Years of Ocean Madness* (New York, 1979), pp. 17–28.

28 A useful account of English resort cliff railways and lifts is Michael J. Burrell, *Cliffhangers* (Sidcup, 2000).

29 Smets, 'Promenade', p. 6.

30 Ward, Lock & Co., *A Pictorial and Descriptive Guide to Ramsgate* (London, 1910), pp. 7–8.

31 Quoted in Levi and Eisenberg, *Atlantic City*, pp. 20–25.

32 Quoted in C. H. Bishop, *Folkestone: The Story of a Town* (Folkestone, 1973), p. 120.

33 Ted Lightbown, *Blackpool: A Pictorial History* (Chichester, 1994) and Brian Turner and Steve Palmer, *The Blackpool Story* (Cleveleys, Lancs., 1976).

34 Quoted in Edmund M. Gilbert, *Brighton: Old Ocean's Bauble* (London, 1954), p. 169.

35 Levi and Eisenberg, *Atlantic City*, and Charles Denson, *Coney Island Lost and Found* (Berkeley, CA, 2002).

36 Frederick Treves, *The Riviera of the Corniche Road* (London, 1921), pp. 15–6.

37 Darwin Porter and Danforth Prince, *Frommer's France 2003* (New York, 2002), p. 560.

38 Mel Gooding, *Promenade: An Architectural Collaboration for Bridlington* (Beverley, 2001).

39 Smets, 'Promenade', p. 6.

CHAPTER SIX: ARCHITECTURE FOR SEA AND BEACH

1 From the engraving by Samuel and Nathaniel Buck, *The South Prospect of Scarborough, in the County of Yorkshire* (London, 1745).

2 John F. Travis, *The Rise of the Devon Seaside Resorts, 1750–1900* (Exeter, 1993), p. 9.

3 Tobias Smollett, *The Expedition of Humphry Clinker* (Harmondsworth, 1967), p. 213.

4 I. Stell, *A Guide to Hastings* (Hastings, 1794), p. 69.

5 Quoted in John Whyman, *The Early Kentish Seaside, 1736–1840* (Gloucester, 1985), pp. 186–7.

6 Ward, Lock & Co., *A Pictorial and Descriptive Guide to Ilfracombe and North-West Devon* (London, c. 1909), p. 5.

7 L. Upcott Gill (publisher), *Seaside Watering Places* (London, 1888), p. 168.

8 Quoted in Whyman, *The Early Kentish Seaside*, p. 165.

9 Andrea Inglis, *Beside the Seaside: Victorian Resorts in the Nineteenth Century* (Carlton South, Victoria, 1999).

10 John Travis, 'Continuity and Change in English Sea-Bathing, 1730–1900: A Case of Swimming with the Tide', in *Recreation and the Sea*, ed. Stephen Fisher (Exeter, 1997), pp. 8–35.

11 Anonymous, *A Tour of Worthing; or, Idle Hours Not Idly Spent* (London, 1805), pp. 72–3.

12 John Bolwell, *The Worthing Guide* (Worthing, 1817), p. 30.

13 Anon., *A Week in Worthing* (London, 1823), pp. 46–8.

14 Emlyn Thomas and Ron Iden, 'John Marsh and the Seaside', *West Sussex History*, 11 (1993), p. 5.

15 Quoted in Whyman, *The Early Kentish Seaside*, p. 179.

16 Charles Dickens, 'The Tuggses at Ramsgate', in *Dickens' Journalism: Sketches by Boz and Other Early Papers*, ed. Michael Slater (London, 1994), p. 336.

17 Christiana Payne, 'Seaside Visitors: Idlers, Thinkers and Patriots in Mid-Nineteenth-Century Britain', in *Water, Leisure and Culture: European Historical Perspectives*, ed. Susan C. Anderson and Bruce H. Tabb (Oxford, 2002), pp. 87–104.

18 Ruth Manning-Sanders, *Seaside England* (London, 1951).

19 Sarah Howell, *The Seaside* (London, 1974), p. 24.

20 Travis, *Devon Seaside Resorts*, p. 178.

21 Philip Henry Gosse, *Tenby: A Sea-Side Holiday* (London, 1856), pp. 12–13.

22 For a twentieth-century version, see Sylvia Endacott, *'Our Mary': Mary Wheatland, the Grace Darling of Berstead* (Bognor Regis, 1987).

23 Quoted in Whyman, *The Early Kentish Seaside*, p. 183.

24 Edward Cresy, *Report to the General Board of Health on a Preliminary Inquiry into the Sewerage, Drainage, and Supply of Water, and Sanitary Condition of the Inhabitants of the Town of Worthing* (London, 1850), p. 17.

25 Travis, *Devon Seaside Resorts*, p. 180.

26 Travis, *Devon Seaside Resorts*, p. 180.

27 Travis, 'Continuity and Change', p. 23.

28 Borough of Worthing, *Byelaws with Respect to Public Bathing* (Worthing, 1902).

29 Gordon H. Luck, 'Walter Fagg's "Railway" – a "Transport" Oddity', *Bluebell News*, XV/1(1983), pp. 20–24.

30 Travis, *Devon Seaside Resorts*, p. 121.

31 Travis, *Devon Seaside Resorts*, p. 121.

32 Travis, *Devon Seaside Resorts*, p. 178.

33 Towner Art Gallery, *The Modesty Machine* (Eastbourne, 1992), p. 9.

34 Quoted in George Ryley Scott, *The Story of Baths and Bathing* (London, 1939), p. 170.

35 *Brighton Herald*, 16 May 1896.

36 H. F. Hoden, 'The Boy's Own Portable Bathing Tent', *Boy's Own Paper*, XIV/686 (1892), pp. 381–3.

37 Travis, 'Continuity and Change', p. 25.

38 Travis, 'Continuity and Change', p. 26.

39 Travis, *Devon Seaside Resorts*, p. 182.

40 Quoted in *Worthing and District Advertiser*, 30 November 1988.

41 J. Davis, *Hastings and St Leonards Visitors Guide* (Hastings, 1905).

42 For the United States, see Lena Lencek and Gideon Bosker, *Making Waves: Swimsuits and the Undressing of America* (San Francisco, CA, 1989); for Australia, Geoffrey Dutton, *Sun, Sea, Surf and Sand – The Myth of the Beach* (Melbourne, 1985) and Inglis, *Beside the Seaside*.

43 Quoted in *Bexhill Observer*, 18 September 1954.

44 Travis, 'Continuity and Change', p. 30.

45 Ivor Brown, *The Heart of England* (London, 1935), pp. 18–19.

46 Scott, *The Story of Baths and Bathing*, p. 261.

47 *Illustrated Handbook of the Bay: For Those Seeking Recreation During the*

Summer Months (Melbourne, 1876–7), p. 26, quoted in Inglis, *Beside the Seaside*, p. 63.

48 *Illustrated Handbook of the Bay*, p. 27, quoted in Inglis, *Beside the Seaside*, pp. 63–4.

49 Graham McInnes, *The Road to Gundagai* (London, 1965), pp. 68–9, quoted in Dutton, *Sun, Sea, Surf and Sand*, pp. 51–2.

50 Inglis, *Beside the Seaside*, p. 63.

51 Thomas Mann, *Death in Venice and Other Stories* (London, 1996), p. 223.

52 Mann, *Death in Venice*, p. 241.

53 John Hooker Packard, *Sea-Air and Sea-Bathing* (Philadelphia, 1880), p. 35.

54 Melissa E. Baldock, 'Preserving the Honky-Tonk: Coney Island's Future in its Amusement Past', unpublished M.SC. thesis, Columbia University, New York, 2003, p. 28.

55 Anthony Hern, *The Seaside Holiday: The History of the English Seaside Resort* (London, 1967).

56 John K. Walton, *The British Seaside: Holidays and Resorts in the Twentieth Century* (Manchester, 2000).

57 Felicity Stafford and Nigel Yates, *The Later Kentish Seaside* (Gloucester, 1985), p. 113.

58 Alan Baxter & Associates, *Tinside Pool, the Hoe and Hoe Foreshore: A Conservation Plan* (London, 2002).

59 David Scurrell, Felicity Stafford and John Whyman, *Margate: A Resort History* (Margate, 1986), pp. 57–8.

60 Ward, Lock & Co., *A Pictorial and Descriptive Guide to Margate and North-East Kent* (London, 1933), pp. 14–15 and p. 13.

61 Scurrell, Stafford and Whyman, *Margate: A Resort History*, p. 62.

62 Southport Corporation, *Sunny Southport: Official Guide, 1938–39* (Liverpool, 1938), p. 17.

63 'Developments at Poole', *Municipal Review* (September 1932), pp. 378–9.

64 Poole Borough Council, *Official Guide to Poole* (Poole, 1934).

65 Ward, Lock & Co., *A Pictorial and Descriptive Guide to Bournemouth, Poole and District* (London, 1937), p. 67.

66 *The Guardian*, 17 April 2004.

67 Walton, *The British Seaside*, p. 100.

68 *The Guardian*, 24 June 1995.

69 *Daily Telegraph*, 16 June 2001.

70 *The Guardian*, 4 January 2002.

71 *The Guardian*, 14 May 2005.

72 *The Guardian*, 5 January 2002.

73 *Daily Mail*, 30 July 2004.

74 *Sunday Telegraph*, 24 August 2003.

75 Mel Gooding, *Promenade: An Architectural Collaboration for Bridlington* (Beverley, 2001), p. 95.

76 Mandalay Bay Las Vegas, 'Hotel Brochure' (2002).

77 *Daily Telegraph*, 22 May 2004

78 Phil Vallack, *Naked as the Day* (Hastings, 1983).

79 *West Sussex Gazette*, 11 October 1984.

80 *West Sussex Gazette*, 21 February 1985.

81 *West Sussex Gazette*, 28 February 1985.

82 *The Guardian*, 18 July 1989.

83 Michael Collins, *The Feminists Go Swimming* (London, 1996), p. 2.

CHAPTER SEVEN: FROM BATH HOUSE TO WATER PARK

1 John Whyman, *The Early Kentish Seaside, 1736–1840* (Gloucester, 1985), pp. 160–61.

2 For the earlier history of baths and pools away from the seaside, see Thomas A. P. van Leeuwen, *The Springboard in the Pond: An Intimate History of the Swimming Pool* (Cambridge, MA, 1999).

3 Sue Farrant, *Georgian Brighton, 1740–1820* (Brighton, 1980).

4 Edmund M. Gilbert, *Brighton: Old Ocean's Bauble* (London, 1954), pp. 66–7, and Timothy Carden, *The Encyclopedia of Brighton* (Lewes, 1990), entry 7.

5 Unless otherwise stated the following account of Brighton's eighteenth- and nineteenth-century baths is derived from Gilbert, *Brighton*, pp. 66–75, and Carden, *Encyclopedia of Brighton*, entry 7. Details of baths in Kent resorts are provided by Whyman, *The Early Kentish Seaside*, pp. 165–76.

6 Whyman, *The Early Kentish Seaside*, pp. 171–2.

7 Michael H. Fisher, *The First Indian Author in English: Dean Mahomed (1759–1851) in India, Ireland and England* (Delhi, 1996), p. 292.

8 Charles Wright, *The Brighton Ambulator* (London, 1818), p. 138.

9 George Ryley Scott, *The Story of Baths and Bathing* (London, 1939), p. 143.

10 Fisher, *The First Indian Author*, pp. 279–82.

11 Fisher, *The First Indian Author*, pp. 321–2.

12 Gilbert, *Brighton*, p. 71.

13 Gilbert, *Brighton*, p. 68.

14 Southport Corporation, *Sunny Southport: Official Guide, 1938–39* (Southport, 1938), p. 103.

15 'Open Air Baths: Completion and Opening of Pools and Hastings and Guildford', *Municipal Review* (July 1933), p. 263.

16 Hastings Corporation, *Hastings For Health: Official Handbook, 1939–40* (Hastings, 1939), p. 41.

17 'New Public Baths: Completion of Bournemouth's £78,000 Sea Front

Scheme', *Municipal Review*, (April 1937), pp. 149–50.

18 Weston-super-Mare, *The New Swimming Pool Weston-super-Mare, Souvenir Programme* (Weston-super-Mare, 1937), p. 15.

19 These details come from 'Open Air Baths: Completion and Opening of Pools and Hastings and Guildford', *Municipal Review*, (July 1933), p. 263.

20 'Open-Air Baths: Brighton Corporation's Proposed £75,000 Scheme', *Municipal Review*, (April 1934), p. 123.

21 'Open-Air Baths, Brighton Corporation', *Municipal Review*, p. 123.

22 'Open-Air Baths. New Pools Opened at Croydon and Ramsgate', *Municipal Review* (September 1935), pp. 371–2.

23 Steven Braggs and Diane Harris, *Sun, Fun and Crowds: Seaside Holidays Between the Wars* (Stroud, 2000).

24 Hastings Corporation, *Hastings and St Leonards: Official Handbook, 1935* (Hastings, 1935), p. 25.

25 Hastings Corporation, *Hastings For Health: Official Handbook, 1939–40* (Hastings, 1939), p. 5.

26 Scott, *Baths and Bathing*, p. 181.

27 Southport Corporation, *Sunny Southport*, p. 17.

28 'Open-Air Baths: New Pools Opened at Croydon and Ramsgate'.

29 S. D. Adshead and H. V. Overfield, *The Further Development of Scarborough* (Scarborough, 1938), p. 42.

30 'Coastal Developments at Brighton: Completion of Marine Drive and Undercliff Promenade', *Municipal Review* (September 1935), p. 368.

31 John Hassan, *The Seaside, Health and the Environment in England and Wales since 1800* (Aldershot, 2003), pp. 109–11.

32 Ward, Lock & Co., *Scarborough and District* (London, 1922), p. 22.

33 Anon., *Scarborough: The Glory of the English Coast* (n.p., *c*. 1925), p. 11.

34 Alan Powers, ed., *Farewell My Lido* (London, 1991).

35 These details come from 'Blackpool's Amenities: Its Promenades, Public Walks and Magnificent Park', *Municipal Review* (June 1932), pp. 231–2.

36 Southport Corporation, *Sunny Southport*. p. 16.

37 Felicity Stafford and Nigel Yates, *The Later Kentish Seaside* (Gloucester, 1985), pp. 116–17.

38 Powers, *Farewell My Lido*, p. 4.

39 These details come from 'Open Air Baths: Completion and Opening of Pools in Hastings and Guildford', *Municipal Review* (July 1933), p. 263.

40 Alan Baxter & Associates, *Tinside Pool, the Hoe and Hoe Foreshore: A Conservation Plan* (London, 2002).

41 Weston-super-Mare, *The New Swimming Pool*, p. 15.

42 Powers, *Farewell My Lido*, p. 26.

43 Saltdean Estate Company, *The Ocean Hotel* (Brighton, *c*. 1937), p. 10. See

also Carden, *The Encyclopedia of Brighton*, entry 171.

44 Carden, *The Encyclopedia of Brighton*, entry 171.

45 Adshead and Overfield, *The Further Development of Scarborough*, p. 42.

46 Ward, Lock & Co., *Scarborough and the Yorkshire Coast* (London, 1950), p. 95.

47 County Borough of Blackpool, *The Official Holiday Journal* (Blackpool, 1994), p. 14.

48 *Scarborough Evening News*, 4 March 2002.

49 Colin Ward and Dennis Hardy, *Goodnight Campers! The History of the British Holiday Camp* (London, 1986), p. 130.

50 Scarborough Borough Council, *Scarborough, Whitby and Filey Holiday Guide* (Scarborough, 2002).

51 *Guardian Magazine*, 8 May 1999.

52 *Daily Telegraph*, 17 June 2000.

53 Powers, *Farewell My Lido*, p. 14.

54 See, for example, Ian Parker, 'Last of the Lidos', *Independent Magazine*, 1 July 1992, and *Daily Telegraph*, 17 June 2000.

55 Powers, *Farewell My Lido*, p. 2.

56 Ken Worpole, *Here Comes the Sun: Architecture and Public Space in Twentieth-century European Culture* (London, 2000), p. 125.

57 Marilyn Blaisdell, *San Francisciana Photographs of Sutro Baths* (San Francisco, 1987), p. 26. Unless otherwise indicated., this account uses contemporary quotes from the introductory essay by Robert Ehler Blaisdell.

58 John Allen quoted in Ariel Rubissow Okamoto, *A Day at the Seaside: San Francisco's Sutro Heights, Cliff House, and Sutro Baths* (San Francisco, 1998), p. 63.

59 Okamoto, *A Day at the Seaside*, quote p. 67.

60 Blaisdell, *Sutro Baths*, p. 46.

61 Okamoto, *A Day at the Seaside*, quote p. 75.

62 *Everyone is Different: Short Breaks at Centre Parcs 2005* (Newark, 2005), p. 26.

63 Blackpool Borough Council, *Blackpool* (Blackpool, 1989), p. 17.

64 George Orwell, 'Pleasure Spots', in *Collected Essays*, vol. IV (Harmondsworth, 1970).

65 David Boyle, *Authenticity: Brands, Fakes, Spin and the Lust for Real Life* (London, 2003).

66 David Boyle, 'Ocean Dome . . . The Most Artificial Place on Earth?', *The Ecologist*, XXXIII/8 (2003), p. 31.

67 Edmund Gosse, *Father and Son: A Study of Two Temperaments* (London, 1974), p. 78.

68 Orlando Tourism Bureau, *Orlando Destination Imagination* (Orlando, 2000), p. 15.

69 *The Times*, 1 July 2000.

70 For an analysis of the related Sea World theme parks, see Susan G. Davies, *Spectacular Nature: Corporate Culture and the Sea World Experience* (Berkeley, CA, 1997).

CHAPTER EIGHT: WALKING ON WATER

1 Alain Corbin, *The Lure of the Sea: The Discovery of the Seaside in the Western World, 1750–1840* (Cambridge, 1994), p. 263.

2 Jane Austen, *Persuasion* (London, 1932), p. 81.

3 Austen, *Persuasion*, p. 94.

4 Marian Lane, *Piers of the Isle of Wight: A Nostalgic View* (Isle of Wight, 1996).

5 Quoted in David Scurrell, Felicity Stafford and John Whyman, *Margate: A Resort History* (Margate, 1986), p. 18.

6 John George Bishop, *The Brighton Chain Pier: In Memoriam* (Brighton, 1897), p. xviii.

7 Corbin, *The Lure of the Sea*, p. 265.

8 *New Monthly Magazine*, LXI (1841), p. 168, quoted in Edmund M. Gilbert, *Brighton: Old Ocean's Bauble* (London, 1954), p. 129.

9 John. H. Clapham, *An Economic History of Modern Britain: The Early Railway Age, 1820–1850* (Cambridge, 1959), p. 8.

10 Bishop, *The Brighton Chain Pier*, p. 23.

11 Stella Beddoe, '"Hung Like a Fairy Fabric O'er the Sea . . ." The Brighton Chain Suspension Pier', in *Brighton Revealed Through Artists' Eyes, c. 1760 – c. 1960*, ed. David Beevers (Brighton, 1995), p. 40.

12 *The Times*, 2 December 1823.

13 Beddoe, 'The Brighton Chain Suspension Pier'.

14 William Makepeace Thackeray, *The Newcomes* (London, 1893), pp. 102–3.

15 John Walton, 'Introduction', in Richard Fischer and John Walton, *British Piers* (London, 1987), p. 12.

16 E. W. Shepherd, *The Story of Southend Pier . . . and its Associations* (Letchworth, 1979).

17 John. H. Clapham, *An Economic History of Modern Britain: Free Trade and Steel, 1850–1886* (Cambridge, 1952), p. 518.

18 John K. Walton, *The English Seaside Resort: A Social History, 1750–1914* (Leicester, 1983), p. 173.

19 Quoted in Simon H. Adamson, *Seaside Piers* (London, 1977), p. 40.

20 Clapham, *Free Trade and Steel*, p. 518.

21 Adamson, *Seaside Piers*.

22 Walton, *The English Seaside Resort*, pp. 164–6.

23 John Field, 'The Battle of Southsea', *Portsmouth Papers*, 34 (1981).

24 John F. Travis, *The Rise of the Devon Seaside Resorts, 1750–1900* (Exeter, 1993), p. 184.

25 David Cannadine, *Lords and Landlords: The Aristocracy and the Towns, 1774–1967* (Leicester, 1980), p. 355.

26 Unless otherwise indicated, this section draws on Fred Gray, *Walking on Water: The West Pier Story* (Brighton, 1998).

27 *Brighton Herald*, 4 July 1863.

28 The account of the pier's opening and details of its architecture and engineering come from *The Brighton Guardian*, 10 October 1866 and *Brighton Examiner*, 9 October 1866.

29 *The Builder*, 13 October 1866.

30 *Brighton Herald*, 8 April 1865.

31 *Brighton Herald*, 1 April 1865.

32 *The Builder*, 13 October 1866.

33 *Brighton Examiner*, 9 October 1866.

34 *The Times*, 4 August 1868.

35 Richard Jefferies, *The Open Air* (London, 1948), p. 116.

36 *Illustrated Times*, 15 April 1865.

37 Ernest Ryman, *The Romance of the Old Chain Pier at Brighton* (Brighton, 1996).

38 *Brighton Gazette*, 9 March 1893.

39 *Sussex Daily News*, 14 October 1893.

40 *Daily Telegraph*, 20 October 1893.

41 *The Times*, 28 May 1912.

42 *Brighton Herald*, 25 March 1916.

43 Beevers, *Brighton Revealed*.

44 Brighton Corporation, *Brighton Official Handbook, 1934–35* (Brighton, 1934).

45 Harold Clunn, *Famous South Coast Pleasure Resorts Past and Present* (London, 1929), p. 65.

46 Graham Greene, *Brighton Rock* (London, 1938).

47 Ron Cunningham, *The Crowd Roars: Tales from the Life of a Professional Stuntman* (Brighton, 1998).

48 Patrick Hamilton, *The West Pier* (London, 1951), pp. 57–8.

49 Brighton Corporation and Hove Corporation, *Brighton and Hove Official Guidebook* (Brighton, 1968), p. 62.

50 Frank Gray, 'Oh! What a Lovely War', in Royal Pavilion, Libraries and Museums, Brighton and Hove, *Kiss and Kill: Film Visions of Brighton* (Brighton, 2002), pp. 22–9.

51 Ian Nairn and Nikolaus Pevsner, *The Buildings of England: Sussex* (Harmondsworth, 1965), p. 450.

52 English Tourist Board, *Brighton Tourism Study* (London, 1983), p. 79.

53 Hugh Casson, *Observer Magazine*, 8 July 1984.

54 Helen Zahavi, *Dirty Weekend* (London, 1991), p. 171.

55 Georg Simmel, 'The Ruin', in *Essays on Sociology, Philosophy and Aesthetics: Georg Simmel*, ed. Kurt H. Wolff (New York, 1959), pp. 259–66, p. 266.

56 E. Cohen, 'Contemporary Tourism – Trends and Challenges: Sustainable Authenticity or Contrived Post-modernity?', in *Change in Tourism: People, Places, Processes*, ed. Richard W. Butler and Douglas D. Pearce (London, 1995), p. 15.

57 David Lowenthal, *The Heritage Crusade and the Spoils of History* (Cambridge, 1998), p. 91.

58 *The Guardian*, 25 January 2003.

59 *The Times*, 30 December 2002, *The Guardian*, 29 March 2003, and *The Guardian*, 12 May 2003.

60 Richard Morrice, 'A Report into Recent Practice Following Catastrophic Damage at Historic Places, with Particular Reference to Brighton's West Pier', English Heritage report (December 2003), p. 18, and English Heritage, 'Saving Brighton's Seafront Treasure', *Heritage Today*, (June 2004), p. 7.

61 *The Times*, 29 January 2004.

62 *The Independent*, 30 July 2004.

63 *Daily Telegraph*, 31 July 2004.

64 Tim Mickleburgh, *Glory Days: Piers* (Shepperton, Surrey, 1999)

65 English Tourist Board, *Turning the Tide: A Heritage and Environment Strategy for a Seaside Resort* (London, 1993), English Tourism Council, *Sea Changes: Creating World-Class Resorts in England* (London, 2001), and English Heritage and Commission for Architecture and the Built Environment, *Shifting Sands: Design and the Changing Image of English Seaside Towns* (London, 2003).

66 John Urry, *The Tourist Gaze* (London, 2002), pp. 30–35.

67 Matthew Parris, 'Why Britain's Piers Should be Allowed to Slip Beneath the Waves', *The Spectator*, 29 November 1997, p. 10.

68 Walton, 'Introduction', p. 30.

69 Fred Gray, 'Pier Pressures', *Geographical*, LXXI 4 (2000), pp. 14–22.

70 Fred Gray, 'Learning from the Seaside', *Journal of Access, Policy and Practice*, II/1 (2004), pp. 83–92.

71 Vicki Gold Levi and Lee Eisenberg, *Atlantic City: 125 Years of Ocean Madness* (New York, 1979).

72 George Sternlieb and James W. Hughes, *The Atlantic City Gamble* (Cambridge, MA, 1983).

73 Jim Futrell, *Amusement Parks of New Jersey* (Mechanicsburg, PA, 2004).

74 Jeffrey Stanton, *Venice California: 'Coney Island of the Pacific'* (Los Angeles, CA, 1993).

75 Karal Ann Marling, ed., *Designing Disney's Theme Parks: The Architecture of Reassurance* (New York, 1997).

76 Stanton, *Venice California*, and Fred E. Basten, *Paradise by the Sea: Santa Monica Bay* (Los Angeles, CA, 1997).

77 Jeffrey Stanton, *Santa Monica Pier: A History from 1875 to 1990* (Los Angeles, CA, 1990).

78 Basten, *Paradise by the Sea*.

79 Fred Gray and Mary Hoar, 'Marcher sur l'eau: une histoire des jetées promenades de Brighton et Trouville', in *Bains de Mer et Thermalisme en Normandie. Actes du 36ᵉ congrès organisée par la Fédération des Sociétés Historiques et Archeologiques de Normandie Caen*: 2002, pp. 93–105, and Emmanuelle Gallo, *Les Roches noires Trouville-sur-Mer* (Cabourg, 2000), pp. 38–45.

80 Guy Junien Moreau, *Le Casino de la Jetée-Promenade* (Nice, 1993).

81 Wilhelm Huls and Ulf Böttcher, *Bäderarchitektur* (Rostock, 1998).

CHAPTER NINE: PAVILIONS AND AMUSEMENT PARKS

1 A detailed study is provided by Lynn F. Pearson, *The People's Palaces: Britain's Seaside Pleasure Buildings of 1870–1914* (Buckingham, 1991).

2 Timothy Carden, *The Encyclopedia of Brighton* (Lewes, 1990), entry 3.

3 Ward, Lock & Co., *A Pictorial and Descriptive Guide to Bournemouth* (London, c. 1937), p. 36.

4 'Seaside Pavilion Gets New Life', *Architects Journal* (6 January 1993), pp. 27–36.

5 John Williams and Andy Salvage, *A History of Margate's Winter Gardens* (Thanet, Kent, c. 1992).

6 Corporation of Folkestone, *Folkestone Official Guide* (Folkestone, c. 1947).

7 'Folkestone and its Foreshore', *Architectural Review*, LXXXIII (1938), p. 19.

8 Bill Curtis, *Blackpool Tower* (Lavenham, 1988).

9 James Laver, 'Blackpool', in *Beside the Seaside*, ed. Yvonne Cloud (London, 1934), pp. 163–6.

10 Edmund Vale, *North Country* (London, 1937), p. 50.

11 John K. Walton, 'The Re-making of a Popular Resort: Blackpool Tower and the Boom of the 1890s', *Local Historian*, XXIV/4 (1994), pp. 194–205.

12 *The Times*, 2 August 1996.

13 Fred Gray, ed., *Bexhill Voices* (Falmer, Sussex, 1994).

14 Alastair Fairley, *Bucking the Trend: The Life and Times of the Ninth Earl De La Warr, 1900–1976* (Bexhill, 2001).

15 Alan Powers, *Serge Chermayeff: Designer, Architect, Teacher* (London, 2001), p. 72.

16 'Leisure at the Seaside', *Architectural Review*, LXXX (1936), p. 23.

17 Powers, *Serge Chermayeff*, p. 77.

18 *The Independent*, 11December 1991.

19 Russell Stevens and Peter Willis, 'Earl De La Warr and the Competition for the Bexhill Pavilion, 1933–34', *Architectural History*, XXXIII (1990), p. 146.

20 Stevens and Willis, 'Earl De La Warr', p. 143.

21 Stevens and Willis, 'Earl De La Warr', p. 143.

22 *The Guardian*, 18 October 1997.

23 Bexhill Corporation, *Bexhill-on-Sea, For... Health & Happiness, Holidays and Homes: The Official Guide of the Corporation* (Bexhill, 1935), p. 15.

24 Bexhill Corporation, *Bexhill-on-Sea*, p. 134.

25 Leisure at the Seaside', *Architectural Review*, p. 18.

26 Bexhill Corporation, *Bexhill-on-Sea Official Guide* (Bexhill, 1939), p 31.

27 R. B. White, *Qualitative Studies of Buildings: The De La Warr Pavilion, Bexhill-on-Sea. National Building Studies Special Report 39* (London, 1966).

28 *Daily Telegraph*, 25 October 2003.

29 Stephen Bayley, 'Patrons of the Modern Movement', *Architectural Design*, XLIX, 10–11 (1979), pp. 90–95, p. 90.

30 Paul Theroux, *The Kingdom by the Sea* (London, 1983), pp. 40–41.

31 *The Independent*, 4 August 2001.

32 *The Guardian*, 16 April 2002.

33 *The Observer*, 19 March 2000.

34 *Daily Telegraph*, 25 October 2003.

35 De La Warr Pavilion, *Building for the Future* (Bexhill, 2001), p. 4.

36 Stevens and Willis, 'Earl De La Warr', p. 143.

37 Accounts are provided by Charles Denson, *Coney Island: Lost and Found* (Berkeley, CA, 2002) and Michael Immerso, *Coney Island: The People's Playground* (New Brunswick, NJ, 2002).

38 Robert Lewis, 'Seaside Holiday Resorts in the United States and Britain: A Review', *Urban History Yearbook, 1980* (Leicester, 1980), p. 48.

39 Melissa E. Baldock, 'Preserving the Honky-Tonk: Coney Island's Future in its Amusement Past', unpublished M.SC. thesis, Columbia University, New York, 2003.

40 An account of Dreamland's history is provided in Nick Evans, *Dreamland Remembered: 140 Years of Seaside Fun in Margate* (Whitstable, 2003).

41 Ward, Lock & Co., *A Pictorial and Descriptive Guide to Margate and North-East Kent* (London, c. 1933), p. 15.

42 Quoted in Felicity Stafford and Nigel Yates, *The Later Kentish Seaside* (Gloucester, 1985), p. 149.

43 Stafford and Yates, *The Later Kentish Seaside*, pp. 150–51.

44 Quotes in Stafford and Yates, *The Later Kentish Seaside*, p. 120.

45 Kaye Webb, 'By the Sea', *Leader Magazine*, X/29 (1948), pp. 20–21.

46 Nick Laister, 'Fairgrounds for Recognition', *Heritage Today* (March 2004), pp. 19–20.

47 The history of the Pleasure Beach is told in Peter Bennett, *Blackpool Pleasure Beach: A Century of Fun* (Blackpool, 1996) and Brian Turner and Steve Palmer, *The Blackpool Story* (Cleveleys, Lancs., 1976).

48 See, for example, Vale, *North Country*.

49 Laver, 'Blackpool', pp. 171–2.

50 T. A. Bennett, 'A Thousand and One Troubles: Blackpool Pleasure Beach', in *Formations of Pleasure*, ed. Formations Editorial Collective (London, 1983), p. 139.

51 Bennett, 'A Thousand and One Troubles', p. 153.

52 Quoted in Bennett, *Blackpool Pleasure Beach*, p. 62.

53 Bennett, 'A Thousand and One Troubles', p. 145.

54 David Bennett, *Roller Coaster: Wooden and Steel Coasters, Twisters and Corkscrews* (London, 1998), p. 130.

CHAPTER TEN: SLEEPING BY THE SEA

1 Charles Wright, *The Brighton Ambulator* (London, 1818), p, 25.

2 F. Scott Fitzgerald, *Tender is the Night* (Harmondsworth, 1982), pp. 35–6.

3 John Piper, 'The Nautical Style', *Architectural Review*, LXXXIII (1938), p. 13. The building of Regency Brighton is detailed in Antony Dale, *Fashionable Brighton, 1820–1860* (London, 1947).

4 Mary Blume, *Côte d'Azur: Inventing the French Riviera* (London, 1992) and Shirley Johnson, *The Villas of the Riviera: Magnificence and Majesty on the Côte d'Azur* (London, 1998).

5 Gilles Plum, *Villas Balnéaires du Second Empire* (Cabourg, 2001).

6 Wilhelm Hüls and Ulf Böttcher, *Bäderarchitekur* (Rostock, 1998).

7 Sidmouth Urban District Council, *Official Guide and Souvenir of Sidmouth* (Gloucester, c. 1959), pp. 57–9.

8 John Hooker Packard, *Sea-Air and Sea-Bathing* (Philadelphia, PA, 1880), pp. 27–8.

9 Alastair Gordon, *Weekend Utopia: Modern Living in the Hamptons* (New York, 2001).

10 *The Guardian*, 25 June 2001. See also Mark Darley and Pilar Viladas, *California Beach Houses: Style, Interiors, and Architecture* (San Francisco, CA, 1996).

11 Ian Nairn and Nikolaus Pevsner, *The Buildings of England: Sussex* (Harmondsworth, 1965), p. 528.

12 The bungalow is superbly analysed in Anthony D. King, *The Bungalow: The Production of a Global Culture* (New York, 1995).

13 Quoted in Felicity Stafford and Nigel Yates, *The Later Kentish Seaside* (Gloucester, 1985), p. 56.

14 Quoted in Stafford and Yates, *The Later Kentish Seaside*, p. 59.

15 Quoted in Stafford and Yates, *The Later Kentish Seaside*, pp. 59–60.

16 John Buchan, *The Thirty-Nine Steps* (London, 1991), p. 110.

17 Ward, Lock & Co., *A Pictorial and Descriptive Guide to Ramsgate and North East Kent* (London, c. 1910), pp. 35–6.

18 *Daily Telegraph*, 25 May 2002.

19 Dennis Hardy and Colin Ward, *Arcadia for All: The Legacy of a Makeshift*

Landscape (London, 1984), p. vii.

20   Ella Carter, ed., *Seaside Houses and Bungalows* (London, 1937), p. 14.

21   Quoted in Gerard Young, *A History of Bognor Regis* (Chichester, 1983), p. 218.

22   Ward, Lock & Co., *Worthing* (London, *c.* 1931), p. 47.

23   N.E.B. Wolters, *Bungalow Town: Theatre & Film Colony* (Shoreham-by-Sea, 1985), p. 27.

24   Peter Dickens, 'A Disgusting Blot on the Landscape', *New Society* (17 July 1975), pp. 127–9.

25   S.P.B. Mais, 'A Plain Man Looks at England', in *Britain and the Beast*, ed. Clough Williams-Ellis (London, 1937), p. 216.

26   Howard Marshall, 'A Rake's Progress', in *Britain and the Beast*, p. 166.

27   Nairn and Pevsner, *Sussex*, p. 578.

28   English Heritage, *Shifting Sands: Design and the Changing Image of English Seaside Towns* (London, 2003), p. 22.

29   Ginny Anderson, 'Bach to the Future', *Wallpaper* (June 2004), pp. 56–9.

30   Marsha Dean Phelts, *An American Beach for African Americans* (Gainesville, FL, 1997) and Russ Rymer, *Sea, Sand and Strife: A Saga of Race, Wealth and Memory* (New York, 1998). See also Cindy S. Aron, *Working At Play: A History of Vacations in the United States* (New York, 1999), pp. 214–16.

31   *Jacksonville Homebuyer* (Summer 2003).

32   Jill Drover, *Good Clean Fun: The Story of Britain's First Holiday Camp* (London, 1982).

33   Colin Ward and Dennis Hardy, *Goodnight Campers! The History of the British Holiday Camp* (London, 1986).

34   The most thoughtful history of the British holiday camps is Ward and Hardy, *Goodnight Campers!*

35   *Holiday Camp Review* (21 May–3 June 1949), p. 5.

36   Sue Read, *Hello Campers!* (London, 1986).

37   See, for example, Johnny Lancaster, *If It Hadn't Been Hi-de-Hi, It Wouldn't Have Been Funny!* (London, 1994).

38   *Holiday Camp Review* (21 May–3 June 1949), p. 4.

39   Prestatyn Holiday Camp, *Souvenir and Guide* (1953), p. 7.

40   Ward and Hardy, *Goodnight Campers!*, p. 147.

41   *Holiday Camp Review* (21 May–3 June 1949), p. 4.

42   Godfrey Winn, *Holiday Camp* (London, 1947), postscript.

43   See the early post-war discussion of holiday camps in J.A.R. Pimlott, *The Englishman's Holiday: A Social History* (Hassocks, 1976), pp. 246–53.

44   George Orwell, 'Pleasure Spots', in *Collected Essays*, vol. IV (Harmondsworth, 1970), p. 102.

45   This discussion draws on Stefano de Martino and Alex Wall, *Cities of Childhood: Italian Colonie of the 1930s* (London, 1988).

46   De Martino and Wall, *Cities of Childhood*, p. 12.

47   Hasso Spode, 'Ein Seebad für zwanzigtausend Volksgenossen: Zur Grammatik und Geschichte des Fordistischen Urlaubs', in *Reisekultur in Deutschland: Von der Weimarer Republik zum 'Dritten Reich'*, ed. P. J.

Brenner (Tübingen, 1997), pp. 7–47; Orvar Löfgren, *On Holiday: A History of Vacationing* (Berkeley, CA, 1999), pp. 241–4; and Christopher Stocks, 'Mein Camp', *Wallpaper* (October 1999), pp. 181–4.

48   Jan de Graaf with D'Laine Camp, *Europe: Coast Wise: An Anthology of Reflections on Architecture and Tourism* (Rotterdam, 1997), pp. 98–111, and *The Guardian*, 21 March 2005.

49   Fred Pontin, *My Happy Life, Always … Thumbs Up!* (London, 1991).

50   The heyday and subsequent dereliction of Butlin's Filey camp is recorded in Paul Wray, *Butlin's Filey: Thanks for the Memories* (Beverley, 1992).

51   Ward and Hardy, *Goodnight Campers!*, p. 156.

52   Ken Worpole, *Here Comes the Sun: Architecture and Public Space in Twentieth-century European Culture* (London, 2000), p. 38.

53   *Butlins Summer Holiday and Winter Breakaways* (Bognor Regis, 2003), p. 7.

54   *The Guardian*, 25 August 1997.

55   *The Times*, 5 December 2004.

56   The caravan park phenomenon is discussed in John K. Walton, *The British Seaside: Holidays and Resorts in the Twentieth Century* (Manchester, 2000), pp. 43–4.

57   André Rauch, 'Vacationing on France's Côte d'Azur, 1950–2000', in *Water, Leisure and Culture: European Historical Perspectives*, ed. Susan C. Anderson and Bruce H. Tabb (Oxford, 2002), pp. 223–38.

58   An account of the development and evolution of British resort accommodation is provided by John K. Walton, *The English Seaside Resort: A Social History, 1750–1914* (Leicester, 1983), and Walton, *The British Seaside*.

59   Edmund M. Gilbert, *Brighton: Old Ocean's Bauble* (London, 1954), p. 102.

60   For a locality-based study of the context and role of boarding houses and their landladies, see John K. Walton, *The Blackpool Landlady: A Social History* (Manchester, 1983).

61   Sarah Howell, *The Seaside* (London, 1974), pp. 126–33. For negative comments on lodging houses, see Pimlott, *The Englishman's Holiday*, pp. 126–7.

62   An example of the poetic damming of boarding houses is John Betjeman's 'Beside the Seaside' in his *Collected Poems* (London, 1979), pp. 157–65.

63   Derek Taylor and David Bush, *The Golden Age of British Hotels* (London, 1974).

64   A history of Eastbourne's Grand Hotel is provided by Peter Pugh, *Grand Hotel* (Eastbourne, 1987); an account of Torquay's Imperial Hotel in Gabor Denes, *The Story of the Imperial: The Life and Times of Torquay's Great Hotel* (Newton Abbot, 1982).

65   Kenneth Lindley, *Seaside Architecture* (London, 1973), pp. 79–90.

66   Emmanuelle Gallo, *Les Roches noires Trouville-sur-Mer* (Cabourg, 2000).

67   Blume, *Côte d'Azur*.

68 Vicki Gold Levi and Lee Eisenberg, *Atlantic City: 125 Years of Ocean Madness* (New York, 1979).

69 *New Riviera Côte D'Azur* (August–October 2003).

70 *Sunday Telegraph*, 13 July 2003.

71 *Daily Telegraph*, 28 June 2003.

72 *Daily Telegraph*, 28 June 2003.

73 The contemporary 'seaside style' of the purpose-built beach house is illustrated in Angelika Taschen, ed., *Seaside Style: Living on the Beach* (Cologne, 2002).

74 *Sunday Telegraph*, 22 June 2003.

SELECT BIBLIOGRAPHY

Adamson, Simon, *Seaside Piers* (London, 1977)

Akhtar, Miriam, and Steve Humphries, *Some Liked It Hot: The British on Holiday at Home and Abroad* (London, 2000)

Anderson, Susan C., and Bruce H. Tabb, eds, *Water, Leisure and Culture. European Historical Perspectives* (Oxford, 2002)

Aron, Cindy S., *Working at Play: A History of Vacations in the United States* (New York, 1999)

Bainbridge, Cyril, *Pavilions on the Sea: A History of the Seaside Pleasure Pier* (London, 1986)

Ballard, J. G., *Super-Cannes* (London, 2000)

Baranowski, Shelley, and Ellen Furlough, eds, *Being Elsewhere: Tourism, Consumer Culture, and Identity in Modern Europe and Northern America* (Ann Arbor, MI, 2001)

Basten, Fred E., *Paradise by the Sea: Santa Monica Bay* (Los Angeles, CA, 1997)

Beatty, Christina, and Stephen Fothergill, *The Seaside Economy: The Final Report of the Seaside Towns Research Project* (Sheffield, 2003)

Bell, Jo, Suzanne Clisby, Gary Craig, Lynda Measor, Stephanie Petrie and Nicky Stanley, *Living on the Edge: Sexual Behaviour and Young Parenthood in Seaside and Rural Areas* (Hull, 2004)

Bennett, David, *Roller Coaster: Wooden and Steel Coasters, Twisters and Corkscrews* (London, 1998)

Bennett, Peter, *Blackpool Pleasure Beach: A Century of Fun* (Blackpool, 1996)

Benson, John, *The Rise of Consumer Society in Britain, 1880-1980* (London, 1994)

Berry, Sue, 'Pleasure Gardens in Georgian and Regency Seaside Resorts: Brighton, 1750-1840', *Garden History*, XXVIII/2 (2000), pp. 222–30

Blaisdell, Marilyn, *San Francisciana Photographs of Sutro Baths* (San Francisco, CA, 1987)

Blume, Mary, *Côte d'Azur: Inventing the French Riviera* (London, 1992)

Blume, Mary, and Martine D'Astier, *Lartigue's Riviera* (Paris, 1997)

Boyle, David, *Authenticity: Brands, Fakes, Spin and the Lust for Real Life* (London, 2003)

Braggs, Steven, and Diane Harris, *Sun, Fun and Crowds: Seaside Holidays Between the Wars* (Stroud, 2000)

Brenner, P. J., ed. *Reisekultur in Deutschland. Von der Weimarer Republik zum 'Dritten Reich'* (Tübingen, 1997)

Buckland, Elfreda, *The World of Donald McGill* (Poole, 1984)

Butler, Richard W., and Douglas D. Pearce, eds, *Change in Tourism: People, Places, Processes* (London, 1995)

Cannadine, David, *Lords and Landlords: The Aristocracy and the Towns, 1774–1967* (Leicester, 1980)

——, *Ornamentalism: How the British Saw their Empire* (London, 2001)

Carden, Timothy, *The Encyclopedia of Brighton* (Lewes, 1990)

Cole, Beverley, and Richard Durack, *Happy as a Sand-Boy: Early Railway Posters* (York, 1990)

——, *Railway Posters 1923–1947* (London, 1992)

Collas, Philippe, and Éric Villedary, *Edith Wharton's French Riviera* (Paris, 2002)

Conner, Patrick, *Oriental Architecture in the West* (London, 1979)

Connolly, Joseph, *Beside the Seaside* (London, 1999)

Corbin, Alain, *The Lure of the Sea: The Discovery of the Seaside in the Western World, 1750–1840* (Cambridge, 1994)

Crinson, Mark, *Empire Building, Orientalism and Victorian Architecture* (London, 1996)

Cross, Gary, ed., *Worktowners at Blackpool: Mass-Observation and Popular Leisure in the 1930s* (London, 1990)

Crouch, David, and Nina Lübbren, eds, *Visual Culture and Tourism* (Oxford, 2003)

Curtis, Bill, *Blackpool Tower* (Lavenham, 1988)

Dale, Anthony, *Fashionable Brighton 1820–1860* (London, 1947)

——, *The History and Architecture of Brighton* (Brighton, 1950)

Darley, Mark, and Pilar Viladas, *California Beach Houses. Style, Interiors, and Architecture* (San Francisco, CA, 1996)

Davies, Susan G., *Spectacular Nature: Corporate Culture and the Sea World Experience* (Berkeley, CA, 1997)

de Graaf, Jan, with D'Laine Camp, *Europe, Coast Wise: An Anthology of Reflections on Architecture and Tourism* (Rotterdam, 1997)

de Martino, Stefano, and Alex Wall, *Cities of Childhood: Italian Colonie of the 1930s* (London, 1988)

Dean, David, *The Thirties: Recalling the English Architectural Scene* (London, 1983)

DeLa Vega, Timothy T., ed., *200 Years of Surfing Literature: An Annotated Bibliography* (Hawai'i, 2004)

Denson, Charles, *Coney Island: Lost and Found* (Berkeley, CA, 2002)

Dickens, Peter, *Society and Nature: Changing Our Environment, Changing Ourselves* (Cambridge, 2004)

Dinkel, John, *The Royal Pavilion Brighton* (London, 1983)

Douglas, Jack D., and Paul K. Rasmussen with Carol Ann Flanagan, *The Nude Beach* (Beverley Hill, CA, 1977)

Drover, Jill, *Good Clean Fun: The Story of Britain's First Holiday Camp* (London, 1982)

du Maurier, Daphne, *Vanishing Cornwall* (London, 1967)

Dutton, Geoffrey, *Sun, Sea, Surf and Sand – The Myth of the Beach* (Melbourne, 1985)

English Heritage and Commission for Architecture and the Built Environment, *Shifting Sands: Design and the Changing Image of English Seaside Towns* (London, 2003)

English Tourism Council, *Sea Changes: Creating World-Class Resorts in England* (London, 2001)

English Tourist Board, *Turning the Tide: A Heritage and Environment Strategy for a Seaside Resort* (London, 1993)

Evans, Nick, *Dreamland Remembered: 140 Years of Seaside Fun in Margate* (Whitstable, 2003)

Farrant, Sue, *Georgian Brighton, 1740 to 1820* (Brighton, 1980)

Fischer, Richard, and John Walton, *British Piers* (London, 1987)

Fisher, Michael H., *The First Indian Author in English: Dean Mahomed (1759–1851) in India, Ireland and England* (Delhi, 1996)

Fisher, Stephen, ed. *Recreation and the Sea* (Exeter, 1997)

Fiske, John, *Reading the Popular* (London, 1989)

Flint, Kate, *The Victorians and the Visual Imagination* (Cambridge, 2000)

Fowles, John, *The French Lieutenant's Woman* (London, 1969)

Franklin, Adrian, *Nature and Social Theory* (London, 2002)

Futrell, Jim, *Amusement Parks of New Jersey* (Mechanicsburg, PA, 2004)

Gallo, Emmanuelle, *Les Roches Noires Trouville-sur-Mer* (Cabourg, 2000)

Garner, Philippe, *A Seaside Album: Photographs and Memory* (London, 2003)

GESAMP and Advisory Committee on the Protection of the Sea, *A Sea of Trouble* (New York, 2001)

Gilbert, Edmund M., *Brighton: Old Ocean's Bauble* (London, 1954)

Gooding, Mel, *Promenade: An Architectural Collaboration for Bridlington* (Beverley, 2001)

Gordon, A., *Weekend Utopia: Modern Living in the Hamptons* (New York, 2001)

Gordon, Ian, and Brian Goodall, 'Resort Cycles and Development Processes', *Built Environment*, XVIII/1 (1992), pp. 41–56

Grasse, Marie-Christine, *Coups de Soleil & Bikinis* (Toulouse, 1997)

Gray, Fred., ed., *Bexhill Voices* (Falmer, 1994)

——, *Walking on Water: the West Pier Story* (Brighton, 1998)

——, 'Learning from the Seaside', *Journal of Access, Policy and Practice*, II/1 (2004), pp. 83–92

Greene, Graham, *Brighton Rock* (London, 1959),

Hamilton, Patrick, *The West Pier* (London, 1951)

Hardy, Dennis, and Colin Ward, *Arcadia for All: The Legacy of a Makeshift Landscape* (London, 1984)

Hartmut Berghoff, Barbara Korte, Ralf Schneider and Christopher Harvie, eds, *The Making of Modern Tourism: The Cultural History of the British Experience, 1600–2000* (Basingstoke, 2002)

Hassan, John, *The Seaside, Health and the Environment in England and Wales since 1800* (Aldershot, 2003)

Hastings Modern History Workshop, *Hastings Childhoods* (Falmer, 1987)

Head, Raymond, *The Indian Style* (Chicago, 1986)

Hern, Anthony, *The Seaside Holiday: The History of the English Seaside Resort* (London, 1967)

Hiaasen, Carl, *Strip Tease* (London, 1993)

——, *Tourist Season* (New York, 1986)

Hillman, Tony, and Beverley Cole, *South for Sunshine: Southern Railway Publicity and Posters, 1923 to 1947* (Harrow Weald, Middx, 1999)

Hinde, John, *Our True Intent Is All for Your Delight: The John Hinde Butlin's Photographs* (London, 2002)

Howell, Sarah, *The Seaside* (London, 1974)

Huls, Wilhelm, and Ulf Böttcher, *Bäderarchitektur* (Rostock, 1998)

Immerso, Michael, *Coney Island: The People's Playground* (New Brunswick, NJ, 2002)

Inglis, Andrea, *Beside the Seaside: Victorian Resorts in the Nineteenth Century* (Carlton South, Victoria, 1999)

Jackson, Peter, and Nigel Thrift, 'Geographies of Consumption', in *Acknowledging Consumption: A Review of New Studies*, ed. Daniel Miller (London, 1995), pp. 204–37

Johnson, Shirley, *The Villas of the Riviera: Magnificence and Majesty on the Côte d'Azur* (London, 1998)

Karn, V. A., *Retiring to the Seaside* (London, 1977)

King, Anthony D., *The Bungalow: The Production of a Global Culture* (New York, 1995)

Lansdell, Avril, *Seaside Fashions, 1860–1939* (Princes Risborough, 1990)

Lencek, Lena, and Gideon Bosker, *Making Waves: Swimsuits and the Undressing of America* (San Francisco, CA, 1989)

——, *The Beach: The History of Paradise on Earth* (London, 1998)

Levi, Vicki Gold and Lee Eisenberg, *Atlantic City: 125 Years of Ocean Madness* (New York, 1979)

Lewis, Robert, 'Seaside Holiday Resorts in the United States and Britain: A Review', *Urban History Yearbook 1980* (Leicester, 1980), pp. 44–52

Lightbown, Ted., *Blackpool: A Pictorial History* (Chichester, 1994)

Lindley, Kenneth, *Seaside Architecture* (London, 1973)

Lowenthal, David, *The Heritage Crusade and the Spoils of History* (Cambridge, 1998)

MacKenzie, John M., *Orientalism: History, Theory and the Arts* (Manchester, 1995)

Macnaghten, Phil, and John Urry, *Contested Nature* (London, 1998)

Manning-Sanders, Ruth, *Seaside England* (London, 1951)

Manwaring Baines, J., *Historic Hastings* (St Leonards on Sea, 1986)

Marling, Karal Ann, ed., *Designing Disney's Theme Parks: The Architecture of Reassurance* (New York, 1997)

Mickleburgh, Tim, *Glory Days: Piers* (Shepperton, 1999)

Moreau, Guy Junien, *Le Casino de la Jetée-Promenade* (Nice, 1993)

Morgan, Nigel J., and Annette Pritchard, *Power and Politics at the Seaside: The Development of Devon's Resorts in the Twentieth Century* (Exeter, 1999)

Mukerji, Chandra, 'Reading and Writing with Nature: Social Claims and the French Formal Garden, *Theory and Society*, XIX (1990), pp. 651–79

Musgrave, Clifford, *Royal Pavilion: An Episode in the Romantic* (London, 1959)

Muthesius, Stefan, *The High Victorian Movement in Architecture, 1950–1870* (London, 1972)

National Portrait Gallery, *We Are The People: Postcards from the Collection of Tom Phillips* (London, 2004)

O'Connell, James C., *Becoming Cape Cod: Creating a Seaside Resort* (Lebanon, NH, 2003), pp. 80–93

Okamoto, Ariel Rubissow, *A Day at the Seaside: San Francisco's Sutro Heights, Cliff House, and Sutro Baths* (San Francisco, CA, 1998)

Orvar, Löfgren, *On Holiday: A History of Vacationing* (Berkeley, CA, 1999)

Paris, Michael, *Warrior Nation: Images of War in British Popular Culture, 1850–2000* (London, 2002)

Parr, Martin, *The Last Resort: Photographs of New Brighton* (Wallasey, Cheshire, 1986)

——, *Boring Postcards* (London, 1999)

Peak, Steve, *Fishermen of Hastings: 200 Years of the Hastings Fishing Community* (St Leonards on Sea, 1985)

Pearson, Lynn F., *The People's Palaces: Britain's Seaside Pleasure Buildings of 1870–1914* (Buckingham, 1991)

Phelts, Marsha Dean, *An American Beach for African Americans* (Gainesville, FL, 1997)

Phillips, Tom, *The Postcard Century: 2000 Cards and their Messages* (London, 2000)

Pilcher, Rosamunde *The Shell Seekers* (London, 1987)

Pimlott, J.A.R., *The Englishman's Holiday: A Social History* (Hassocks, 1976)

Plum, Gilles, *Villas Balnéaires du Second Empire* (Cabourg, 2001)

Powers, Alan, ed., *Farewell My Lido* (London, 1991)

——, *Serge Chermayeff: Designer, Architect, Teacher* (London, 2001)

Racine, Michel, Ernest J.-P. Boursier-Mougenot and Françoise Binet, *The Gardens of Provence and the French Riviera* (Cambridge, MA, 1987)

Read, Sue, *Hello Campers!* (London, 1986)

Reynolds, Stanley, *A Poor Man's House* (Oxford, 1982)

Richards, Thomas, *The Commodity Culture of Victorian England: Advertising and Spectacle, 1851–1914* (London, 1991)

Robertson, E. Graeme, and Joan Robertson, *Cast Iron Decoration: A World Survey* (London, 1977)

Rojek, Chris, *Ways of Escape: Modern Transformations in Leisure and Travel* (London, 1993)

Royal Pavilion, Libraries and Museums, Brighton and Hove, *Kiss and Kill: Film Visions of Brighton* (Brighton, 2002)

Russell Stevens and Peter Willis, 'Earl De La Warr and the Competition for the Bexhill Pavilion, 1933–34', *Architectural History*, XXXIII (1990), pp. 135–66

Rutherford, Jessica, *A Prince's Passion: The Life of the Royal Pavilion* (Brighton, 2003)

Rymer, Russ, *Sea, Sand and Strife: A Saga of Race, Wealth and Memory* (New York, 1998)

Said, Edward W., *Orientalism* (London, 1978)

Shaw, Gareth, and Allan Williams, eds, *The Rise and Fall of British Coastal Resorts: Cultural and Economic Perspectives* (London, 1997)

Shields, Rob, *Places on the Margin: Alternative Geographies of Modernity* (London, 1991)

Smets, Marcel, 'Promenade, Past and Present', *Topos*, XLI (2002), pp. 6–17

Smith, Alison, ed., *Exposed: The Victorian Nude* (London, 2001)

Soane, J.V.N., *Fashionable Resorts Regions: Their Evolution and Transformation* (Wallingford, Oxon, 1993)

Somerville, Christopher, *Britain Beside the Sea* (London, 1989)

Sprawson, Charles, *Haunts of the Black Masseur* (London, 1992)

Stafford, Felicity, and Nigel Yates, *The Later Kentish Seaside* (Gloucester, 1985)

Stanley, Allen, and Christopher Newall, *Pre-Raphaelite Vision: Truth to Nature*, exh. cat., Tate Britain, London (2004)

Stanton, Jeffrey, *Santa Monica Pier: A History from 1875 to 1990* (Los Angeles, CA, 1990)

——, *Venice California: 'Coney Island of the Pacific'* (Los Angeles, CA, 1993)

Stephen Bayley, 'Patrons of the Modern Movement', *Architectural Design*, XLIX, 10–11 (1979), pp. 90–95

Sternlieb, George, and James W. Hughes, *The Atlantic City Gamble* (Cambridge, MA, 1983)

Stokes, H. G., *The English Seaside* (London, 1947)

Taschen, Angelika, ed., *Seaside Style: Living on the Beach* (Cologne, 2002)

Taylor, Derek, and David Bush, *The Golden Age of British Hotels* (London, 1974)

Theroux, Paul, *The Kingdom by the Sea* (London, 1983)

Travis, John F., *The Rise of the Devon Seaside Resorts, 1750–1900* (Exeter, 1993)

Tressell, Robert, *The Ragged Trousered Philanthropists* (London, 1965)

Tunstall, Sylvia M., and Edmund C. Penning-Rowsell, 'The English Beach: Experiences and Values', *The Geographical Journal*, 164/3 (1998), pp. 319–32

Turner, Brian and Steve Palmer, *The Blackpool Story* (Cleveleys, Lancashire, 1976)

Urry, John, *The Tourist Gaze: Leisure and Travel in Contemporary Societies* (London, 1990)

——, *Consuming Places* (London, 1995)

——, *The Tourist Gaze* (2nd edn, London, 2002)

van Leeuwen, Thomas A. P., *The Springboard in the Pond: An Intimate History of the Swimming Pool* (Cambridge, MA, 1999)

Venturi, Robert, Denise Scott Brown and Steven Izenour, *Learning from Las Vegas* (Cambridge, MA, 1977)

Wallace, Catherine, *Under the Open Sky* (Truro, 2002)

Walton, John K., *The Blackpool Landlady: A Social History* (Manchester, 1983)

——, *The English Seaside Resort: A Social History, 1750–1914* (Leicester, 1983)

——, 'The Re-making of a Popular Resort: Blackpool Tower and the Boom of the 1890s', *The Local Historian*, XXIV/4 (1994), pp. 194–205

——, *The British Seaside: Holidays and Resorts in the Twentieth Century* (Manchester, 2000)

Walton, John K., and James Walvin, eds, *Leisure in Britain, 1780–1939* (Manchester, 1983)

Walvin, James, *Besides the Seaside* (London, 1978)

Ward, Colin, and Dennis Hardy, *Goodnight Campers! The History of the British Holiday Camp* (London, 1986)

Ward, Stephen V., *Selling Places: The Marketing and Promotion of Towns and Cities, 1850–2000* (London, 1998)

Watson, Elwood, and Darcy Martin, 'The Miss America Pageant: Pluralism, Femininity, and Cinderella All in One', *Journal of Popular Culture*, XXXIV/1 (2000), pp. 105–26

Weightman, Gavin, *The Seaside* (Devizes, 1993)

Whyman, John, *The Early Kentish Seaside (1736–1840)* (Gloucester, 1985)

Wigg, Julia, *Bon Voyage! Travel Posters of the Edwardian Era* (London, 1996)

Wolters, N.E.B., *Bungalow Town: Theatre & Film Colony* (Shoreham-by-Sea, 1985)

Worpole, Ken, *Here Comes the Sun: Architecture and Public Space in Twentieth-century European Culture* (London, 2000)

Wray, Paul, *Butlin's Filey. Thanks for the Memories* (Beverley, 1992)

Young, Gerard, *A History of Bognor Regis* (Chichester, 1983)

Young, Kenneth, *Music's Great Days in the Spas and Watering-Places* (London, 1968)

ACKNOWLEDGEMENTS

The purpose of this book is to piece together some elements of the making, using and representing of Western seaside architecture. The beginnings of the book, in a professional sense, date back to the late 1980s, while at a personal level its origins stretch back five decades to my own childhood experiences of the English seaside. Although the errors and misinterpretations are my own, the book has depended on a group of sometimes unwitting collaborators.

The book's themes have been developed in a variety of academic and public contexts. I am especially grateful to students at the University of Sussex Centre for Continuing Education who have discussed and criticized my ideas. Particular thanks are also due to the following individuals: Eamon and Michel of Seafront Image, Brighton; Hilary Lane for help with my understanding of the De La Warr Pavilion, Bexhill; Sylvia Endacott for the information about Hothamton, perhaps the first planned resort; Jessica Rutherford, David Beevers and their colleagues in The Royal Pavilion, Libraries & Museums of Brighton & Hove City Council; Bob Bradley for opening the resources of Margate Museum to me; Philip Godwin for information about Cromer and Norfolk; Tim Loe for the material on, and tour of, Tinside Lido, Plymouth; Sue Berry for her insights into the early history of Brighton as a resort and English seaside parks and gardens; Andy Durr and Steve Peak for helping to explain the relationship of the fishing industry to holidaymaking in, respectively, Brighton and Hastings; Zena Thompson of Brighton, Jinty Rouke of Tauranga City Libraries, New Zealand, Margaret Evans of the Queenscliffe Historical Museum, Victoria, Australia, and Christian Deflandre of the Musée de la Carte Postale, Antibes, France, for providing access to some important images for the book; and David Sawyers for his deep understanding of the significance of swimming in Brighton.

Mary Hoar has made a sustained and delightful contribution from the early 1990s to my own understanding of seaside architecture; Geoffrey Mead supplied a wonderful array of resources for the book and gave freely of his knowledge of all things Brighton; my other Centre for Continuing Education colleagues Mike Boice, Pam Coare, David Rudling and Martin Ryle provided some excellent seaside titbits; Richard Riding, John Muir, Martin Easdown, Tony Wills and other friends from the National Piers Society instructed me about British seaside pleasure piers; Rachel Clark and Geoff Lockwood involved me with the struggle for the survival of Brighton's wondrous West Pier; John Field told me about his own studies of class conflict at the seaside; Ted Lightbown bestowed many brilliant Blackpool images, some of which are reproduced in this book, and showed me Britain's most popular resort; Richard Morrice helped develop the early ideas for the book; Marie-Noël Tournoux told me about French seaside architecture, particularly on the Channel coast; Margrit Kühl allowed me to appreciate better the inter-war seaside architecture of Germany and Italy; Bernd Fischer guided me around some of the architectural glories of Germany's Baltic coast; Melissa E. Baldock deepened my fascination with the iconic Coney Island and Allen 'Boo' Pergament, a historian of Atlantic City, New Jersey, provided wonderful insights into that resort's rich history; John K. Walton, the supreme historian of the seaside, made insightful comments on sections of the draft text; Doris Parfitt provided a collection of seaside postcards; and David and Nickie, Justin and Jo, Lyn and Steve, and Mark and Fi shared the pleasures of experiencing the south coast of seaside England.

Last, my gratitude to Carol, Jack and Holly for enjoying so much seaside architecture with me and for putting up with the fixation that has so often led us on coastal diversions in various parts of the Western world in search of a pavilion, pier or lido by the sea. This book is for them.

PHOTO ACKNOWLEDGEMENTS

The author and publishers wish to express their thanks to the below sources of illustrative material and/or permission to reproduce it. Every effort has been made to trace and acknowledge holders of copyright of the illustrations used in this book, and the publishers would be pleased to hear from copyright holders concerning any errors or omissions.

A. H. & S. Paragon Series: p. 252 (top); © AROS Limited: p. 244 (top); Art Gallery of New South Wales (© Margaret Stephenson-Meere): p. 120 foot (photo Jenni Carter for the Art Gallery of New South Wales); photos by the author: pp. 6, 8 (top), 9 (top), 11, 16, 19, 25, 36 (top right), 37, 38, 42, 45, 48 (top), 56 (foot), 57, 60, 71 (top and middle), 72 (foot), 78 (top right and foot), 94 (right), 96 (foot), 99, 100, 105 (top), 111 (top right), 112 (left), 121, 125 (foot), 126, 127, 129 (foot), 130, 136 (foot), 137, 138, 140, 143 (foot), 144 (foot), 145 (foot), 146, 150, 153, 172, 173, 175, 190 (top), 192 (foot), 193 (right), 194, 195, 196, 198, 202, 223, 224, 225, 228, 229, 230, 237, 238, 239, 240, 241, 243, 249, 250 (top left and top right), 251 (left), 255, 261, 271, 276, 277, 278, 280, 281, 282, 283, 286, 287, 299, 300 (bottom right), 301 (foot), 304 (foot), 307 (foot), 308 (top), 309, 310 (top); postcards, photographs, newsprint and other illustrative material collection of the author: pp. 8 (foot), 12, 21, 23 (top right and foot), 24 (top), 27, 28, 30 (top), 31, 32 (foot), 33 (foot), 35 (foot), 39, 46, 47 (foot), 48 (foot), 49, 51 (top right), 54 (foot), 55, 56 (top), 77, 84, 85, 86, 87, 88, 89, 90, 95, 96 (top), 97 (foot), 98 (top), 101 (top), 104 (top), 105 (foot), 108 (foot), 111 (top left), 115, 117, 123 (top), 129 (top), 132 (top), 133 (foot), 135, 136 (top), 139 (top left and right), 141 (top), 142, 145 (top), 152 (foot), 154 (foot), 155, 158, 159, 161 (top), 166 (foot), 169, 171 (foot), 182, 188 (top), 189, 190 (foot), 210, 213 (top), 214, 215, 216, 217 (top), 219, 220 (foot), 232 (top), 242 (top), 246, 247, 248, 250 (foot), 252 (top), 256, 264 (foot), 273, 291, 294 (top), 298, 301 (top), 303, 305, 306 (foot), 307 (top), 310 (foot); poster Hervé Baille, 1955, for the S.N.C.F.: p. 59; courtesy of Melissa E. Baldock: pp. 265, 267 (top); courtesy The Society of Bexhill Museums: pp. 258, 260; courtesy of Blackpool Tourism: pp. 72 top (from the County Borough of Blackpool's 1964 Official Holiday Journal), 75 left (cover illustration by Rushton for the 1989 Blackpool Official Guide, Built for Fun), 75 right (cover illustration for the 2004 Blackpool Official Guide Blackpool. So Much Fun You Can Taste It); courtesy of Blackpool Pleasure Beach: pp. 97 (top and middle), 148 (foot), 272, 274, 275 (top); courtesy Mike Boice: p. 165 (foot); photos courtesy of Bondi Surf Bathers' Life Saving Club: pp. 36, 163, 164; courtesy of Brighton Fishing Museum: p. 177; Brighton Museum & Art Gallery: pp. 22 (photos © The Royal Pavilion, Libraries & Museums, Brighton and Hove): pp. 22, 24 (foot), 50 (top), 116, 156, 179, 208, 209, 213 (foot); cover illustration to the

1934–35 Brighton Official Handbook (illustration by H. G. Gawthorn): p. 219; courtesy of Brighton West Pier Trust: p. 220 (top); courtesy of Butlins: pp. 54 (top), 294 (foot), 295, 296, 300 (top left, middle left, top right); photo courtesy of City of Coral Gables Historical Resources Department: pp. 30 (foot), 103 (foot); the Clock Tower Studio, Marine Terrace, Margate: p. 89 (top); courtesy F. Coakley Collection: p. 290; H. Coates, Wisbech: p.55 (top); courtesy of Conway County Borough Council: p. 66 (front cover of the Lllandudno Publicity Association's 1939 Llandudno Official Guide); Donlion Productions: p. 248; courtesy of Eastbourne Borough Council: p. 74 left and right (front and back covers of Eastbourne Corporation Publicity Committee's 1963 Official Guide to Eastbourne); photo courtesy of the Sylvia Endacott collection: p. 47 (top); courtesy of the English Riviera Tourist Board: pp. 78 (top left), 122 (foot), 254; reproduced by permission of English Heritage. NMR / © Crown Copyright. NMR: pp. 53 (middle), 221, 268; courtesy of Folkestone Library Local History Collection: pp. 157, 252 (foot), 267 (foot); illustration © FOA (Foreign Office Architects): p. 244 (foot); courtesy Jack Gray: p. 94 (left); courtesy Carol Gray: p. 275 (foot); Greaves, Scarborough: 182 (top); photo courtesy of Hastings Borough Council: pp. 32 top, 187 foot (front cover and inside illustration from Hastings and St Leonards Borough Association's 1935 Hastings and St Leonards Official Handbook); courtesy of Hill and Knowlton: p. 113; photo Anne Howard: p. 222; Interborough News: p. 264 (foot); courtesy of Isle of Wight Record Office: p. 18; 'Jarrolds': p. 250 (foot), photo courtesy Jay Jopling/White Cube (London), © the artist (Tracey Emin): p. 174; courtesy of Judges ©: p. 33 (top); courtesy of Karis Developments: p. 63 (foot); from John Leech, Pictures of Life & Character, first series (London, c. 1860): p. 152 (top); courtesy of Leisure Parcs Ltd: pp. 51 (foot), 98 (foot), 204 (foot), 205, 257; photos Library of Congress, Washington, DC (Prints & Photographs Division): pp. 13 top (LC-DIG-ppmsc-09020), 13 foot (LC-DIG-ppmsc-05634), 14 (Chadbourne collection of Japanese prints, gift of Mrs E. Crane Chadbourne, LC-USZC4-10639), 101 lower right (LC-USZ64-126575), 103 top (Detroit Publishing Company Photograph Collection, LC-D418-68093), 111 foot (LC-USZ62-128079), 166 top (LC-USZ62-100334), 197 (LC-USZ62-70341), 263 top (LC-USZ62-92172), 263 foot (Grantham Bain Collection, LC-DIG-ggbain-09282), 264 top (George Grantham Bain Collection, LC-B2-2240-13); courtesy of Ted Lightbown: pp. 61 (left), 109, 143 (top), 186 (top); Los Angeles County Museum of Art (gift of Peter Paanakker): p. 120 top (photo courtesy of D. C. Moore Gallery, New York); photos courtesy of the photographer, E. Ludwig, and John Hinde Ltd: pp. 270 (top), 297 (foot); courtesy of Margate Museum: pp. 20, 53 (top), 53 (foot), 61 (right), 69 (foot), 112 (right), 125 (top), 132 (foot), 149, 154 (top), 168,

178, 187 (top), 192 (top), 269, 270 (lower left, lower right); from the collection of Geoffrey Mead: p. 251 (right); photos courtesy of the Musée de la Carte Postale, Antibes: pp. 35 (top), 58, 128, 165 (top), 242 (foot); photo courtesy of the photographer, E. Nägele, and John Hinde Ltd: p. 9 (foot); photo © National Museum of Photography, Film & Television (Daily Herald Archive/Science & Society Picture Library): p. 288;photos © National Railway Museum/Science & Society Picture Library: pp. 10, 67, 68, 183, 253, 292, 306 (top); photo courtesy of the photographer, D. Noble, and John Hinde Ltd: p. 297 (top) courtesy North Somerset Museum Service: p. 193 (left); Paragon Series, Margate: p. 182 (foot); courtesy Penzance Jubilee Pool Association: p. 188 (foot); courtesy of Allen 'Boo' Pergament: pp. 69 (top), 232 (foot), 233, 234, 235, 308 (foot); photo © Phoenix Seagaia Resort: p. 199; The Photochrom Co. Ltd: pp. 256, 294 (top); courtesy of the Borough of Poole: pp. 35 top left (from Poole Borough Council's 1934 *Official Guide to Poole*), 170 (from Poole Borough Council's 1932 *Official Guide to Poole*); photo reproduced with the kind permission of Portsmouth Museums and Records Service: p. 30 (middle); courtesy of Queenscliffe Historical Museum, Victoria, Australia: p. 162; courtesy of Rother District Council: pp. 69 (middle), 124 (from Bexhill Corporation's 1935 guide *Bexhill-on-Sea. For . . . Health & Happiness, Holidays and Homes*); The Royal Collection © 2005 Her Majesty Queen Elizabeth II: p. 119 foot (photo Royal Collection Picture Library); photos © The Royal Pavilion, Libraries & Museums, Brighton and Hove: p. 50 (foot), 70 (top), 92, 93, 106, 118, 141 (foot), 211, 217 (foot), 218; courtesy David Rudling: p. 161 (foot); courtesy of J. Salmon Ltd: pp. 108 (top), 134; Saltzburg's Merchandise Co.: p. 232 (top); courtesy of

Scarborough Borough Council: p. 191 top (from D. Adshead and H. V. Overfield, *The Further Development of Scarborough*, Scarborough, Yorkshire, 1938); courtesy of Scarborough Museums and Gallery: pp. 119 top, 148 top (detail from *The South prospect of Scarborough in the County of Yorkshire*, 1745), 185, 304 (top); photos Science & Society Picture Library: pp. 81 top (© Tony Ray-Jones/NMPFT), 144 top (© Science Museum), 288 (© National Museum of Photography, Film & Television/Daily Herald Archive/Science & Society Picture Library); photos © Seafront Image, Brighton: pp. 71 (foot), 81 (foot); illustration from *Seaside, Aunt Louisa's London Toy Books* (London, c. 1860s): p. 117 (top); courtesy of Sefton MBC and Southport Tourism: pp. 70 foot, 191 foot (front cover and inside illustration from Southport Corporation's 1957 *Southport Official Guide*); reproduced with permission of, and ©, Sidmouth Museum, Devon: p. 34 (top), courtesy of the architects Snøhetta/Spence: p. 63 (top); courtesy of Southend-on-Sea Borough Council (photo, Borough of Southend Publicity Officer): p. 204 (top); from Southport Corporation's *1938–39 Sunny Southport. Official Guide*: pp. 52, 104 (foot), 186 (foot); Sunbeam Photo Ltd, Margate: p. 89 (foot); Tate, London (photo © Tate, London, 2005): p. 26; photos courtesy of Tauranga City Libraries: p. 133 (top), 289; courtesy of Tendring District Council: p. 73; courtesy of Zena Thompson: p. 23 (top left), 122 (top), 123 (foot), 131; courtesy Torbay Council: p.139 bottom left (front cover of Paignton Urban District Council's 1949 *Official Guide to Paignton Glorious South Devon*); courtesy of Trump Taj Mahal: p. 102; courtesy of West Sussex County Council Library Service: p. 171 (top); photo courtesy of Worthing Borough Council: p. 41.

INDEX